Economic Aid and American Policy toward Egypt, 1955–1981

Economic Aid and American Policy toward Egypt, 1955-1981

William J. Burns

with a foreword by
Ambassador Hermann Frederick Eilts

State University of New York Press
ALBANY

The views expressed in this book are those of the author and do not necessarily represent those of the United States State Department, the United States Government or any other organization.

Published by
State University of New York Press, Albany

© 1985 State University of New York

For information, address State University of New York
Press, State University Plaza, Albany, N.Y. 12246

Library of Congress Cataloging in Publication Data

Burns, William J. (William Joseph), 1956–
   Economic aid and American policy toward Egypt, 1955–1981.
   Bibliography: p. 263
   1. Economic assistance, American—Egypt. 2. Egypt—Foreign relations—
United States. 3. United States—Foreign relations—Egypt. I. Title.
HC830.B87   1984   338.91'73602   83–20181
ISBN 0-87395-868-3
ISBN 0-87395-869-1 (pbk.)

10 9 8 7 6 5 4 3 2

*For Lisa
and
for my parents*

Contents

Acknowledgments

This work would not have been possible without the kind support of a number of individuals and institutions. I am particularly indebted to the Marshall Scholarship Commission; Wilfrid Knapp, Hedley Bull, and Albert Hourani of Oxford University; Barry Rubin of Georgetown University's Center for Strategic and International Studies; the staff of SUNY Press; and Thomas Carothers of Harvard Law School and Mark Foulon of the Department of State, who provided careful criticism of earlier drafts of this manuscript. I am also deeply grateful to the former policymakers whom I interviewed in the course of my research, especially former Ambassadors Henry Byroade, Raymond Hare, Mustapha Kamel, and Roger Makins. I wish to express special thanks to former Ambassador Hermann Eilts, who graciously offered to write the Foreword for this study.

Foreword

Few phenomena in the sphere of foreign relations have these past thirty years evoked as much controversy and commentary as American economic aid to Egypt. In a real sense, providing or withholding such aid has been a weather vane of U.S.-Egyptian relations. Since 1976, American economic aid to Egypt has totalled over 1 billion a year. Egypt, along with Israel, is currently the largest United States economic aid recipient.

By definition, economic aid should be for economic development purposes, but in the case of Egypt various psychopolitical aspects have usually been pervasive. These have included an evolving American understanding of economic aid as a foreign policy tool; the applicability of this perception in Egypt at any given time; the Egyptian need for and, as a separate matter, their perception of foreign aid; the role of economic aid in the superpower competition between the United States and the Soviet Union for influence in the Middle East; and endemic structural problems in both the American and Egyptian governments which affect giving or utilizing foreign aid, respectively, in each of the two countries. These constantly interact with one another in kaleidoscopic fashion, producing at different times variant patterns.

With the post World War II emergence of the United States as a superpower, and largely because of the demonstrable effectiveness of the Marshall Plan in rebuilding shattered European economies, economic aid came to be recognized as a potentially useful component of American foreign policy. Initial assumptions as to its utility were strangely naive, however, and reflected in large measure America's heretofore limited involvement in foreign affairs. It was believed, for example, that communism flourished mainly in abjectly poor societies; hence, if economic aid were provided to poor polities, the anticipated

resultant prosperity would surely bring about a rejection of
leftist ideologies. President Harry Truman's Point IV program
was largely the product of such a political philosophy. Moreover,
there was little initial appreciation of the need for technologically-trained and managerially competent indigenous human
infrastructure to make such foreign aid optimally effective. The
absence of communism, it was further assumed, would bring
with it political stability. By the mid-fifties, that simplistic thesis
had been disproven as it became increasingly evident that
economic development itself could create, as a by-product,
political instability.

Still another American belief in the fifties was that economic
aid offered political leverage to persuade recipient states to
follow foreign policies consistent with those of the United States.
Through economic (and military) aid, they could be induced
to accept the then prevailing Manichaean-type dichotomy that
divided the world between forces of light, as represented by
the so-called "free world," and forces of darkness, as represented by the Soviet Union and its satellites. Neutralism between
these opposing poles was, in the American view, anathema,
even immoral. American economic aid was thus used to pressure
recipient states to support United States foreign policy objectives. Conversely, it was withheld when putative recipients
balked and pursued policies at odds with those of Washington,
but which they believed best suited their national interests. Not
until the sixties did a more sophisticated appreciation of the
use of foreign aid, one that did not tie such aid directly to the
recipient's foreign policy behavior, but rather to creating an
improved climate of confidence in which differences of view
could more constructively be discussed, enter American foreign
policy thinking. By that time the wreckage of earlier American
attempts to use economic aid as a bludgeoning device in Egypt
and elsewhere had become palpably apparent.

If American administrations were learning the hard way
the potential use and nonuse of economic aid, so were recipient
states throughout the world. Many such states had only recently
acquired their independence. They were still in the process of
seeking to fuse disparate elements in their societies into some
single nationality, were administratively poorly organized with
sharply limited technologically-trained human infrastructure,
and were above all keenly sensitive to any suggestion, real or

imagined, of foreign doners seeking to encroach upon their foreign sovereignty. They needed and indeed wanted foreign economic aid, withal looked suspiciously at any offers lest these somehow have hidden strings attached. It was difficult for American administrations, especially after the positive United States record of having pressed the British, French and Dutch to decolonize, to understand the feelings of newly independent peoples and governments that Congressionally required procedural restrictions on American economic aid could by any stretch of the imagination be interpreted as "neo-imperialism." Conceptions of what was involved in economic aid between the United States doner and the putative foreign recipient were in each such instance a function of the different historical experiences of the parties involved.

The Soviet Union, emerging from the massive destruction it had sustained during World War II, was slow to enter the foreign economic aid arena. By the mid-fifties, however, it had also come to realize the potential political value of such aid in its dealings with newly independent African and Asian nations. While it could hardly outbid the United States in any area where American economic aid was being actively offered, it could seize upon instances where American aid was being withheld as a pressure device and, by substituting Soviet economic aid, could reduce the recipient state's reliance upon the United States. The Soviets, too, suffered from the misguided belief that economic aid translated into political influence. While its economic aid procedures are considerably more expeditious than those of the United States, it went through the same painful learning process that economic aid and political influence are separate matters.

The Egyptian case represents a prime example of the congruence of the aforementioned factors. Nowhere have the pitfalls of economic aid as a political device been more dramatically demonstrated. The Aswan Dam offer of the Eisenhower Administration in the mid-fifties is a classic instance of the political misuse of economic aid offers. After having decided to provide economic aid, along with the World Bank and Great Britain, to Egypt for the construction of a new high dam at Aswan, largely because President Dwight Eisenhower and Secretary of State John Foster Dulles believed this would induce Gamal Abdul Nasser to move toward peace with Israel and to reject further Soviet blandishments (Nasser had already accepted Soviet arms), Dulles abruptly informed the Egyptians that Nasser's international conduct precluded providing such aid. To be sure, it had by then become highly unlikely that Congress was prepared to appropriate needed funds for this purpose, but that critical aspect was lost in the ensuing controversy. Britain and the World Bank, the latter reluctantly, followed suit.

Nasser, and much of the Arab world, saw the American action as a deliberate slap at Egypt's independent policy line; the Soviets saw it as an opportunity to capitalize on the American rebuff to Egypt and to offer their aid to build the dam; Nasser retaliated against the perceived American and British affront by nationalizing the Suez Canal; Great Britain and France (together with Israel) reacted by staging an invasion of Egypt, which was opposed by the United States, and ultimately brought an end to British and French "great power" status in the Middle East; and the political forces in the area were significantly realigned. The adverse chain of events resulting from the withdrawal of the Aswan Dam offer were truly portentious. Many years later, in June, 1974, when President Richard Nixon visited Egypt, he responded to an Egyptian reporter's question about the Aswan Dam affair by stating categorically, "This was one of the greatest mistakes that we made." Granted, that statement may have been tailored for his particular audience at the time— there is no evidence that Nixon, as Vice President under Eisenhower, opposed the withdrawal decision—but there was much truth in it. At a minimum, the matter could have been handled more tactfully.

On the Egyptian side, while few Egyptians would acknowledge this, mistakes were also made in handling the American economic aid offers. One can appreciate Nasser's sense of pride in the achievements of the Egyptian revolution and his unwillingness to accept any limitations on Egyptian sovereignty after having just rid the nation of the British presence. Moreover, with the Israeli raid on Gaza in February, 1955, his ability to negotiate any kind of settlement with Israel had been sharply circumscribed, even if his sometime protestations of wanting to do so were sincere. Still, had there been a better political dialogue between the United States and Egypt—and somehow Ambassador Henry Byroade's frequent, long nocturnal sessions with Nasser usually ended up more as twin monologues than as dialogue—the two sides' pertinent domestic and foreign policy problems in connection with United States aid for an Aswan dam could have been better comprehended by each party. With patience and persistence, ways could have been explored to bridge them.

A part of the problem was that Nasser was feeling his oats; he had managed, often through American political intervention in his behalf, to parlay what could have been disastrous defeats into political victories and had become the hero of Arab nationalism. With the Soviets bidding for his favor, he believed that he could dictate to the United States when his cards were in fact precious few and limited. It was a colossal miscalculation on his part, as in a different sense were the pertinent views of Eisenhower and Dulles, and ultimately lead to the June, 1967, Arab-Israeli war. Nasser died in September, 1970, still leader of Egypt, but in the eyes of his closest associates a broken man.

Apart from political miscalculation, there exists an underlying Egyptian attitude toward foreign aid, which some suggest is historically rooted and which grates on foreign doners. So often, including in my own experience during the subsequent Sadat period, Egyptian officials acted as though there were some kind of an obligation on the part of foreign doners, including the United States, to provide them with economic help. They may have done so unconsciously, but their attitude often brought to mind Pharaonic friezes showing subject peoples bringing tribute to Egyptian rulers. Sadat excepted, there was usually little sign of appreciation on the part of Egyptian officials and an obvious reluctance to give public credit to the foreign doner for the burden borne by the latter's taxpayers. I recall once mentioning this, only half jocularly, to an Egyptian deputy prime minister. His initial reaction was indignantly to deny it; then he smiled and agreed that there might be something to this.

In the wake of the Aswan Dam fiasco, and especially under the Kennedy Administration, President Kennedy and sensitive American and Egyptian ambassadors sought to ameliorate the tensions between the two countries and temporarily succeeded in doing so. American economic aid to Egypt, including Public Law 480 Title I wheat assistance, was resumed in modest quantities. Indeed, during the Kennedy Administration, a three-year PL 480 wheat agreement was signed with Egypt as a means of enabling the Egyptian government to do some forward economic planning. It was felt desirable by President Kennedy and by many members of the State Department to "propitiate" Nasser, as one State Department official candidly described it, since the Egyptian leader had by then become the lodestone of Arab nationalism. Other State Department officials, while not opposing economic aid to Egypt, felt that the Kennedy multi-year aid gesture was unwise and would go unrequited. It did. Nasser, treating American aid with disdain and having a Soviet string do his bow, pursued policies in Yemen and elsewhere in the Arab world in utter disregard of American concerns. Propitiation—or "pacification," as Dr. Burns calls it— of a foreign leader through multi-year United States economic aid programs was bound to end in failure. After the June, 1967, military defeat suffered by Egypt at the hands of Israel, President Lyndon Johnson adopted a hard-line policy toward Egypt. Despite frequent hints that Nasser wished to renew diplomatic relations with the United States, if only some "gesture" were made by Washington, Johnson would have none of it. That may have been wise or unwise, but it was a natural reaction.

The situation did not change until President Anwar al-Sadat assumed office in late September, 1970. Sadat, although a Nasser protege, had come to recognize more clearly than his former chief that the prostrate Egyptian economy needed American help and that this could be obtained only through the medium of some kind of constructive diplomatic dialogue with the United States, aimed at achieving a Middle East peace and United States-Egyptian cooperation in the area. It required patience and mutual understanding by the American and Egyptian sides to do this, but, happily, the leaderships in both Washington and Cairo were prepared to work together to achieve common objectives. The Egyptian-Israeli peace treaty and the exclusion of Soviet influence in Egypt were the results.

American economic aid to Egypt was restored by Congressional action in December, 1974, but only after strong objections from pro-Israeli members of the Congress had been overcome by President Gerald Ford. By the end of 1975, aggregate United States aid to Egypt had increased to a billion dollar annual level. Although the political problems that bedeviled past American economic aid to Egypt have not recurred, there are other problems flowing from Egypt's limited absorptive capability to utilize such large amounts of assistance in short time frames. There is also an American conviction that the government of Egypt needs restructuring in order to use more effectively such United States aid. And, since the advent of the Reagan Administration, a view exists in Washington that more American economic aid should be chanelled into the Egyptian private instead of public sector. This latter view, whatever its merits, if pushed too insensitively by the Reagan Administration, could well evoke an Egyptian reaction similar to the Aswan Dam fiasco.

When the Aswan Dam offer was first considered in Washington in the mid-fifties, then Secretary of the Treasury George Humphrey questioned the desirability of providing such help on the grounds that any long-term American economic interface with Egypt would only bring frictions between the two countries. He was prescient. Despite the massive American economic aid to Egypt, there is probably no single aspect of current United States-Egyptian relations that receives as much excoriation from Egyptian officials as the economic aid program, now underway for ten years. This is partly a function of excessive red tape on the part of the Agency for International Development, partly of American efforts to persuade reluctant Egyptians to restructure their governmental machinery, partly because of the limited visibility on the ground of American-financed aid projects, partly of the unwillingness of the United States simply to turn over economic assistance monies to Egypt (as it does with Israel) in order to use as that country's leaders see fit, and partly because of excessive Congressional interference in the AID program for Egypt.

Dr. Burns' study of the origins and evolution of American economic aid to Egypt represents a detailed recital of some of the issues raised above. It is meticulously researched, including highly effective use of interviews and oral histories by participants in the process or persons affected by it over the years, and is spritely written. With the passage of time, some of the factors leading to the Aswan crises and to subsequent, badly strained American-Egyptian relations, have come to be obscured. A mythology of who did what to whom has developed, which is often skewed. Dr. Burns' painstaking research sets the record straight. Both sides must share blame.

In my judgment, Dr. Burns' book will stand as one of the more careful and balanced accounts of the critical economic aid element in the American-Egyptian relationship in the fifties and sixties. In briefer form he carries the story into the Sadat and Mubarak eras and offers useful perspectives on the impact of American economic aid on overall United States-Egyptian relations. Not only will it serve students and teachers, but officials of the United States government—including in AID—might usefully ponder it if they are to avoid some of the mistakes that were made in the past and which at times they seem to be close to repeating.

Ambassador Hermann Frederick Eilts

Introduction

Gamal Abdel Nasser's decision to barter Egyptian cotton for Soviet bloc weaponry in September 1955 thrust Egypt onto center stage in the unfolding drama of the Cold War in the Middle East. In the wake of the 1955 Czech-Egyptian arms agreement, what Egypt needed most, and what the United States was uniquely equipped to provide, was economic aid.[1] For the Egyptian government—eager to take rapid strides toward economic development but crippled by a burgeoning population, a paucity of arable land, and a meager reserve of foreign exchange—American economic aid promised to serve as an enormously important crutch. For American policymakers who perceived that Egypt's "greatest weakness was its dependence on Western help to maintain the pace of economic development," economic assistance appeared to be an ideal means of developing American influence in Egypt.[2]

Few aid relationships in the last three decades can match the drama and significance of the U.S.-Egyptian experience. The Eisenhower Administration's cancellation of its offer to help finance the Aswan High Dam in July 1956 triggered the Suez Crisis, and has been called "a turning point in the political relationship of the West and the Arab peoples."[3] Between 1958 and 1965, Egypt was the world's largest per capita consumer of U.S. food aid.[4] With the demise of the food aid program in the mid-1960s, not long after Nasser had told Lyndon Johnson that he could take his aid and "drink from the sea," U.S. relations with Nasser's Egypt reached their nadir. But his successor, Anwar Sadat, proved far more cooperative than Nasser ever had. By the mid-1970s, the United States had unveiled a multibillion dollar economic assistance program in Egypt, the largest of its kind since the Marshall Plan.

This study considers the ways in which the American government attempted to use its economic aid program to induce

1

or coerce Egypt to support U.S. interests in the quarter century following the Czech arms deal. It focuses primarily on aid as a tool of American policy toward the Nasser regime, relying upon recently released government documents and interviews with former policymakers. A later chapter offers a few preliminary observations about the role of the American economic assistance program in the Sadat era. Although it does not pretend to provide a detailed prescription for American aid policy toward Mubarak's Egypt, much less a complete set of rules to govern the use of aid as a political instrument in other developing countries, the book does highlight some useful lessons about the objectives, application, and effects of aid policy drawn from the American experience in the Nasser and Sadat eras.

Objectives

What were the objectives of American aid policy in the Nasser and Sadat eras? The answer to that question is more elusive than it might seem at first glance: Officials involved in the making of policy toward Egypt rarely set down their aims in neat order; moreover, those aims have been constantly juggled to fit foreign and domestic needs. In general terms, however, American objectives can be grouped in three categories: those relating to Egyptian behavior; those relating to American domestic concerns; and those relating to broader international interests, such as Soviet-American competition in the Third World or the need to appease allies.

A constant goal of American aid policy toward Egypt since the 1950s has been, as a 1967 United States Agency for International Development (AID) study put it, "to moderate the behavior of the Egyptian government along lines which are at least not inimical to United States interests." [5] The American government has been most seriously concerned about Egypt's international, rather than domestic, behavior, since until recently it had few commercial interests in Egypt. However, U.S. officials have continually drawn a connection between Egypt's external and internal policies. The Kennedy Administration, for example, was convinced that inducing Nasser to concentrate his energies on Egyptian economic development would produce a gradual mellowing of Egyptian conduct in international affairs. The rationale underpinning this belief was often expressed as a syllogism: economic development promotes the growth of societies that are economically strong, politically stable and able to resist Communist subversion, thereby favoring U.S. national interests; economic aid stimulates economic development; therefore, the United States should offer aid to developing countries.[6] For the most ardent devotees of this sort of reasoning, the "development process" becomes something like a rigged slot machine: if the economic aid token is inserted, it is only a matter of time before a whole host of congenial political results comes tumbling out.

For officials who did not share the Kennedy Administration's enthusiasm about the long-run political benefits of economic modernization, aid could still be useful as a means of political barter. Herbert Hoover, Jr., Undersecretary of State under John Foster Dulles, had no great faith in the political advantages of development, but he thought that aid for the Aswan project, enormously important to Nasser, could be traded for a signature on a peace agreement with Israel. Here again, the underlying premise was that Egypt's internal and external policies were intimately connected. Hoover assumed, like Kennedy, that Nasser's determination to modernize his economy was such that he would modify his other major ambitions in order to attract foreign assistance.

Shifts in American aid policy toward Egypt cannot, however, be explained solely in terms of an interest in influencing Egyptian behavior. Any assistance program requires an outlay of funds from Congress and is connected to domestic economic conditions. In the case of the Public Law 480, or Food for Peace, program in Egypt, one subsidiary goal of American policy was simply to dispose of unwanted surplus agricultural commodities. Hard currency grants and loans to Egypt had to be balanced against the needs of other countries important to the United States; one of the objectives of the Eisenhower Administration's cancellation of aid for the Aswan Dam was, for example, to preserve its aid program in Yugoslavia against threatened Congressional attacks. Aid to Egypt was particularly vulnerable to American domestic political infighting because of the size and influence of the pro-Israeli interest groups arrayed against it. None of the fluctuations in aid policy toward Egypt in the last thirty years can be understood without at least some reference to American domestic concerns.

Similarly, aid policy toward Egypt has always been shaped to some extent by foreign policy interests transcending bilateral relations with Egypt. Chief among these has been competition with the Soviet Union for the allegiance of Third World states. America's offer to help build the Aswan Dam was a symbol of its commitment to support developing countries; the withdrawal of that offer was intended to demonstrate that Third World leaders could not play off East against West and still reap the benefits of American largesse. U.S. allies also had a voice in aid policy toward Egypt. Their complaints that Nasser was being rewarded for behavior that ran against the interests of loyal American allies were often a key factor in the calculations of American policymakers.

One further distinction to be drawn when considering objectives is that between publicized and unpublicized goals.[7] At various times in the 1950s and 1960s, the American government—whether because of its own determination to clarify the issues for Nasser, domestic political concerns, perceived Cold War imperatives, or pressure from allies—made the aims of its aid policy public. At other times, U.S. goals received little publicity. It is worth remembering this distinction, since publicity or the lack of it has had a powerful effect on Egyptian reactions to American aid policy.

Application

How has aid been applied to promote American objectives? The alternatives available to the U.S. government have been fairly straightforward. Aid could be offered as an incentive to reinforce certain desirable behavior patterns on the part of the recipient country; or aid could be denied as a political sanction for behavior considered contrary to U.S. interests. A whole hierarchy of inducements existed, based upon the quantity, quality, and duration of the aid promised or provided. Similarly, there were various levels of sanctions: requests for increased aid or modification of the conditions attached to aid could be tabled or denied; the delivery of current aid could be partially or completely suspended; current aid levels could be reduced; or aid could be terminated completely.

In practice, the distinctions between inducements and sanctions were rarely as clear-cut as they might seem in theory. American tactics usually combined economic carrots and sticks in an effort to maximize political leverage in Egypt, within the limits imposed by domestic and international concerns. For example, at the same time the Johnson Administration suspended aid to Egypt at the beginning of 1965, it held out the promise of a new aid agreement if Egyptian behavior conformed to American expectations.

The task of applying aid to fit the jumble of American objectives has been a difficult one. When John Foster Dulles paused to consider cancelling the American offer of aid for the Aswan Dam in 1956, he realized that an abrupt and public withdrawal of assistance would probably have a negative effect on U.S.-Egyptian relations, at least in the short-run. But he also believed that outright cancellation of the Aswan offer would provide domestic political benefits, and he thought that rebuking Nasser would reassure anxious allies and provide an object lesson for other budding neutralists. As Dulles discovered in 1956, it was not easy to devise tactics satisfying simultaneously all of the aims of American aid policy.

Effects

What were the effects of aid policy? American policymakers have tended, naturally enough, to view the effects of aid policy through the prism of the objectives they were pursuing. When Egyptian conduct was the prime target, American officials measured "success" by the degree to which Egyptian behavior conformed to the pattern of behavior desired by the U.S. government. But this concept of "success" was an unwieldy proposition, since there was no reliable way to prove the connection between aid policy and Egyptian conduct. Economic aid was not the only instrument of American policy toward Egypt in the 1950s and 1960s. Despite inhibitions on their use, other policy tools—including actual or threatened military intervention, covert intervention, military aid, alliance building, and trade sanctions—lay at the disposal of the U.S. government, and their existence was certainly a factor in the Nasser regime's calculations. Moreover, Egyptian motives for conforming to patterns of behavior desired by the United States may have had little to do with American diplomacy. To cite one example, it is unclear whether Nasser's relatively passive international stance in late 1961–early 1962 had more to do with appeasing the United States, or with consolidating his grip on power in Egypt in the wake of the disintegration of the Syrian-Egyptian union.

The notion of "success" is further complicated by the heterogeneous nature of American goals. Cancellation of Aswan aid may have saved the assistance program in Yugoslavia, and thus been successful in light of domestic and broader international aims, but it had a decidedly adverse effect on relations with the Nasser regime. No single aid policy can be assessed in isolation from its myriad side effects, both long-run and short-run. President Johnson's suspension of assistance to Nasser in 1965 may have staved off a Congressional revolt and contributed to a temporary modification of Egyptian policies, but in the long-run it probably reinforced Nasser's suspicions about the United States and deepened his hostility toward the Johnson Administration. Determining whether aid policy was "successful" or "unsuccessful," in short, involves a long series of qualifications.

A Final Note

One last point: in the account that follows, it is easy to forget that the problem of influencing Third World leaders like Gamal Abdel Nasser was a new phenomenon for the United States in 1955. The American government had had little contact with the new breed of Third World leaders spawned by rapid decolonization, rising Afro-Asian political consciousness, and Cold War rivalry when it began to reconsider its policy toward Nasser's Egypt after the Czech arms agreement. Attempts to use economic aid as a political lever in Egypt in subsequent years were in many ways a learning process for Eisenhower and his successors; indeed, the Aswan affair was, in Hugh Thomas's words, "the first time that aid to underdeveloped countries had been openly used by the West as an instrument of policy." [8] Given the American government's unfamiliarity with both the targets and the tools of its policy in the Third World, it should not be surprising to learn that American officials held some rather unrealistic expectations about the efficacy of economic aid as a political lever. As a prominent former American diplomat later explained: "Some of our expectations about the political value of economic aid in Egypt seem incredible in retrospect. But you must remember that we were new to the game." [9]

CHAPTER ONE

Farewell to Arms:
The United States and Egypt's
Search for Military Aid, 1952–55

1955: Egypt buys Czech arms

Gamal Abdel Nasser's dramatic announcement of the Czech-Egyptian arms deal in September 1955 was in many ways a watershed in U.S.-Egyptian relations. In the first few years after the Egyptian revolution, many American policymakers had regarded Nasser as a potential ally; after the Czech arms agreement, he was regarded increasingly by the American government as a potential enemy. The Egyptian decision to purchase weaponry from the Soviet bloc, which was to have a profound effect not only on U.S.-Egyptian relations but on the entire course of the Cold War, was bound up with the Eisenhower Administration's ill-fated attempt to use the lure of American military aid to entice Egypt into the Western alliance system. The tangled story of the U.S.-Egyptian military aid negotiations in the early 1950s reveals a great deal about the difficulties involved in using aid as a political lever in Egypt and sets the stage for discussion of the Aswan Dam affair.

Revolutionary Egypt's Quest for Arms

The army is a basic factor in Egyptian life. Our revolution was stimulated in the army by a lack of equipment. If our officers feel we still have no equipment, they will lose faith in the government.

Nasser to Cyrus Sulzberger
August 1955[1]

The three hundred "Free Officers" who overthrew the Egyptian monarchy in July 1952 had no formal ideology and no civilian collaborators. Their common interest was to correct the conditions that had subjected them to the humiliation of many decades of British occupation and the 1948 defeat by Israel. Egypt had been an obvious target for foreign influence, they reasoned, because of its strategic position, but it had been peculiarly vulnerable because its people were downtrodden and its government impotent and corrupt. In their eyes, it was not enough to throw out Farouk and the British; the army must stay in power until the Egyptians became strong enough to rule themselves and keep potential intruders out.[2]

The dozen officers who sat on Egypt's Revolutionary Command Council (RCC) in the early 1950s had two broad foreign policy objectives. The first was to end the British occupation of the Suez Canal Zone and to strengthen the foundations of Egyptian independence against the threat of foreign domination. The second was to find the capital resources necessary for economic progress. No Egyptian government at midcentury could afford to ignore internal pressures to work for both of those aims, by one means or another.[3]

Both aims implied, as a natural corollary, a policy of nonalignment toward the great powers, in order to enhance the likelihood of obtaining support from one against dangers posed by the other. The basic Egyptian commitment to some form of nonalignment in the Cold War was clearly not a special product of revolutionary ideology. The prerevolutionary Egyptian government had asserted its neutralism in 1950 by refusing to side with the West in the United Nations Security Council vote on Korea, and in 1951 by repudiating the 1936 Anglo-Egyptian Treaty and by rejecting Western proposals for a Middle East Defense Organization. The policy of nonalignment did not prevent the Egyptian government from leaning to one side or the other for tactical reasons during the 1950s; indeed, the RCC gave every sign in 1952–54 of wanting a loose association with the Western alliance system, provided that the British withdrew from the Suez Canal Zone. But the policy of nonalignment did effectively preclude any formal alliance with either the West or the Soviet bloc.

A second corollary of the Egyptian government's broad foreign policy objectives was that Egypt should cultivate its influence, and work to restrict that of others, in the geographical areas surrounding it.[4] As Mohamed Heikal later observed, Egyptian activism in the Arab world, and more generally in the emerging Afro-Asian world, was "one of the country's best investments."[5] By making itself a force to be reckoned with in regional affairs, Egypt could turn its strategic location from a liability into an asset, and could attract attention and aid from the great powers.

Born of a common language, a common religion, and a shared sense of colonial injustice, Egypt's interest in involving itself in Arab affairs was given focus by the tactical desirability of controlling an independent Arab foreign policy. Like their predecessors, the Free Officers saw Egyptian hegemony in the Arab world as a means of preserving Egypt's freedom of action from great power encroachment. Control over the external policies of the Arab states offered Egypt access to the growing wealth of the Persian Gulf, helped buttress Egypt's national independence, and served as a magnet for great power financial assistance. Stripped of its influence in the Arab world, Egypt lay exposed to foreign domination. For the Revolutionary Command Council, an activist foreign policy in the Arab world, and throughout the Afro-Asian world, became one of the keys to the consolidation of Egyptian independence and to the promotion of Egyptian economic development.[6]

The revolutionary regime's quest for modern weaponry grew partly out of a perceived need to give credibility to an activist Egyptian foreign policy. Without a well-equipped army and air force, it was unlikely that Egypt would ever wield much influence in regional affairs. Moreover, the creation of a modern military force was an important symbol of independence and sovereignty in Egypt, contributing to the development of a sense of national identity as well as reinforcing the authority and legitimacy of the ruling elite.[7] Of perhaps even more fundamental importance in the RCC's thinking was the fact that the Egyptian officer corps, the only real power base that the regime had, demanded rapid acquisition of advanced military equipment. Having failed to broaden the political base of the regime, largely because there was not yet a middle class or a peasantry or an industrial proletariat aware of its group interests, the RCC was compelled to pay close attention to the needs of the military.[8] And what the professional officer corps wanted above all, in the aftermath of Egypt's disastrous performance in the 1948 Palestine War, was modern military equipment.

The RCC's interest in obtaining military aid—Egypt was not capable of producing advanced weaponry itself, nor could it afford to make large-scale commercial purchases from Western suppliers—was deeply rooted in the political needs and ambitions of the regime. Modernization of the Egyptian military was believed to be absolutely vital to the survival of the RCC and to the success of the revolution. On 7 August 1952, barely two weeks after the overthrow of King Farouk, Major General Mohamed Naguib, the titular head of the RCC, announced: "We must obtain modern weapons of war somewhere. I cannot say who will supply us if America and the Western democracies refuse their aid." [9]

The American Response to the Egyptian Revolution

The overthrow of the feeble Farouk regime was greeted with barely concealed relief in Washington.[10] In the early 1950s, the Truman and Eisenhower Administrations, mindful of the growing importance of Middle East oil for the Western world, were transfixed by fear of Soviet expansionism in the region.[11] "It's hard to put ourselves back in this period," recalled Raymond Hare, a Foreign Service officer who became U.S. ambassador to Egypt in 1956. "There was really a definite fear of hostilities, of an active Russian occupation of the Middle East physically, and you could practically hear the Russian boots clumping down over hot desert sands." [12] As a bulwark against this perceived Soviet threat, the United States needed a strong, stable, sympathetic Egyptian government; the prerevolutionary Egyptian regime had been neither strong, nor stable, nor particularly sympathetic to Western interests. The Free Officers, on the other hand, immediately impressed the Truman Administration with their determination to stamp out the feudal excesses of the Farouk era, with their apparently genuine interest in improving the lot of the Egyptian *fellahin,* and with their decidedly moderate approach to foreign affairs. The American ambassador, Jefferson Caffery, quickly established close relations with General Naguib and with the small group of junior officers—led by Lieutenant Colonel Gamal Abdel Nasser—who wielded real power in Naguib's shadow.[13] In early August 1952, Caffery reported optimistically to Washington that "the new Egyptian regime's pro-Western potentialities . . . are emerging more clearly in each day's developments."[14]

By the winter of 1952–53, enthusiasm had begun to build within the Washington foreign affairs bureaucracy for a concerted effort to court the Free Officers' regime. The State Department's Arabists had become increasingly concerned during the late 1940s and early 1950s about the erosion of American prestige in the Arab world that had been caused by American involvement in the creation of the state of Israel.[15] As one veteran Foreign Service officer later put it: "The area experts to a man were scandalized by what happened in 1948. We had made a tremendous effort to lay the ground for good relations with the Arabs and all of a sudden, when we were in a good position, all of our hopes were dashed."[16] To the Middle East specialists in the State Department, a strong U.S. relationship with the new Egyptian government seemed to offer a means of reviving American influence in the Arab world. Similarly, the Defense Department—alarmed by the increasing strategic vulnerability of the Western position in the Middle East—was a forceful advocate of closer U.S.-Egyptian ties.[17]

The Central Intelligence Agency established itself as the patron of the Free Officers in Washington shortly after the revolution.[18] In January 1953, Kermit ("Kim") Roosevelt, the director of CIA covert operations in the Middle East, flew to Cairo and met with Nasser and his colleagues on the Revolutionary Command Council. Throughout 1953 and 1954, Roosevelt and the members of the permanent CIA station in Cairo kept in close contact with the leaders of the new regime. During the early years of the "double-Dulles era"—so called because of the intimate working relationship between John Foster Dulles, the Secretary of State, and his brother Allen, the Director of Central Intelligence—the CIA "launched an enormous operation in Egypt, perhaps the largest of its kind since the inception of the agency."[19] Although the CIA's influence in Egypt in this period has been greatly exaggerated, the net effect of the CIA's special relationship with the new Egyptian government was to feed American hopes that a de facto U.S.-Egyptian alliance was a practical possibility.[20]

The Lure of Military Aid and the Suez Base Negotiations

Given the sympathetic American view of the Egyptian revolution and the subsequent growth of American interest in a close relationship with the revolutionary regime, it is not surprising that the initial American response to Egyptian requests for military aid was generally favorable.[21] There was, to be sure, some skepticism within the U.S. Embassy in Cairo about the extravagance of the RCC's military shopping list.[22] Colonel Joseph Greco, the Air Force attaché, argued in a memorandum for Ambassador Caffery that the Egyptian request for immediate delivery of a squadron of advanced U.S. jet fighters was "ridiculous", adding that "a jet squadron is not handed over to a rather green outfit as though it were a fleet of automobiles."[23] But Caffery and his superiors in the State Department agreed on the importance of providing a modest quantity of military equipment—to include tank parts, armored cars, ammunition, and radio sets—as an immediate sign of American good faith.[24] Kim Roosevelt echoed Caffery's arguments.[25] On 3 September 1952, President Truman made a public statement which expressed broad support for the new Egyptian government and hinted at American readiness to provide military aid to the Free Officers.[26] In November 1952, Deputy Secretary of Defense William C. Foster visited Cairo and apparently assured Naguib and Nasser that U.S. arms aid would be forthcoming. On his own initiative, Foster invited an Egyptian mission to come to Washington to discuss the details of a U.S. military assistance program.[27]

There was, however, one very large stumbling block in the path of U.S.-Egyptian talks—the impasse in Anglo-Egyptian negotiations over the future of Britain's sprawling military base at Suez.[28] Until Britain evacuated the Suez Base, the Egyptian government was unwilling to make anything more than very vague pledges about future Egyptian association with an anti-Communist Middle East defense system. Without definite Egyptian assurances about participation in Western regional defense schemes, the American government was uneager to provide substantial military aid to the RCC. Moreover, the British government lobbied tirelessly and effectively in Washington to block American arms aid to Egypt while the Suez Base issue was unresolved—and while the provision of weapons to the revolutionary regime posed a threat to British troops in the Canal Zone.[29]

The delicate American position in the Anglo-Egyptian dispute over the Suez Base held out both opportunities and dangers for the U.S. government. Successful mediation of the conflict might stabilize the whole Western defense structure in the Middle East. On the other hand, the United States ran the risk of alienating both Britain and Egypt. The Conservative government that came to power in Britain in October 1951 made no secret of its resentment of America's efforts to distance itself from identification with British policy in the Middle East.[30] At the same time, the revolutionary Egyptian regime was disturbed by the American government's reluctance to condemn publicly British efforts to retain control of the Suez Base. In November 1952, Nasser bluntly told William Lakeland, one of Caffery's political officers, that "the British are losing this country and you with them because you are tied to their policy."[31]

Under these circumstances, the U.S. government eventually decided to postpone military aid to Egypt until after the Suez issue had been settled. While American mediators encouraged the British government to consent to evacuation of the Suez Base, the State Department used the promise of military aid as bait to entice the RCC into agreeing to the return of British forces to Suez in time of crisis or war. The American policy of dangling the carrot of military aid out in front of Egypt proved enormously frustrating for the Free Officers. When an Egyptian delegation led by Wing Commander Ali Sabri flew to Washington in December 1952 as Deputy Secretary of Defense Foster had suggested, it discovered that neither the lame duck Truman White House nor the newly elected Eisenhower Administration was prepared to make any firm commitments about military assistance to Egypt. Exasperated by American prevarication, Sabri returned to Cairo in January 1953.[32] Both Sabri and the Egyptian military attaché in Washington, Brigadier General Abdel Hamid Ghaleb, deeply resented U.S. foot dragging; Ghaleb later complained to Miles Copeland, a CIA operative in Cairo, that "we were treated like children." [33]

Nasser told William Lakeland privately during this period that he was "beginning to despair of tangible assistance from the West," and reiterated his plea for military aid to ensure the "continued loyalty of the Armed Forces officers." [34] In a series of cables during the winter and spring of 1953, Ambassador Caffery warned the State Department that General Naguib, whom he considered "more cautious and pro-Western" than the younger officers on the RCC, was losing influence rapidly, and that further delays in furnishing military aid to Egypt would destroy Naguib's position.[35] Meanwhile, the Suez talks remained stalemated, as domestic pressures in both Egypt and Britain impeded compromise. Disturbed by Caffery's reports, and more generally by the lack of progress on the Suez negotiations, Secretary of State Dulles decided to travel to the Middle East to take a first hand look at the situation.

Dulles arrived in Cairo on 8 May 1953, "with the hope and expectation that quite a lot could be built around the foundation of Egypt. . . ." [36] Dulles assured Naguib and Nasser that the United States would intensify its efforts to win British concessions in the Suez Base talks, and promised "substantial" U.S. military aid to Egypt as soon as a Suez agreement was reached.[37] Dulles realized after his talks with Egyptian leaders that the Egyptian government was not prepared to associate itself formally with Western defense plans in the Middle East. Determined to "avoid becoming fascinated with concepts that have no reality," Dulles shelved his ideas about building an anti-Communist defense organization around Egypt and concentrated his energies upon formation of a defense pact among the states of the region's "Northern Tier." The American Secretary of State remained hopeful that Egypt might develop an interest in becoming involved in the Western defense system once a Suez treaty was signed.[38]

In the spring of 1954, after another year of stalemate in the Suez talks, Nasser effectively stripped Naguib of his influence on the RCC. Both the CIA and the State Department moved quickly to solidify their relationships with the new Egyptian leader. "Nasser," wrote Ambassador Caffery on 31 March 1954, "is the only man in Egypt with strength enough and guts enough to put over an agreement with Britain." [39]

Despite continued opposition from extremist groups, Nasser finally agreed to a compromise which the British, under considerable pressure from the Eisenhower Administration, were willing to accept.[40] On 27 July 1954, British and Egyptian representatives initialled a treaty which provided for phased British withdrawal from the Canal Base, but which permitted British reoccupation of the base in the event of a Soviet attack on Turkey or any of the Arab states.

With the conclusion of the Suez Agreement, the American government unveiled its long-awaited program of aid to Egypt. On the afternoon of 27 July 1954, shortly after the Anglo-Egyptian accord had been signed in Cairo, Foster Dulles telephoned Harold Stassen, Director of the Mutual Security Agency, and asked him to assemble a package of military and economic aid for Egypt. Dulles told Stassen: "The President thinks it would be nice to be able to follow up right away. It does not have to be big. Things are beginning to break." [41] On 2 August, Ambassador Caffery presented Egyptian Foreign Minister Mahmoud Fawzi with draft proposals for $20 million in military aid and an equal amount in economic assistance.[42]

The Wrangle Over MAAG

Discussion of the American draft proposals quickly bogged down. No sooner had the Suez dispute been resolved than two equally formidable obstacles to the provision of U.S. military aid to Egypt emerged. The first of these barriers was Egyptian resistance to the stringent conditions which Congress had attached to American military assistance.[43] The Mutual Security Act of 1954, under which military aid was administered, required recipient governments to make binding commitments that American weapons would be used only for legitimate defense and for internal security (that is, not for an attack upon neighboring countries). This same condition was imposed under the terms of the 1950 Tripartite Declaration.[44] In addition, Congress required that U.S. arms assistance be accompanied by a Military Assistance Advisory Group (MAAG) that could, to some extent, supervise the proper use of American weapons and ensure that recipients kept their promises.

The Egyptian government refused to accept the MAAG. Having endured a storm of domestic criticism over the concessions made to secure British withdrawal from the Suez Base, Nasser was not prepared to acquiesce to even the most modest sort of formal foreign military presence in Egypt. In an interview published in an American periodical in August 1954, Nasser appealed to the Eisenhower Administration to understand his predicament.

> Because of our history we have complexes in this country about some words—especially those that imply that we are being tied to another country. Words like "joint command" "joint pact," and "training missions" are not beloved in our country because we have suffered from them. . . . I think your men who deal with this area should understand the psychology of the area. You send military aid, but if you send ten officers along with it, nobody will thank you for your aid but instead will turn it against you.[45]

Weighed down by disagreements over the MAAG, U.S.-Egyptian arms talks ground to a halt at the end of August 1954. On 28 August, Foreign Minister Fawzi informed Ambassador Caffery that "after careful consideration the Egyptian government has decided not to ask military aid from the United States at this time." Fawzi emphasized that the Egyptian government's decision was "based solely on internal political conditions."[46] On 31 August, Egypt's ambassador in Washington, Ahmed Hussein, told William C. Burdett, the chief of the State Department's Office of Near East Affairs, that "Nasser has informed [me] that the RCC is in the midst of an intense bitter fight with the Moslem Brotherhood, aided by the Communists and the Wafd. Nasser feels that this is a crucial battle for the RCC. He believes that it is impossible for the RCC to give the opposition another point on which to attack it, such as would be provided by the type of military aid agreement required by Mutual Security Act legislation."[47] At Caffery's urging, the Eisenhower Administration agreed to try to temporarily defuse Egyptian resentment of U.S. military aid policy by increasing American economic assistance, thus freeing funds in Cairo for commercial military purchases.[48]

The CIA sponsored an "informal approach" to Nasser in November 1954, in hopes that some sort of compromise over the MAAG issue could be worked out. Two American Army officers, Colonel H. Alan Gerhardt and Major Wilbur Eveland, accompanied by Miles Copeland, met secretly with Nasser and a few of his colleagues in the Cairo suburb of Maadi. Unfortunately, it quickly became clear to the Pentagon negotiators that the Egyptians were still unwilling either to subscribe to Western regional defense plans or to accept a modified version of the MAAG.[49] The RCC was still extremely sensitive to domestic pressures; indeed, Nasser himself had narrowly escaped assassination in Alexandria on the night of 26 October 1954, when a nervous Moslem Brotherhood gunman had fired several shots at the lightbulbs above the platform on which the Egyptian Prime Minister was speaking.[50]

The Lure of Military Aid and an Egyptian-Israeli Peace Settlement

Had the Eisenhower Administration been eager to reward Egypt for the Suez Agreement, it is at least conceivable that a mutually acceptable formula for military assistance could have been devised after the Nasser regime consolidated its domestic position in the winter of 1954–55. But by the end of 1954 Foster Dulles had decided that aid used as leverage to gain an Anglo-Egyptian agreement on Suez could be used to entice Egypt into a settlement of its differences with Israel.[51] Lack of progress toward such a settlement thus became a second obstacle in the path of U.S. military aid to Egypt.

Dulles feared that the provision of arms to Egypt would trigger renewed Israeli requests for U.S. military assistance— requests which the Eisenhower Administration, under pressure from the American Jewish community, would find it difficult to refuse. Dulles did not want to ignite an arms race in the Middle East, particularly at a time when the removal of the British buffer along the Suez Canal had heightened tensions along the Israeli-Egyptian frontier. Any increase in the level of Arab-Israeli friction, Dulles realized, would create further opportunities for Soviet meddling in the region, and would greatly complicate the already vexing problem of regional defense.

The Israel Lobby and the Eisenhower Administration

The Eisenhower Administration's interest in deferring military aid to Egypt until after some progress toward an Arab-Israeli settlement had been made was reinforced by widespread domestic hostility to the idea of providing arms to Egypt which might someday be used against Israel. Although the Israel lobby was not nearly the political force in Washington in the 1950s that it was to become in the 1960s and 1970s, Israel's backers in the United States made their presence felt during the Eisenhower era, particularly when the issue of aid to Arab governments surfaced. Sherman Adams, Eisenhower's White House chief of staff, later noted that "any attempt to give aid to the Arabs always met with opposition behind the scenes in Washington, where the members of Congress were acutely aware of the strong popular sentiment in this country for Israel. . . . Consideration for the great body of private opinion in the United States favoring Israel was a large factor in every governmental decision on Middle East issues." [52] Given the importance of pro-Israeli sentiment in the American policy-making process, particularly in the process through which military aid policy toward Egypt was made, it might be useful at this juncture to digress briefly in order to provide a thumbnail sketch of the Israel lobby. [53]

The political influence of the Israel lobby derived from three factors: the internal cohesion of the lobby itself; broad public sympathy for Israel in the United States; and the success of the lobby in gaining access to Washington decision makers. [54] In the 1950s, about 45 percent of the world's Jewish community lived in the United States. [55] During the struggle to establish the state of Israel, a strong Zionist consensus had developed amongst American Jews, which was gradually translated into effective political leverage by the Israel lobby's two umbrella organizations, the Conference of Presidents of Major American Jewish Organizations, and the America Israel Public Affairs Committee (or AIPAC, known throughout most of the 1950s as the America Zionist Public Affairs Committee). Under the brilliant leadership of Isaiah ("Si") Kenen, AIPAC quickly became the organizational spearhead of the Israel lobby in Washington. Although the interest of American Jews diverged on a number of other issues, Kenen and his colleagues helped shape the American Jewish community into an extraordinarily cohesive, articulate force on issues affecting Israel. "Without this lobby," Kenen said later, "Israel would have gone down the drain." [56]

Without widespread public sympathy for Israel in the United States, it is unlikely that the Israel lobby would ever have developed into a potent political entity. Support for Israel in the years after the 1948 war can be traced to a number of sources, including memories of the Holocaust, association of Jews with the Bible, the natural affinity of two democratic regimes, and respect for Israel's pioneering spirit and strength. [57] By contrast, the American public evinced little interest in or sympathy for the Arab world in the 1950s. When Eisenhower came into office, "few Americans could have told the difference between the Arab League and the Arab Legion, or whether Iraq was a misprint for Iran or what." [58] Clearly, the limited success that the Israel lobby had in influencing U.S. policy in the Middle East in the 1950s, and the far greater success that it had in the 1960s, were made possible by the compatibility of its goals with the friendly predispositions of the American public. [59]

The internal cohesion of the Israel lobby and the high degree of sympathy for its aims in the United States helped explain the lobby's remarkable ability to gain access to key Washington decision makers. The relatively small size of the Jewish community in the United States—in the 1950s the five million American Jews comprised about 3.5 percent of the American population—belied the political clout that the Israel lobby possessed. The American Jewish population was heavily concentrated in electorally important urban areas in the East and Midwest; in 1955, for example, 26.4 percent of the population of New York City was Jewish. [60] Given the potential electoral power of Jewish voters themselves, and pervasive pro-Israel sentiment amongst non-Jewish voters, no candidate for national office, and few candidates for state office, could afford to entirely ignore the Israel lobby.

Nevertheless, the Eisenhower Administration greeted most of the Israel lobby's requests in the 1950s "with a long, dark silence." [61] Eisenhower had won only 36 percent of the Jewish vote in 1952;[62] he did not spend many sleepless nights during his first term worrying about "losing" the Jewish vote in 1956 since he had never really possessed it. More importantly, Eisenhower was determined to resist the Zionist pressures that he believed Truman had exploited solely for domestic political gain.[63] Eisenhower told a group of American Jewish leaders privately in 1954: "I don't know what I would have done had I been President when the question of Israel's independence came up." [64] Eisenhower added, however, "Israel is now a sovereign nation to which we do have obligations. We shall keep them." [65] Although Eisenhower and Dulles—who shared the President's suspicion of the Zionist lobby—committed themselves to preservation of Israel, they were adamantly opposed to the Truman Administration's close identification of U.S. interests in the Middle East with Israel.[66] Max Rabb, Secretary to Eisenhower's Cabinet, and Sherman Adams maintained links to the American Jewish community during the 1950s, but the Israel lobby had much less influence in the White House in the Eisenhower era than it had enjoyed during the Truman years.[67]

Frustrated by the Eisenhower Administration's unsympathetic attitude, the Israel lobby found fertile soil for its views on Capitol Hill. Like a good number of their constituents, many Senators and Representatives were inclined to favor Israel in the Arab-Israeli conflict; when this generally sympathetic outlook was combined with the Israel lobby's ability to raise campaign contributions, define issues, and mobilize public opinion, a strong pro-Israel consensus began to develop in Congress.[68] No effective counterbalance to the Israel lobby emerged in the corridors of Congress during the 1950s and 1960s. The Arab embassies in Washington did not, by and large, make much of an effort to sell their case to the American public or its representatives in Congress; "Congressional relations" in most Arab embassies consisted almost entirely of "giving large parties where a sprinkling of Senators and Congressmen enjoyed the wine, the lamb, and the stuffed grape leaves before heading home." [69] The oil lobby, whose interests coincided in many respects with those of the Arabs, followed a very low-key strategy in Congress after the overthrow of Mossadeq in Iran, and was in any case rarely willing to sacrifice its political capital on Capitol Hill to campaign actively for aid to Egypt, which was not an oil exporter. The Israel lobby was thus well situated for an attack on any proposal that the Eisenhower Administration made in Congress for aid to Egypt, especially after Republican setbacks in the 1954 midterm elections, which were widely interpreted in Washington as an indictment of Dulles's "even-handed" policies in the Middle East.[70] In the fall of 1954, Eisenhower and Dulles were well aware of the fact that any attempt to provide military assistance to Egypt would drag the Administration into an extremely difficult, costly battle in Congress.

The Alpha Project

Disturbed by the probable foreign and domestic repercussions of arming Egypt in the absence of any progress toward an Arab-Israeli settlement, Dulles finally decided in late December 1954 to postpone indefinitely military aid to Egypt.[71] In the meantime, Dulles set out to exploit both the relatively amicable atmosphere of U.S.-Egyptian relations after the Suez Agreement and the Nasser regime's eagerness to secure American military assistance as means of extracting Egyptian concessions in the Arab-Israeli dispute. Dulles's hopes for obtaining such concessions were bolstered by persistent Egyptian hints during 1953–54 that the revolutionary regime was prepared to accept Israel's right to exist in return for a Negev corridor arrangement linking Egypt to the eastern Arab states and compensation for displaced Palestinians.[72] The Israeli government of Moshe Sharett, for its part, had indicated privately during the same period that it was prepared to consider some minor modifications of the 1949 armistice lines and to accept limited responsibility for compensating the Palestinian refugees, if Nasser publicly declared that Egypt had no aggressive intentions toward Israel, and if the Western powers formally guaranteed Israel's frontiers. The Israelis added a note of urgency, however; if the United States did not capitalize upon the "honeymoon period" in U.S.-Egyptian relations that followed completion of

the Suez Agreement, it was unlikely that Nasser would ever
be persuaded to take positive steps toward a resolution of
Egypt's differences with Israel.[73]

Filled with high hopes of inducing the Egyptians to "make
practical arrangements to improve relations with Israel," [74] Dulles
established a special unit in the State Department, code-named
the "Alpha Group," in October 1954 to coordinate overtures
to the Egyptian and Israeli governments. Dulles appointed
Francis H. Russell, a career Foreign Service officer, to direct the
top-secret operation. In the early stages of the Alpha Project,
Russell worked closely with Evelyn Shuckburgh, a Middle East
specialist in the British Foreign Office. By the beginning of
1955, Russell and Shuckburgh had devised a very general
framework for an Arab-Israeli settlement based upon the sug-
gestions made by the Egyptian and Israeli governments in
1953–54.[75]

The Turning Points: The Baghdad Pact, Gaza, and Bandung

As the American Embassy in Cairo had expected, Nasser
deeply resented the linking of U.S. military aid to the Alpha
Project. Nasser and his colleagues on the RCC had, as a result
of their discussions with Deputy Secretary of Defense Foster
in 1952, Secretary of State Dulles in 1953, and CIA operatives
throughout 1952–54, anticipated something on the order of
$100 million worth of American arms aid after conclusion of
the Suez Agreement. Although it is not clear whether or not
representatives of the American government actually promised
aid of this magnitude to the Egyptians in private conversations,
it is quite clear that the Egyptian government was disappointed
by the U.S. offer of $20 million in military assistance presented
in August 1954.[76] When the Eisenhower Administration tied
even this relatively modest aid offer to progress toward an
Egyptian-Israeli peace accord, the Nasser regime began to question the feasibility of obtaining military aid from the United
States. During the first few months of 1955, three very important
events occurred which deepened Egyptian doubts about the
desirability of relying on the United States as an arms supplier,

and which added a new sense of urgency to Egypt's search for military aid.

The first of these events was the formation of the Baghdad Pact. After his trip to the Middle East in May 1953, Foster Dulles had expressed general interest in the idea of building an anti-Communist defense alliance among the states of the region's "Northern Tier." The British government encouraged Iraqi Prime Minister Nuri Said to seek to associate Iraq with such a grouping, largely as a means of strengthening the British position in Iraq.[77] Dulles instructed the U.S. ambassador in Baghdad to back British efforts to woo the Iraqis, and thus it came as no surprise to the State Department when the governments of Iraq and Turkey announced on 12 January 1955 that they intended to conclude a mutual defense pact.[78] The treaty was formally signed in Baghdad on 24 February 1955, and on 4 April the British government officially joined the Iraqi-Turkish alliance. In a thinly disguised attempt to sidestep Egyptian criticism, the American government informed the British in early April 1955 that it would postpone its entry into the Baghdad Pact.

Nasser was violently displeased by the Baghdad Pact. Nothing seemed more remote to the Egyptian government in early 1955 than the threat of Soviet invasion, and nothing seemed more menacing to the architects of the Egyptian revolution than a direct challenge, supported by the West, to Egyptian hegemony in the Arab world. The Free Officers believed firmly that Egypt's international bargaining position depended upon their ability to keep the other Arab states in line. Throughout 1953 and 1954, the Nasser regime had sought to convince the United States and Britain that informal cooperation with an Arab League collective security organization dominated by Egypt was the only practicable way to protect Western interests in the Arab world, and had sought to use Cairo's control of an independent Arab foreign policy as a lever to obtain military aid from the West. When Nuri upset the RCC's strategy by breaking ranks and striking a separate bargain with the West, Nasser complained that both the West and the Iraqis had "violated a gentleman's agreement that Egypt would be permitted to take the lead in constructing a purely Arab defense alliance free from formal links with outside powers."[79] The Egyptian government was profoundly concerned about the pos-

sibility that the other Arab states—beginning with Jordan and
Lebanon—would follow Iraq into the Western alliance system,
leaving Egypt isolated and impotent. Moreover, Iraq's defection
came at a time when the RCC, having only just muffled the
attacks of the Moslem Brotherhood and the other domestic
critics of the regime, could ill afford any damage to its prestige.

Nasser held the Eisenhower Administration responsible for
the Baghdad Pact, since he did not believe that the British
could have engineered Iraq's entry into the Western defense
system without American support. When seen in juxtaposition
to the U.S. government's restrictive military aid policy, formation
of the Pact appeared to Nasser to be part of a general Western
effort to keep Egypt weak and isolated.[80]

The Israeli raid on Gaza in late February 1955 posed a far
more immediate threat to Egyptian security than did the creation
of the Baghdad Pact.[81] The Israeli government had complained
bitterly throughout 1954 about terrorist attacks on Israeli border
settlements from the Egyptian-controlled Gaza Strip by the
Moslem Brotherhood and the followers of the exiled Grand
Mufti of Jerusalem. Despite the Nasser regime's efforts to clamp
down on the Moslem Brothers and the Mufti's men, the attacks
had continued, resulting in fifty Israeli civilian deaths during
1954.[82] The Gaza-based *fedayeen* raids added to Israel's mounting sense of insecurity. The Eisenhower Administration's outspoken "even-handedness" in the Middle East and its efforts
to build a close relationship with Egypt proved deeply unsettling
in Israel. As Abba Eban, then the Israeli ambassador in Washington, put it: "Eisenhower's policies had given the Israeli public
the impression that American friendship for Israel had been a
fleeting and accidental circumstance of history, linked organi-
cally with the Truman Administration." [83] Out of this sense of
uncertainty and isolation, there had arisen growing support
within the Israeli government for the policy of militant self-
reliance advocated by former Prime Minister David Ben Gurion
and Defense Minister Pinhas Lavon.[84] When Lavon was forced
to resign from the Cabinet in mid-February 1955 because of
his involvement in a botched plot to sour Egyptian relations
with the United States and Britain by sabotaging American and
British-owned businesses in Cairo and Alexandria, Ben Gurion
returned to the government to replace him.[85]

Within a week after his return, Ben Gurion authorized a large-scale reprisal raid on Gaza. On the evening of 28 February 1955, two Israeli paratrooper platoons stormed an Egyptian army encampment in Gaza, killing thirty-seven Egyptian soldiers. Although the Israelis claimed that they had attacked the Gaza outpost only after Egyptian forces had ambushed an Israeli patrol inside Israeli territory, United Nations adjudicators branded Israel the aggressor in the Gaza incident. For Ben Gurion and his supporters, the Gaza raid served as an opportunity not only to exact revenge for *fedayeen* attacks, but also to expose the military weakness of the Arabs, and to forestall any attempt by the United States to impose a compromise peace settlement on Israel.[86]

Anwar Sadat later wrote that the Gaza raid "marked a turning point in the history of Egypt, the Revolution, and the Middle East. . . ."[87] Sadat's claim is not as much of an overstatement as it might seem at first glance. For a regime that had come to power partly in response to the revelation of Egypt's unpreparedness in the 1948 war with Israel, the knowledge that Egypt was still quite inadequately equipped to deal with any aggressive moves that Israel might make was a source of grave concern.[88] After Gaza, Nasser was under intense pressure from his chief domestic constituency, the Egyptian officer corps, to secure modern weaponry for the Egyptian military. The Gaza raid aggravated Egyptian resentment of U.S. military aid policy, and—as a contemporary State Department study put it—"catalyzed a certain amount of unrest among many Egyptian army officers with the result that the regime seems inclined to assume a position more independent of the West."[89]

Egypt's disenchantment with the West after the formation of the Baghdad Pact and the Gaza raid was given focus by Nasser's experience at the Bandung Conference of Non-Aligned Peoples in the spring of 1955. Nasser had been powerfully impressed when Yugoslav President Tito and Indian Prime Minister Nehru, the leading lights of the nonaligned movement, had visited Cairo separately in February 1955 to express their support for Nasser's struggle against the Baghdad Pact. The moral backing of these elder statesmen strengthened the Nasser regime politically, and stimulated renewed Egyptian interest in nonalignment—or neutralism (the two terms were used interchangeably in this period)—as an approach to foreign policy. Neutralism, which had as its lowest common denominator the refusal to join in formal alliances with the Great Powers, seemed to an increasing number of Egyptian officials to provide an ideal means of counteracting Western pressure without sacrificing Egyptian and Arab independence.[90]

Intrigued by the potential value of neutralism, but somewhat hesitant in view of Egypt's still insecure position in the Arab world and his own lack of experience in international affairs (his only previous venture outside Egypt had been his attendance at the August 1954 Islamic Conference in Saudi Arabia), Nasser decided to join the leaders of twenty-seven other Afro-Asian states at the Bandung Conference in April 1955.[91] Nasser's "diplomatic reconnaissance" was a spectacular success. As Tom Little, the director of the Arab News Agency, wrote at the time, Nasser "came to Bandung known only by name by the great majority of delegates and left as an accepted leader in Afro-Asian affairs." [92] Nehru, Sukarno, and Chou En-lai publicly recognized Nasser as the spokesman for Arab nationalism, and endorsed Egyptian positions on French colonialism in North Africa and on the Palestine problem. Nasser soon discovered that the support of the emerging Afro-Asian bloc greatly enhanced Egypt's bargaining position in the eyes of the Great Powers; at the same time, he discovered that neutralism had enormous popularity in Egypt and throughout the Arab world. The whole Bandung experience was, Nasser said later, "a turning point in my political understanding. I learned and realized that the only wise policy for us would be [one] of positive neutralism and nonalignment." [93]

The creation of the Baghdad Pact, the Gaza Raid, and the Bandung conference—all occurring within a span of four months in early 1955—had a tremendous cumulative impact upon Egypt's interest in obtaining military equipment, and more generally upon the direction of Egyptian foreign policy. To compete with the Iraqis for leadership in the Arab world, to deter Israeli attacks, and to give credibility to its newfound eminence in the Third World, the Revolutionary Command Council believed that it desperately needed modern weaponry. Western policy in the Middle East, of which U.S. military aid policy was seen to be symptomatic, seemed designed to isolate and weaken Egypt. Neutralism offered the Egyptians a way out of their isolation and weakness—a way to turn the tables on the West and use Cold War rivalry to advance Egyptian interests and enhance Egyptian prestige.

A Marriage of Convenience: Egypt, the Soviet Union, and Military Aid

The dramatic improvements in Soviet-Egyptian relations in the mid-1950s were, as a CIA Special Report later concluded, "the result of a temporary congruence of interest between the two countries." [94] Until the death of Stalin, the Soviet leadership had taken a rather dim view of "bourgeois nationalist" leaders like Nasser and had dismissed the Free Officers as a group of reactionaries who were under the thumb of the Western powers. After Stalin's demise in March 1953, however, a faction within the Kremlin led by the new First Secretary of the Soviet Communist Party, Nikita Khrushchev, began to campaign for a more conciliatory policy toward selected developing countries, both as a means of denying political influence to the West and as a means of laying the foundation for future ideological gains. Despite opposition from more orthodox Politburo members like Foreign Minister V. M. Molotov, Khrushchev and his supporters gradually transformed Soviet policy in the Third World in 1954–55. [95]

Like the Nasser regime, the Soviet government was deeply disturbed by the formation of the Baghdad Pact. Anchored to NATO in the West and SEATO in the East, the Baghdad Pact completed the Western Powers' encirclement of the Soviet bloc. Had they been able to use forward bases along the Northern Tier of the Middle East just outside the flying range of Soviet fighters and light tactical bombers, U.S. strategic bombers could have posed a serious threat to Soviet security in the pre-ICBM age. When Nasser condemned the Baghdad Pact, it was not surprising that Khrushchev actively began to explore means of cooperating with Egypt to undermine Western defense plans in the region.

The Egyptian government's need to obtain arms provided the lever that Khrushchev was looking for. Enroute to Bandung

in the spring of 1955, Nasser met Chinese Premier Chou En-
lai at Rangoon and confided that he doubted that he would
ever receive modern weaponry from the West. Chou suggested
that the Egyptian leader seek arms aid from the Soviet Union.
On 18 May 1955, after his return from the non-aligned conference, Nasser asked the Soviet ambassador in Cairo, Daniel
Solod, about the possibility of obtaining arms from the U.S.S.R.
Three days later, having been forewarned of Nasser's interest
by the Chinese, the Soviet government conveyed its willingness
to supply Egypt with military equipment in exchange for cotton,
"with no strings attached."[96] Soon afterward, the Soviet military attaché in Cairo, Colonel Nimoschenko, began secret talks
with Ali Sabri and two representatives of the Egyptian Defense
Ministry, General Mohamed Hafez Ismail and General Hasan
Ragab, to draw up an Egyptian military shopping list.[97]

Playing off East Against West

In early June, Nasser deliberately leaked news of the Soviet-
Egyptian arms talks to Jefferson Caffery's successor in Cairo,
Henry A. Byroade.[98] Foster Dulles, still smarting from Nasser's
conversion to neutralism at Bandung, concluded that the Egyptians were bluffing, and were feigning interest in Soviet arms
in order to pressure the West into providing military aid on
easy terms. Both Secretary of State Dulles and Undersecretary
of State Herbert Hoover, Jr., ignored Byroade's repeated requests
for serious consideration of a $27 million military aid package
drawn up by the Egyptian government and the American
Embassy in Cairo. Dulles and Hoover offered instead to allow
Egypt to make limited commercial purchases of American arms,
fully aware that the Egyptian government's hard currency shortage would preclude such purchases.[99]

The CIA, which had learned of Solod's general offer of aid
to Nasser on 25 May, did not share the complacency that
prevailed at the highest levels of the State Department.[100] Using
the CIA's "back channel" to the Egyptian government, Kim
Roosevelt escorted Nasser's personal representative, Major Hassan Touhamy, around Washington in June 1955 in search of
military supplies. The Pentagon responded with a plan that
would have permitted the Egyptians to buy sixteen aircraft and

twenty tanks from the U.S. government with local currency, but Foster Dulles refused to approve the scheme.[101]

Dulles was convinced that the Soviet government would not jeopardize the slow improvement in East-West relations that had begun after the death of Stalin merely to gain a foothold in Egypt. At the Geneva summit conference in July 1955, Khrushchev told Dulles flatly that there would be no Soviet arms sales to Egypt.[102] Dulles, Eisenhower, and newly elected British Prime Minister Anthony Eden discussed the rumored Soviet-Egyptian arms deal at a breakfast meeting in Geneva on 20 July 1955, and decided that Khrushchev's denial that such a deal was in the offing was probably truthful.[103]

The Czech Arms Deal

While Western leaders reassured each other at Geneva about the improbability of Soviet military aid to Egypt, Dmitri Shepilov, editor of *Pravda* and one of Khrushchev's most prominent protégés, arrived in Cairo to iron out the details of an arms agreement with Egypt. Khrushchev had used the first few days of the Geneva Summit to gauge the probable reaction of the Western powers to an arms agreement between Egypt and the Soviet bloc, and had deduced that neither the United States nor Britain would do anything more dramatic than offer strong diplomatic protests. After making this deduction, Khrushchev authorized Shepilov to finalize an aid arrangement with the Egyptian government.[104] Meanwhile, Nasser had determined that the tactic of playing East off against West and using a general Soviet offer of military aid as a lever to obtain Western arms on favorable terms was not likely to be a great success. Dulles still believed that Nasser was bluffing. The British government—upset by Nasser's attacks on the Baghdad Pact—continued to withhold delivery of some sixty Centurion tanks purchased by the Egyptian government shortly after the Suez Agreement. Although the French government had signed a basic arms agreement with the Egyptians early in July 1955, by the end of the month it appeared that Franco-Egyptian differences over the political future of the Maghreb and over

French arms sales to Israel would prevent any actual transfer of arms from France to Egypt.[105]

Under intense pressure from the Egyptian military, Nasser reached agreement with Shepilov on delivery dates, types and quantities of armaments, and payment terms. Nasser agreed to conduct further negotiations through the Czech government— a subterfuge suggested by the Soviets in an attempt to minimize the adverse impact of the arms deal on Soviet-American relations. At the end of July 1955, an Egyptian delegation led by General Ragab flew to Prague to complete the technical arrangements for the shipment of Soviet bloc arms to Egypt, and shortly thereafter a squadron of Soviet MIG–15 jet aircraft was crated and readied for delivery to Cairo.[106]

On 15 August 1955, Ahmed Hussein, who had returned to Cairo for consultations, described Nasser's conversations with Shepilov to Ambassador Byroade.[107] Byroade relayed this latest information to the State Department, adding that, in his view, Nasser "would be thrown out of power by the military if he didn't soon accept the Soviet offer." [108] Kim Roosevelt echoed Byroade's views in a two-page memorandum which he handed to Foster Dulles in late August. Roosevelt asserted emphatically that a Soviet-Egyptian arms deal was imminent, if not already a reality. Dulles read the memorandum hastily in Roosevelt's presence, and then dismissed it with an off-handed remark about such a deal being "contrary to the spirit of Geneva." [109]

In mid-September, the Secretary of State was finally convinced by his brother Allen, by Roosevelt, and by Byroade's increasingly exasperated cables that the Egyptian government was on the verge of announcing an agreement to purchase weapons from the Soviet bloc. On 20 September, Soviet Foreign Minister Molotov confirmed the imminence of a Czech-Egyptian arms arrangement to Dulles in New York, where both men were attending the opening session of the United Nations General Assembly.[110] At Undersecretary of State Hoover's suggestion, the Secretary of State immediately dispatched a reluctant Kim Roosevelt to Cairo to "persuade your friend Nasser that he mustn't do this thing." But Roosevelt, as he had expected, was unable to change Nasser's mind.[111] On the evening of 27 September, Nasser announced dramatically that the Revolutionary Command Council had arranged to trade part of the Egyptian cotton crop to Czechoslovakia for about $200 million worth of military equipment.[112]

Meanwhile, on 24 September, President Eisenhower had suffered a mild heart attack while vacationing in Colorado.[113] In a move symptomatic of the fluttery thinking that gripped Foggy Bottom while Eisenhower lay in an oxygen tent in Denver, Dulles and Hoover decided on 28 September to send the Assistant Secretary of State for Near Eastern Affairs, George V. Allen, to Cairo in a last ditch effort to dissuade Nasser from accepting military aid from the Soviet bloc.[114] Allen had no more success than Roosevelt had had; as one American diplomat later put it, "the mission was a flop before Allen left Washington." Nasser perceived Allen's appeal to be an ultimatum and brusquely refused to reconsider the Czech-Egyptian agreement.[115]

The Consequences of the Czech Arms Deal

"When the historians of the future come to write the history of our times," wrote J. C. Hurewitz in December 1956, "they may well select the crucial period from July to September 1955 as marking the turning point in the evolution of the Cold War." [116] Foster Dulles himself remarked in the fall of 1955 that the Czech arms deal was "the most serious development [in international affairs] since Korea, if not since World War II." [117] Even if the apparent hastiness of Hurewitz's judgment and Dulles's weakness for hyperbole are taken into account, it is still difficult to downplay the significance of Egypt's decision to accept military aid from the Soviet bloc. By breaking the Western monopoly on the supply of arms to the countries of the Middle East, the Czech-Egyptian agreement dealt a powerful blow to Dulles's hopes of keeping a lid on the Arab-Israeli arms race. The inevitable result of the Egyptian build-up was not only an intensification of Israel's campaign to obtain arms from the West, especially from the United States, but also a heightening of the possibility of a preemptive Israeli strike aimed at smothering the Nasser regime before it had a chance to absorb and deploy its Soviet weaponry.

Of perhaps even greater concern to the Eisenhower Administration was the fact that the Czech arms deal gave the Soviets an opportunity to leap over the Northern Tier and establish a political base at the heart of the Arab world. Foster Dulles had hoped to prevent Soviet penetration of the Middle East by stage-managing an orderly transition from European colonial domination of the Arab world to a new Arab partnership with the West; now the Soviets seemed poised to frustrate his ambitions.

By daring to thumb his nose at the "imperialist" West, Nasser achieved unprecedented prestige for the RCC in Egypt and throughout the Arab world.[118] The Czech arms deal reinforced the appeal of neutralism in Egypt, and it accelerated the rise of neutralism as an approach to foreign policy throughout the Third World. After September 1955, the task of coming to terms with Nasser's Egypt, and with a whole host of Third World governments that followed Nasser's example of playing East off against West, was an infinitely more complex one for the American government than it had been in the early 1950s.

Aid as Leverage: The Lessons of the American Experience in Egypt, 1952–55

It seems clear in retrospect that there was a huge gap between what the Eisenhower Administration hoped to achieve with its military aid program in Egypt in the early 1950s and the projected size of the program itself. Between 25 May 1950 and 31 December 1955, the United States exported only $1.2 million in arms and only $6.1 million in spare parts and aircraft to Egypt.[119] Although the American government supplemented these sales with a $20 million military aid offer in 1954, in the end the Eisenhower Administration tried, in Barry Rubin's words, "to convince the Egyptians to do too much with too little benefit for the already suspicious Free Officers." [120] Compromise on the Suez Base and Palestine issues, and on the issue of regional defense, entailed tremendous risks for the Nasser regime. Although Foster Dulles's understanding of the pressures facing Nasser was greater than he has usually been given credit for, he ultimately misjudged the strength of Arab nationalism, the urgency of the Egyptian government's need to obtain military aid, and the ability of the United States to shape events in the Middle East with relatively small quantities of aid.

Several other factors served to diminish what leverage the Eisenhower Administration did manage to derive from its promise of military aid. In the first place, the emergence of the Soviet bloc as an alternative source of arms decreased the value of U.S. military aid as a political lever in Egypt. Once competitive bidding for Egypt's favor began, the American bargaining position deteriorated rapidly.

The complexity of America's aid machinery was another anchor on U.S. efforts to use the lure of military assistance as a means of controlling Egyptian behavior. The nature of the American political system made delays, restrictions, and uncertainties an unavoidable part of the aid process, much to the chagrin of the Egyptian government. The three years of unsuccessful U.S.-Egyptian arms talks suffered by comparison with the speedy conclusion of the Czech arms deal. Moreover, Soviet bloc aid programs were unburdened by legislative requirements for military assistance advisory groups and uninhibited by annual public reviews of aid policy. As a member of the CIA Board of National Estimates observed: "The niggling in Congress and its committees about our aid programs and the public debate about "give-aways" contrasts very unfavorably with an executive decision made quickly by the Kremlin." [121]

For an Egyptian regime that was extraordinarily sensitive to foreign attempts to influence or control it, Foster Dulles's sometimes overbearing personal style was a further drain on the effectiveness of American aid policy. "Foster Dulles hadn't had much experience dealing with Third World nationalists like Nasser in 1955," one State Department official said later. "His approach to such leaders often tended to be rather patronizing and pedantic—which was not universally appreciated, least of all by Nasser." [122] In their restless search for dignity, Nasser and his colleagues could hardly react with enthusiasm to Dulles's attempts to tell them why America's restrictive military aid policy was really in the best interests of Egypt.

All of this is not to suggest that a more sophisticated, more generous U.S. arms aid policy would have made Nasser's Egypt a loyal American ally in the Cold War. But such a policy might have given the Eisenhower Administration sufficient leverage to nudge the Egyptian government toward a more pro-Western stance. There does not seem to have been anything predetermined about the pro-Soviet tilt that Egypt's policy of nonalignment later took, or about the Nasser regime's increasingly hostile attitude toward Israel. The central preoccupations of the Egyptian government after the revolution were the consolidation of Egyptian independence and the pursuit of Egyptian primacy in the Arab world. Strict nonalignment and, to a certain extent, an increasingly uncompromising stance vis à vis Israel were seen as means to those ends, not as ends in themselves. It is at least possible that a more flexible American policy toward Egypt, of which a less restrictive military aid policy would have been a key feature, might have led to a much closer U.S.-Egyptian relationship than the one that developed after 1955. Loose American sponsorship of an Egyptian-led Arab bloc might have satisfied the minimum strategic needs of both Egypt and the United States, and might have helped defuse Arab-Israel tensions. A close U.S.-Egyptian relationship along the lines sketched above would no doubt have provoked intense opposition from the Israel lobby, from Nasser's Arab rivals, and from the British government; moreover, it is by no means certain that Nasser's ambitions in the Arab world would have remained manageable for the Eisenhower Administration. Yet the evidence does suggest that there was a "margin for trial" in the early 1950s.[123] The United States may have missed a chance in the first few years after the revolution to build a durable, mutually satisfactory relationship with the Nasser regime; to a considerable extent, the complicated story of America's attempts to use military aid as a political lever in Egypt in the period 1952–55 remains a tale of lost opportunities.

CHAPTER TWO

Pacifying Nasser:
The United States and the Aswan Dam,
October 1955–March 1956

"The Aswan Dam affair," observed one former American diplomat, "is probably the single most important episode in the whole history of American attempts to use economic aid as a political lever in the Third World".[1] In the glare of mounting Soviet-American competition in the developing world, the significance of the Eisenhower Administration's offer—in conjunction with the British government and the World Bank—to help finance construction of the Aswan High Dam was magnified far beyond the size of the offer itself. Alarmed by the Czech arms deal, Foster Dulles hoped to use aid for the High Dam project as an inducement to discourage the Nasser regime from further involvement with the Soviet bloc and to encourage the Egyptians to seek a negotiated settlement of the Arab-Israeli conflict. In a more general sense, Dulles sought to use the Aswan offer as a means of demonstrating American strength in the escalating East-West struggle for influence in the Third World. American efforts to mold Egyptian behavior with the lure of High Dam aid did not, however, meet with much success in late 1955–early 1956. By the end of March 1956, the Eisenhower Administration's frustration with the Nasser regime's conduct, coupled with increasing foreign and domestic pressures, had produced a major shift in American tactics. Having failed to pacify Nasser with promises of economic assistance, Eisenhower and Dulles set out after March 1956 to punish him by suspending those promises.

"A One Shot Deal"

The most dangerous consequences of the Czech-Egyptian arms agreement, from the point of view of the Eisenhower Administration, were the increased influence of the Soviet Union in Egypt and the Arab world and the heightening of Israeli-Egyptian tension. Although deeply concerned about the consequences of the arms deal, Foster Dulles recognized that there was no quick way to turn the clock back and undo the new Soviet-Egyptian relationship. As the State Department's Office of Intelligence and Research put it:

> There would . . . seem to be no possibility that the West could talk Nasser out of the deal or buy him off. Nothing less than making an arms offer as attractive as that of the Soviet Union would accomplish this result, and such an offer would subject [the United States] to blackmail all over the world.[2]

Dulles understood after the failure of the Allen mission that he could not erase the adverse effects of the Czech arms deal, but he still believed that he could limit the damage done to American interests in the Middle East by Nasser's decision to acquire weapons from the Soviet bloc. Ambassador Byroade insisted that the September 1955 Czech-Egyptian arrangement might easily turn out to be a "one shot deal." Nasser, Byroade told Dulles, had been pressured into the Czech arms agreement by the Egyptian military; having now satisfied the officer corps' demands for modern military equipment, he had no further desire to involve himself with the Soviet bloc, nor, for that matter, any further desire to antagonize the United States.[3]

In his effort to contain the damaging effects of the Czech arms deal, Dulles had two courses of action open to him: he could punish the Egyptian government and attempt to coerce it into compliance with American wishes; or he could try to pacify Nasser and use a series of inducements to bring the Egyptian leader to reduce, and eventually end, his reliance on the Soviet bloc. In considering the first option, Dulles told Herbert Hoover, Jr. that "we have a lot of cards to play with Nasser. . . . We can develop the Baghdad group and ruin the cotton market. We can switch this year's economic aid from Egypt to Iraq".[4] But Dulles, like Byroade, was not convinced in the fall of 1955 that Nasser was in any sense a dupe of the Soviets; moreover, the Secretary of State realized that driving Nasser into open hostility toward the West would create a great deal of havoc in the Arab world, and would at least temporarily eliminate all hope of an Arab-Israeli peace settlement. Nasser was still regarded in the fall of 1955 by many Middle East specialists in the State Department and in the CIA, and to a certain extent by Foster Dulles himself, as a sort of errant protégé, who might still be maneuvered into leading the Arabs toward a settlement with Israel and into some kind of loose association with Western defense plans in the Middle East.[5]

Relatively optimistic about the chances of weaning Nasser away from dependence upon the Soviet bloc, Dulles focused his attention upon the second option—the policy of inducement. At a meeting with British Foreign Secretary Harold Macmillan in Washington on 3 October, Dulles emphasized that he "was inclined to temporize regarding Egypt at this stage in order to see how matters developed there . . . we should not take any threatening or drastic step at this time." If the policy of inducement failed, Dulles and Macmillan agreed, "consideration could then be given to the application of progressive pressures . . ."[6]

The immediate aim of the policy of inducement, in Dulles's view, was to establish a "new equilibrium . . . by inducing Nasser to take some other step or steps which would not only be of substantive importance but would also serve as a gauge of Nasser's sincerity when he said he has no intention of reorientating Egypt politically."[7] American opposition to further Arab membership in the Baghdad Pact was clearly one inducement that the Eisenhower Administration could offer the Nasser regime.[8] A second and more visible inducement was economic aid. Nasser's plans for rapid economic development continued, after the Czech arms deal, to depend upon Western capital and technical assistance. This dependence, reasoned Dulles, created a certain amount of leverage for the United States.

By far the most important single project in the Egyptian economic development program in the mid-1950s was the scheme to build a new dam across the Nile near Aswan. For a government interested in using economic aid as bait to influence Egyptian behavior, aid for the Aswan High Dam seemed to be the most powerful economic inducement that could be offered to the Nasser regime.[9] *And for Dam - an attempt to woo Nasser to the West...*

Nasser's New Pyramid

For centuries, Egypt's rulers have preoccupied themselves with the task of maximizing utilization of the waters of the Nile River. By the time the Free Officers seized power in July 1952, several new technological solutions had been proposed to control the high seasonal and annual fluctuations of the Nile, and thus reduce the damaging effects of floods in the high years and droughts in the low ones. The most comprehensive scheme, the "Century Project," featured the overall development of the Nile system, the building of reservoirs on the lakes of the Blue Nile and the White Nile, and of a canal to divert the river from its course through the Sudd swamps of the Sudan. Another proposal involved the creation of a natural reservoir in the large Wadi Rayan depression, located in Egypt's Western Desert.[10] A third proposition, to construct a mammoth new dam near Aswan, about four miles south of a comparatively tiny dam built by British engineers at the turn of the century, quickly proved more attractive to the Revolutionary Command Council than either of the first two schemes.

The original plans for the Aswan High Dam were drawn up by a Greek engineer named Adrien Daninos in 1947. Daninos presented his blueprints to the Farouk government early in 1948, but the High Dam proposal promptly vanished in the labyrinthine Egyptian bureaucracy. On 30 July 1952, four days after Farouk had gone into exile, the tireless Daninos resubmitted his scheme to the Free Officers. As Daninos explained to Ali Sabri, the representative of the revolutionary regime assigned to explore the High Dam proposition, the new dam would have twenty-six times the capacity of the original Aswan Dam, and would require seventeen times as much masonry as the Great Pyramid of Giza. More importantly, the High Dam would, according to Daninos, increase Egypt's cultivable land by one-sixth; would boost Egypt's agricultural exports by as much as 50 percent; would produce a vast increase in Egypt's industrial potential through creation of hydroelectrical power; would increase Egypt's total national income by an estimated 30 percent in the first decade after completion of the project; and would regularize the flow of the Nile.[11]

The High Dam project appealed to Nasser and his colleagues on the RCC for several reasons. First, as Daninos suggested, it appeared to offer immense economic benefits. Second, unlike the Century scheme, the Aswan proposal did not place control of Egypt's life-giving waters outside its national borders and in the hands of potential opponents. Finally, and perhaps most importantly, the High Dam itself held powerful symbolic attractions for Nasser and his fellow revolutionaries. The new dam, advertised as the most ambitious engineering project yet undertaken in the developing world, would symbolize the RCC's commitment to modernization. Construction of the High Dam would not only bolster the legitimacy of the revolutionary regime within Egypt, it would also demonstrate the RCC's boldness and imagination to the Arab world and to the emerging Third World.[12]

The Free Officers needed to resolve three problems before they could begin to build a new Aswan dam: Daninos's technical plans had to be refined; the distribution of the Nile waters had to be negotiated with Sudan; and hard currency had to be found to finance the foreign exchange costs of the project. In the fall of 1952, the RCC commissioned a series of studies aimed at analyzing and improving upon Daninos's original scheme. The Egyptian Water Resources Committee, guided by Dr. H.E. Hurst, assessed the hydrological demands of Egypt and the Sudan, and calculated the necessary storage capacity, given the fluctuations of the Nile and the frequency of lean years. The technical committee of Egypt's Council of National Production explored several alternative construction sites in Upper Egypt. A West German consortium, Hochtief and Dortmund, was employed to review and revise Daninos's design for the dam itself. At the suggestion of World Bank President Eugene Black, a board of international consultants was set up to advise the Egyptian government on questions of feasibility and design.[13]

In December 1954, Hochtief and Dortmund submitted a plan for a rockfill dam at a site near Aswan to the board of international consultants. The West German group estimated that the project would take ten years to complete. The consultants approved the Hochtief design, and the RCC promptly set out to secure a Nile waters agreement from the Sudanese and hard currency assistance from the West.[14]

In its hurry to begin construction of the High Dam, the Egyptian government took a rather cavalier attitude toward the views of the Sudanese; as *The Times* put it early in 1956: "There have been few examples in history of a nation so coolly preparing to convert part of its neighbor into a lake." [15] The High Dam plan drawn up by Hochtief and Dortmund involved the flooding of three hundred miles of the Nile in Egypt and one hundred and fifty in the Sudan, which would submerge the Sudanese border town of Wadi Halfa and displace some 40–50,000 Sudanese inhabitants. The Sudanese government demanded that the Egyptians make firm financial commitments to underwrite the costs of resettlement. Moreover, the Sudanese insisted upon a new Nile waters agreement before consenting to construction of the High Dam. Under the old arrangement, developed by the British in 1929, Egypt was entitled to forty-eight billion gallons of the Nile's average annual flow of eighty-four billion gallons. The Sudanese were entitled to four billion gallons, while thirty-two billion gallons flowed into the Mediterranean. Before the Sudanese government cooperated in further reducing the loss of water, it wanted to be assured of a larger proportion of the water saved through the Aswan project. Preliminary talks between the Egyptian and Sudanese governments on the issues of compensation and water rights made little headway in 1955. Although Sudanese-Egyptian differences over the High Dam did not by any means seem irreconcilable, they were aggravated by broader political tensions between the two countries. The Egyptian government did not, however, seem unduly concerned about the lack of progress toward a new Nile waters agreement at this stage, apparently regarding it more as a nuisance than as a real impediment to the building of the High Dam.[16]

What the RCC did regard as a real impediment to construction of the High Dam was the foreign exchange cost of the project. Cost estimates for the dam were characterized by great uncertainty, but by mid-1955 it was generally agreed that the total cost of the project would be about $1.3 billion, of which about $400 million would have to be in hard currency.[17] Lacking convertible currency, the Nasser regime approached the World Bank for loan capital. After the Hochtief plan was approved by the Egyptian government and its board of international consultants at the end of 1954, the World Bank made its own feasibility study, and determined that the High Dam scheme was technically sound. In August 1955, World Bank President Black informed the Egyptian government that the Bank was prepared to provide financial support for the Aswan project, within the limits of Egypt's capacity to service additional external debt.[18]

Both Nasser and Black realised that loan capital from the World Bank would have to be supplemented with grant capital from foreign donors if the High Dam project was ever to get off the ground. In April 1953, Black wrote a two-page memorandum for President Eisenhower, stressing the merits of the High Dam. Black also suggested that U.S. aid for the Dam might be used as part of a "package deal," in which the American government would provide financial backing for the Aswan scheme in return for Egyptian cooperation in Middle East defense planning and in resolving the Arab-Israeli conflict. Eisenhower was impressed by Black's reasoning.[19] A few months later, in October 1953, Egypt's Minister of Finance, Abdel Galil El Umari, flew to Washington and discussed the High Dam with American officials. After his return to Cairo, Umari reported:

> I have made contacts with the United States government for the purpose of assistance in financing various Egyptian industrial projects; chief among them was the Aswan High Dam. All American circles have shown a positive response in this regard.[20]

But by September 1955, after the World Bank's formal endorsement of the Aswan project, the Egyptian government still had not received a firm American commitment of financial support for the Dam. The Czech arms deal revived American interest in the High Dam.[21] Two weeks after Nasser's announcement of the Czech-Egyptian military aid agreement, the question of aid for the Aswan project acquired a new sense of urgency in the West when the Soviet government, flush with its recent success in the arms deal, was reported to have offered to underwrite the costs of building the High Dam.[22]

The Soviet Bid to Build the High Dam

On 10 October 1955, Soviet Ambassador Daniel Solod hinted in a statement in Cairo that the Soviet Union was prepared to provide substantial financial backing for the new Aswan Dam. Later that same day, the deputy chairman of Egypt's National Production Board, Dr. Mohamed Ahmed Salim, noted that "a Soviet offer on the Dam would be difficult for Egypt to refuse even though Western help would be preferred".[23] On 12 October the Cairo daily *Al Akhbar* reported: "The Soviet Union has expressed its willingness to finance the building of the great Nile dam and take Egypt's national products in exchange. No payment in foreign currency will be required." The *New York Times* confirmed the Soviet High Dam offer on 13 October.[24]

On 17 October 1955, Egyptian Ambassador Ahmed Hussein had a "long and far-ranging talk" with Foster Dulles in Washington, during which he reportedly told the American Secretary of State that the Soviets had offered a loan of $200 million, at 2 percent interest, repayable over a thirty-year period, for the High Dam. Hussein is said to have stressed that the Egyptian government was fearful of becoming overly dependent upon the Soviet bloc, and would prefer Western assistance in the Aswan project.[25] Nasser repeated this theme to Ambassador Byroade at about the same time.[26] Although Mohamed Heikal later claimed that the Soviets did not make a firm offer of aid for the High Dam in the fall of 1955, many American officials— from Byroade in Cairo to Foster Dulles in Foggy Bottom to the Middle East specialists in the CIA—were convinced by the end of October 1955 that there was a serious possibility that the Soviet Union would step in and finance the construction of the High Dam if the Western Powers refused their aid.[27]

Eden's Agitation

British Prime Minister Anthony Eden was deeply disturbed by the possibility that the Soviet government might get a "stranglehold" on Egypt by subsidizing both the Egyptian military and the Aswan project. The West had to act quickly, Eden told Minister of State for Foreign Affairs Anthony Nutting in October 1955, in order to "keep the Russian bear out of the Nile Valley." [28] Eden at this point had a curiously ambivalent attitude towards Nasser. At their only meeting, in February 1955 in Cairo, there had been considerable tension between the two men.[29] Britain's entry into the Baghdad Pact, and Egypt's vociferous opposition to it, had done little to allay that tension. The Czech arms deal further aggravated Anglo-Egyptian strains. But Eden—with a long string of post war diplomatic triumphs behind him—still thought that he could contain, and perhaps eventually resolve, the "Nasser problem." [30]

Anglo-American support for the Aswan project, Eden strongly believed, was necessary: first, to prevent the Soviets from consolidating their position in Egypt and expanding their influence into Africa; and second, to test Nasser's willingness to cooperate with the West in the Middle East. In the latter half of October 1955, Eden began to press this view, which had been endorsed by his Cabinet, on the Eisenhower Administration.[31]

On 21 October 1955, Eden summoned the American Ambassador in London, Winthrop Aldrich, to 10 Downing Street to discuss the rumored Soviet offer of aid for the High Dam. Aldrich later recalled that "Eden was obviously greatly agitated." The British Prime Minister told Aldrich that he feared that Nasser would "go over to the Russians" if the West did not provide financial backing for the Dam. Eden implored the American Ambassador to try to convince his superiors in Washington to counter the Soviets with a Western offer of support for the Aswan project.[32]

Eden's telegrams to the British Embassy in Washington in this period reflected the sense of urgency that he had sought to convey to Aldrich. "Eden," recalls Sir Roger Makins, then the British Ambassador to the United States, "was very keen on the High Dam, and instructed me to push the idea of a joint Anglo-American offer of aid for the Dam in Washington." [33]

On 26 October, British Foreign Secretary Harold Macmillan discussed the High Dam issue with Foster Dulles in Paris, where the two men were meeting to coordinate strategy for the Big Four Foreign Ministers' meeting in Geneva later that week. Macmillan found Dulles sympathetic to British concerns, noting in his diary that "we decided to try to get the Aswan Dam for a Western group, by some means or other." [34]

America and the Aswan Offer: The Preliminary Domestic Debate

Although Foster Dulles himself was intrigued by the idea of using aid for the High Dam to improve the West's bargaining position in Egypt, Makins detected "a certain reluctance on the American side to go into this." [35] President Eisenhower's heart attack and subsequent hospitalization delayed action on the Aswan issue. Moreover, Dulles's views on the desirability of providing aid for the Aswan project were not universally shared within the Executive Branch of the American government.

The International Cooperation Administration (ICA), the successor to the Mutual Security Agency, strongly supported aid for the High Dam, as did Eric Johnston, the influential director of the Eisenhower Administration's Jordan River development project.[36] Opinion among the CIA's Middle East specialists was generally favorable to a Western offer of aid for the High Dam.[37] Opinion in the State Department ran along similar lines, although both Assistant Secretary George Allen and Undersecretary Herbert Hoover voiced reservations about the desirability of a long term commitment to the Aswan project. Allen was particularly worried that the initial euphoria that an American offer of aid for the High Dam would produce would gradually deteriorate into mutual recrimination, as the strain of a decade of concentration on the Dam began to show on the Egyptian economy.[38] Curiously, Foster Dulles did not actively seek out Ambassador Byroade's views on the Aswan project, although Byroade later recalled that he too had feared initially that the protracted U.S.-Egyptian aid relationship that would be necessary to complete the High Dam would degenerate over time into "a tense and unfriendly affair." Byroade was not convinced that "the United States Congress would stay in the foreign aid business for a decade" and he "doubted that U.S.-Egyptian political relations would remain amicable enough to maintain Congressional interest in appropriating money for the Dam year after year." Nevertheless, Byroade recognized the depth of the Nasser regime's commitment to the Aswan project, and supported American aid for the High Dam both as a gesture of American good faith and as a means of forestalling Soviet involvement in the project.[39]

The main opposition to Aswan aid within the Executive Branch came from Secretary of the Treasury George Humphrey. A staunch fiscal conservative, Humphrey was generally suspicious of large foreign aid projects and particularly suspicious of involvement in construction of the High Dam.[40] Humphrey did not believe that the Egyptian economy was strong enough to bear simultaneously the burden of servicing the debt incurred in the Czech-Egyptian arms agreement and the burden of building the High Dam. Humphrey feared that an American offer of aid for the High Dam would eventually develop into an open-ended commitment to construct the Dam for the bankrupt Egyptians; as he later put it, "if you ever got your foot in the door there would be no end to it."[41] Humphrey's opposition to American involvement in the Aswan project was bound to have a powerful effect upon President Eisenhower, who had the highest regard for Humphrey's professional ability, and who shared Humphrey's fiscal conservatism.[42] Humphrey's views on the Aswan issue were also bound to reinforce opposition to the High Dam among the Secretary of the Treasury's many admirers on Capitol Hill—which was not in any case a hot bed of support for foreign aid in the mid-1950s.

Congress and Economic Aid to the Third World

"Economic aid to the developing world," Dwight Eisenhower commented acidly in 1955, "has the political appeal of an ordinary clod in the field."[43] Executive Branch policy makers had had little difficulty drumming up Congressional support for economic aid to friendly European countries threatened by hundreds of Red Army divisions, but they had considerable difficulty obtaining Congressional support for economic aid to neutralist developing countries threatened by nothing more tangible than rates of economic growth that barely kept pace with rates of population growth.[44]

Between 1948 and 1952, the United States provided $13 billion worth of economic aid to a dozen Western European countries. Almost immediately, a whole array of desirable political trends developed: economies revived; Communist parties did not come to power; and stability and democracy were the political results, by and large, in Western Europe. The success of the Marshall Plan seemed to confirm the universal applicability of a set of beliefs about economic, social, and political development that had their roots in the unique historical experience of liberal America.[45] In the United States, economic development (increased industrialization, growth of per capita income) and social development (progress in fields like education, health care, housing, and land tenure) had been relatively easy processes, and had led to the development of stable political institutions. With a little "pump priming" from the United States, the countries of Western Europe had enjoyed similarly remarkable rates of economic, social, and political development.

With the revival of Western European strength and the outbreak of the Korean War, the focus of the Cold War swung from Europe to the developing world. Between 1948 and 1952, 86 percent of all American economic aid had been poured into Europe; between 1953 and 1957, only 25 percent went to Europe.[46] Although it was clear that the economic, social, and political setting that had existed in Europe in the late 1940s did not exist in the developing world in the 1950s, much of the American public and many members of Congress continued to apply the unreachable standards of the Marshall Plan to aid programs in the Third World.

As it became apparent in the early and mid-1950s that United States aid would nòt lead automatically to stability, democracy, anti-Communism, peace, and pro-Americanism wherever it was applied in the developing world, public and Congressional interest in and support for the economic aid program diminished rapidly.[47] Although many powerful domestic interest groups—like the AFL-CIO, the Veterans of Foreign Wars, the American Legion and the U.S. Chamber of Commerce—offered lukewarm support for foreign aid appropriations during the Eisenhower era, the only organizations to campaign actively for economic aid to the developing world were those—like the League of Women Voters and various church groups—that had little clout on Capitol Hill.[48]

Lacking a firm popular mandate, and bereft of significant interest group support, it is not surprising that the economic aid program did not fare well in Congress. The organization of Congress, which generally makes it easier to obstruct legislation than to promote it, posed an additional problem for Executive Branch officials. Custom dictates that appropriation bills originate in the House of Representatives, and thus the lower chamber of Congress assumed the key role in the passage of aid bills during the Eisenhower years. Congressmen were, as a rule, less sympathetic to Presidential aid requests than Senators.[49] Preoccupied with almost continuous re-election campaigning, most Congressmen focused their attention upon legislation that had an immediate impact upon their districts. Since those who benefit most directly from foreign aid do not vote for Congressmen, aid appropriations tended to occupy a rather lowly rung on the ladder of Congressional priorities. With little time for, and even less interest in, the intricacies of the aid program, Congressmen often effectively delegated decision-making powers to a few self-styled experts in the House. Perhaps the most prominent such "expert" in the 1950s was Otto Passman (D-La.), chairman of the foreign aid subcommittee of the House Appropriations Committee.

Passman's attitude toward economic aid programs in the Third World provided an extreme example of Congressional hostility to foreign aid. Passman was an eccentric, even by Washington standards. A high-strung, erratic man, Passman dressed in dapper silk suits and had a penchant for delivering impassioned speeches accompanied by strange gyrations of hip and shoulder known to his colleagues as the "Passman dance." Whittling away at the annual aid budget became something of a personal crusade for the Louisiana legislator. He once confided to a State Department official: "Son, I don't smoke and I don't drink. My only pleasure in life is kicking the shit out of the

[margin handwritten note: Lack of Support in Congress]

foreign aid program of the United States of America."[50] Oblivious to the blandishments of Presidents from Truman to Johnson, Otto Passman voted against every single foreign aid authorization or appropriation presented in Congress in the first two decades after the Second World War.[51] Year after year, Passman played the Grand Inquisitor at the Appropriations subcommittee hearings on the aid budget, and year after year Executive Branch policy-makers stumbled down off Capitol Hill with the tattered remnants of the Administration's aid proposals. With Passman leading the way, Congress cut Executive Branch aid requests by an annual average of 18 percent during the 1950s.[52]

Congress, the Israel Lobby, and Aswan Dam Aid

General Congressional hostility to economic aid was reinforced, in the case of the Aswan Dam, by marked Congressional reluctance to bolster Israel's enemies. In the wake of the Czech arms deal, the Israel lobby launched a two-pronged campaign on Capitol Hill, coupling a high-profile, high-pressure drive to secure American military aid for Israel with a discreet, low-key effort to block aid for the High Dam so long as Egypt continued its military build up.[53] According to Isaiah Kenen, the Israel lobby "tried during the fall of 1955 to recapture the spirit of 1948 in Washington," holding big public rallies attended by such venerable Democratic figures as Harry Truman and Eleanor Roosevelt to demonstrate the strength of American sympathy for Israel. But despite such public displays, and despite a Congressional petition calling for U.S. military aid to Israel signed by forty Republican Congressmen, the Eisenhower Administration refused to consider concessional arms sales to the Israeli government.[54]

Kenen and his supporters had somewhat greater success quietly mobilizing opposition to Aswan Dam aid in Congress than they had had publicly pressing President Eisenhower to agree to the provision of arms assistance to Israel. The Israeli Embassy in Washington cooperated intimately with the Israel lobby in the campaign against High Dam aid. Ambassador Abba Eban later commented that "the Israeli influence, I will

[handwritten margin note: Israel eg. the project as was Israeli lobby]

say quite frankly, was exercised against American support of the Dam. Israel's influence is not a very ponderable thing, but it counts and certainly in that context there were many in the Senate and the House who opposed the Aswan Dam proposal in Israel's interest." [55] By the end of 1955, Congressional opposition to Aswan Dam aid posed a formidable, although not insurmountable, obstacle for the Eisenhower Administration.

Eisenhower and Dulles Weigh the Aswan Issue

When President Eisenhower returned to the White House from his hospital bed in Colorado, he and Foster Dulles carefully considered the advantages and disadvantages of providing financial backing for the Aswan project. Eisenhower and Dulles agreed that the Egyptian government was "determined to advance this project and would probably accept a Soviet offer of assistance if help [was] not obtained from the West." [56] Both men believed that a Western offer of support for the High Dam would at least temporarily blunt the Soviet offensive in Egypt, and might eventually lead Nasser to end his flirtation with the Soviet bloc. Construction of the High Dam would become the Nasser regime's central preoccupation for a decade or more, and American aid for the Dam might give the United States a fairly powerful grip on the Egyptian economy and, Eisenhower and Dulles thought, on the direction of Egyptian foreign policy. The Secretary of State assured Senator Lyndon Johnson, who was skeptical about the desirability of providing economic assistance to Egypt, that American aid for the Aswan project "would make it unlikely that Egypt would change her affiliation with us for the next ten years." [57]

The Aswan issue also seemed to Eisenhower and Dulles to offer a good opportunity to demonstrate Western resolve in the face of the general Soviet economic offensive in the developing world. "At first glance," Eisenhower told Dulles, "it would appear that we are being challenged in the area of our greatest strength." [58] But, Eisenhower noted, the Soviets could overcome their relative economic inferiority by distributing their economic aid selectively in the Third World, concentrating upon highly visible projects in a few key countries. In Eisenhower's view,

Pro Support: stop soviets; aid could be inducement to
end Arab/Israeli conflict
Con: Congress against, Israeli lobby ag, cost a lot.

Pacifying Nasser 51

the best way to counter this Soviet tactic was to make solid long term commitments to similarly visible development projects in a variety of Third World countries.

> I believe if we plan and organize properly, we can do these things without going broke, and that we can do them effectively and with the kind of selectivity and smoothness that will largely rob the Soviets of the initiative.[59]

The disadvantages of making an offer of aid for the High Dam appeared, however, to be formidable. Eisenhower and Dulles worried that the Nasser regime would use a Western offer of aid to drag the United States into a bidding war with the Soviet Union over the High Dam. Dulles noted that the Soviets could "always make an offer we cannot match. Some think Nasser is trying to get a bid and then let the Russians better the terms." [60] Even if Nasser accepted a Western offer, there was still the danger—which George Humphrey stressed repeatedly to the President—that the United States would be sucked into a long, costly, and politically unrewarding donor-recipient relationship with the Egyptian government. Finally, the Administration would have to pay a heavy political price to obtain Congressional approval of an Aswan offer, even though the price on Capitol Hill for economic aid to Egypt was considerably less than it would have been for military aid. 1956 was an election year and neither Eisenhower nor Dulles relished the thought of dragging weighty political baggage like Aswan Dam aid with them through a Presidential election campaign.

As Eisenhower and Dulles saw them late in the fall of 1955, the arguments for and against American involvement in the Aswan project were of roughly equal weight. What tipped the balance in favor of American support for construction of the High Dam, in their eyes, was the notion that Aswan Dam aid could be used as an inducement to encourage the Nasser regime to seek a negotiated settlement of the Arab-Israeli conflict.

Aswan Dam Aid and the Alpha Project

Foster Dulles had not abandoned the Alpha Project after the Gaza Raid; on the contrary, he had redoubled American efforts to resolve the Arab-Israeli dispute. The centerpiece of his renewed attempt to lure the Arabs, particularly the Egyptians, and the Israelis into peace talks was a meticulously crafted speech that he delivered to the Council on Foreign Relations in New York City on 26 August 1955. In his address, Dulles identified three obstacles to a resolution of the Arab-Israeli conflict: the plight of the 900,000 Palestinian refugees; mutual fears of Israeli expansionism and Arab vengefulness; and "the lack of fixed permanent boundaries between Israel and its Arab neighbors." Dulles recognized the difficulties presented by each of the three problems, but he stressed that he considered them "capable of solution." Dulles pledged that the United States, for its part, would provide financial support for repatriation of some refugees, and for compensation of those who were not repatriated; would assist Israel and its Arab neighbors to devise mutually acceptable borders, and would formally guarantee any frontiers that were agreed upon; and would provide financial backing for a regional drive to promote economic development.[61]

The Secretary of State was pleasantly surprised by the reaction to his speech in the Middle East, which—he told Presidential Press Secretary James Hagerty on 29 August—was "somewhat more friendly . . . than we had thought it would be." [62] In a subsequent letter to Eisenhower, Dulles noted that the Israeli reaction "seems more favorable than anticipated." [63] Although Nasser did not express any public enthusiasm for Dulles's proposals, he assured Ambassador Byroade privately that he was interested in arranging a compromise settlement with Israel, and would do his best to persuade the other Arab states to acquiesce to any agreements that Egypt and Israel were able to reach. The refugee problem, Nasser told Byroade, was the real heart of the Arab-Israeli dispute. Nasser emphasized that he could not publicly agree to anything less than unequivocal Israeli acknowledgment of the right of all of the refugees to return to their homes in Palestine. But the Egyptian leader added, according to Byroade, that "practically speaking, there is no danger of Israel being flooded with refugees. Most of the Palestinians won't return home if adequate provision is made for their resettlement elsewhere in the Arab world." If Israel would concede the right of the refugees to return to their abandoned homes, Nasser said, he would be prepared to discuss a general settlement of the Arab-Israeli dispute.[64]

Foster Dulles's effort to promote a negotiated Arab-Israeli settlement was supplemented, after the Czech arms deal, by a similar British peace initiative. At the Prime Minister's annual speech at the London Guildhall on 9 November 1955, Eden proposed a framework for an Arab-Israeli settlement that closely resembled the scheme that Dulles had outlined on 26 August. In a series of meetings with Nasser in the week after Eden's speech, the British ambassador in Cairo, Sir Humphrey Trevelyan, promised that Britain would provide arms aid to Egypt and would refrain from further expansion of the Baghdad Pact if the Egyptian government would take steps to reduce Arab-Israeli tensions.[65]

By the beginning of December 1955, Foster Dulles was more determined than ever to push for an Arab-Israeli settlement. Western aid for the Aswan project, Dulles reasoned, could be used discreetly to pry concessions on the Palestine issue out of the Nasser regime.[66] Dulles understood that the connection between such concessions and Aswan Dam aid "could probably not be openly negotiated," but he believed that it "could be delicately suggested." [67] Herbert Hoover, Jr., was even more enthusiastic than the Secretary of State about the potential rewards of linking Aswan aid to an Arab-Israeli settlement; as Henry Byroade later commented, Hoover "was convinced that the United States could buy an Arab-Israeli peace treaty with aid for the High Dam." [68]

On 8 December 1955, Foster Dulles discussed the idea of tying a Western offer of financial backing for the Aswan project to progress towards a resolution of the Palestine dispute with President Eisenhower at Camp David.[69] Eisenhower agreed that a reduction of Arab-Israeli tensions would mitigate many of the disadvantages of an offer of aid for the High Dam. Progress towards an Arab-Israeli settlement would, Eisenhower and Dulles thought, reduce Nasser's interest in acquiring new weaponry, and would thus remove an opportunity for further Soviet meddling in the region. Any reduction of Arab-Israeli tensions would undoubtedly improve the prospects for some form of Arab cooperation in Western regional defense planning. Moreover, an improvement in Arab-Israeli relations would greatly ease the problem of obtaining Congressional approval for economic assistance to Egypt. Eisenhower felt certain that "our Congress would authorize almost any kind of material aid" for Egypt if "a practicable peace treaty" could be arranged between Israel and the Arab states.[70]

Well aware that public disclosure of the American interest in using Aswan Dam aid as a bargaining chip in Arab-Israeli peace talks would alienate the Nasser regime, Eisenhower, Dulles, and Hoover kept a fairly tight security lid on their discussions. The only breach in the secrecy surrounding the scheme came on 12 December 1955, when the *New York Times* noted in a very brief and otherwise unremarkable article that:

> The United States government is tying its proposals for a ten year aid program to build the High Aswan Dam in Egypt to a settlement of the Egypt-Israel dispute. The hope here is that the negotiations for economic aid to Egypt can lead to a general settlement of the disturbing Near East situation.[71]

The Western Offer of Aid for the High Dam

The groundwork for the Western offer of aid for the Aswan project had been laid during the latter part of November 1955 in talks in Washington between Dr. Abdel Moneim Kaissouny, the Egyptian Finance Minister; World Bank President Eugene Black; Herbert Hoover, Jr.; and Sir Roger Makins.[72] On 16 December, the World Bank, the American government, and the British government formally announced a joint offer of aid for the Aswan High Dam. Under the terms of the offer, the U.S. government pledged $56 million, and the British government $14 million, to cover the foreign exchange costs of the first stage of the Aswan project, which involved the construction of upstream and downstream coffer dams; diversion of the Nile through artificial gorges and tunnels; and the building of irrigation works, using the water surplus held by the upstream coffer dam to create new crop acreage. The first stage was to be completed within five years. The final stages of the project—which would take ten more years to complete—involved construction of a huge rock-fill dam incorporating both coffer dams into itself, erection of a hydroelectric plant and power lines to the Delta, and establishment of new irrigation systems. The World Bank promised to lend the Egyptian government $200 million at 5.5 percent interest to underwrite part of the cost of the final stages, while the United States and Britain asserted that they would give "sympathetic attention" to a further grant of $130 million after the first stage of the Dam was completed. The Eisenhower Administration lacked the legislative authority to make a firm long term pledge of assistance for the High Dam, but President Eisenhower believed that the initial Western offer "all but committed [us] to further support at the completion of the first stage." For its part, the Egyptian government was expected to contribute about $900 million in local currency to the project.[73]

In the joint statement of 16 December and in separate *aides-mémoires* submitted by the United States and Britain to the Egyptian government a few days later, five conditions were set out for the provision of Western economic assistance.[74] First, Egypt was to devote one third of all its annual internal revenue to the High Dam over the fifteen-year construction period. Second, in view of the magnitude of the undertaking and the great strains it would inevitably impose on Egypt's resources, the Egyptian government was required to pledge to avoid new foreign debt obligations. Third, the World Bank would be permitted to monitor the Egyptian economy to ensure that sound fiscal and monetary policies were being followed. Fourth, competitive bidding for the High Dam construction contracts was to be closed to Soviet bloc countries. Finally, the Egyptian government was required to reach agreement with the Sudanese government on the Nile waters question before work was begun on the final stages of the Aswan project.[75]

Nasser's Reaction to the Western Offer

Despite Dr. Kaissouny's general enthusiasm for the Western offer, Nasser had several serious reservations about the conditions which the West had attached to its aid proposal.[76] Haunted by the specter of the Egyptian government struggling to free itself from the bonds of its European creditors in the 1870s, Nasser suspected that the Western conditions were part of an attempt to reintroduce colonial control over Egypt. Although Nasser's suspicions were exaggerated, there is no doubt that Western restrictions concerning additional foreign debts and World Bank supervision of the Egyptian economy would have sharply limited the ability of the Nasser government to make independent financial decisions during the High Dam's fifteen-year construction period. Nasser told Byroade that he was very apprehensive about "giving the West a virtual veto over his national security expenditures."[77]

Nasser also objected to the stipulation that bidding for High Dam contracts be limited to Western firms, seeing Western insistence on this point as yet another potential infringement on Egyptian sovereignty. Finally, and perhaps most importantly, Nasser was disturbed by the vagueness of the Anglo-American commitment to the final stages of the project. Unmoved by the Eisenhower Administration's argument that it lacked the legislative authority to make iron-clad promises of aid after the first stage of the High Dam was completed, Nasser feared that he would run the risk of being refused funding for the second stage of the Aswan project if his domestic and foreign policies did not conform to Western expectations.[78]

Black's Visit to Cairo

The task of easing Nasser's suspicions about the Western offer fell to World Bank President Eugene Black. On 23 January 1956, Secretary of State Dulles told Black that the issue of High Dam aid was "one of the most important things facing the United States government," and urged him to do his utmost to persuade Nasser to accept the Western offer.[79] On 24 January, Black flew to London for two days of talks with Anthony Eden and Harold Macmillan. Eden repeated Dulles's message on the political importance of the High Dam, and expressed a personal hope that Black "wouldn't act like a banker" and bog negotiations down in debate over financial technicalities.[80] On 27 January, Black arrived in Cairo.

Black's first meeting with Nasser was rather stormy. The Egyptian leader stubbornly insisted that the revolutionary regime could never accept the sort of foreign involvement in Egypt's economic planning that the West's High Dam proposal called for, and Black stressed with equal firmness that the conditions attached to the Western offer were regarded by the prospective donors as essential safeguards on their investment.[81] After Kim Roosevelt flew into Cairo and eased some of the initial strains that had developed between Black and Nasser, however, considerable progress was made in the High Dam negotiations.[82]

To convince the Nasser regime of the sincerity of the World Bank's commitment to the Aswan project, Black made three significant concessions. First, Black agreed that the role of the Bank in the management of the Egyptian economy would be advisory and not supervisory. Second, the World Bank President lowered the interest rate on the IBRD loan from 5.5 percent to 5 percent. Finally, Black reportedly substituted a "letter of commitment" regarding the $200 million Bank loan for the original "letter of intent."[83] In return, Nasser pledged that

> The [Egyptian] government's own contribution to the project will be provided in such a way as to avoid inflation and impairment of Egypt's credit worthiness. To this end, the Government and the Bank will reach an understanding on, and will periodically revise, an investment program which will recognise the priority of the High Dam Project and the need for adjusting total public expenditures to the financial resources which can be mobilized.[84]

On 9 February 1956, the Egyptian government and the World Bank issued a joint statement announcing that "substantial agreement had been reached concerning the basis of the Bank's participation . . . in the financing of the foreign exchange cost of the High Dam project, in an amount equivalent to $200 million."[85] The unresolved Sudanese-Egyptian dispute over distribution of the Nile waters remained an obstacle in the path of the Aswan project, but Black assured Nasser that the Western donors were willing to finance preparatory construction work while a new Nile waters agreement was hammered out.[86]

Nasser's doubts about the long term reliability of the U.S. and British governments as partners in the Aswan project continued, despite Black's efforts, to impede progress towards a final agreement between the Egyptian government and the Western donors.[87] Nasser wanted the United States and Britain to turn their grants over to the World Bank, so that the Bank would be the sole party with which Egypt would have to deal. Nasser thought that such an arrangement would reduce the probability of political manipulation of Western aid. Convinced by Black that the American and British governments were unlikely to agree to his scheme, Nasser submitted a contre-mémoire to Washington and London, requesting a larger Anglo-American grant covering the entire period of construction.[88]

On the whole, Black had good reason to be pleased with his two weeks of talks in Cairo. During a brief stop over at Rome airport on 10 February 1956, on his return journey to the United States, Black told Henry Byroade, who was en route to Cairo after a month of consultation in Washington, that he thought that Nasser was now prepared to accept the Western High Dam offer, with a few minor modifications. Byroade congratulated Black on the apparent success of his mission to Cairo, but warned him that the Eisenhower Administration's interest in High Dam aid had rather suddenly begun to wane. Byroade said that "an amazing thing has happened. There's been a change of feeling about [Aswan aid]. And when you get back to Washington you had better see if you can't get this thing back on the track." [89]

A Preview of "Shuttle Diplomacy": The First Anderson Mission

What had happened to derail the Eisenhower Administration's interest in High Dam aid, in the two weeks that Black had been in Cairo, was that Eisenhower, Hoover, and Foster Dulles had begun to realize that there was little chance that financial backing for the Aswan project would produce enough political leverage to pressure the Nasser regime into a negotiated settlement of the Arab-Israeli conflict. The source of this disillusionment was the apparent failure of former Deputy Secretary of Defense Robert B. Anderson's secret mission to Cairo and Tel Aviv in the latter part of January 1956.

In December 1955, President Eisenhower and Secretary of State Dulles decided to supplement public promotion of the Alpha Project with a confidential approach to Prime Ministers Nasser and Ben Gurion. The man chosen to make the approach was Robert B. Anderson, a forty-five-year old Texan who had left the Pentagon in the summer of 1955 to return to private business. Anderson knew very little about the Middle East, but Eisenhower considered him one of the ablest public servants that he had ever encountered. "My confidence in him is such," Eisenhower noted in his diary in early January 1956, "that at the moment I feel nothing could give me greater satisfaction than to believe that next January 20, I could turn over this office to his hands. His capacity is unlimited and his dedication to this country is complete." [90]

The details of Anderson's mission were arranged in deepest secrecy by Foster Dulles and his brother Allen. The logistical planning for the Anderson operation was handled primarily by the CIA; all of Anderson's later cables from the Middle East were transmitted through special CIA communications channels, not through the State Department. James Jesus Angleton, a CIA counter-intelligence expert with extensive contacts in Israel, coordinated preparations for Anderson's visit in Tel Aviv, and Kermit Roosevelt played a similar role in Cairo. Ambassador Byroade was excluded from the preliminary planning. [91] To clear the way for Anderson and Roosevelt, Byroade was recalled to Washington for consultation shortly after Christmas of 1955. Foster Dulles then informed him of Anderson's impending trip to Cairo. Disturbed about "being kept in the dark by the Dulles brothers," Byroade insisted upon a meeting with Anderson. After his talk with Anderson, Byroade was even more disturbed. Extremely pessimistic about Anderson's chances of reconciling the Egyptian and Israeli positions, Byroade told the Secretary of State that "what really scares me is that no matter how this fails, Nasser will get the blame." [92]

Eisenhower and Foster Dulles were rather more optimistic than Byroade about Anderson's prospects for success. On the afternoon of 11 January 1956, the President and the Secretary of State met with Anderson at the White House to review the Alpha Project. Dulles noted that "so far as the immediate issue between Israel and the Arab states is concerned, I [feel] that money could deal basically with the problem of the refugees." [93] The Eisenhower Administration was prepared to underwrite much of the cost of indemnifying and resettling the Palestinian refugees. Eisenhower and Dulles anticipated that some of the refugees would be resettled in Israel, but thought that the majority would be resettled in the Arab states bordering Israel, and in Iraq and Iran. The Johnston Plan for development of the Jordan River basin, said Dulles, could be used to gain the support of the Jordanian, Syrian, and Lebanese governments for the resettlement program.[94]

"The most difficult problem," Dulles told Anderson, "was the Negev and the question of Israel's access to the Gulf of Aqaba and Egypt's access to Jordan and Arabia." [95] To solve the Egyptian-Israeli boundary problem, the Secretary of State unveiled a complicated scheme based upon converging triangles of Egyptian, Israeli and Jordanian territory in the Negev. The Egyptian and Jordanian triangles would be joined by an east-west Arab highway, with an overpass over a north-south Israeli highway leading to the port of Eilat on the Gulf of Aqaba. The United States government, according to Dulles's plan, would formally guarantee the national boundaries resulting from the converging triangle arrangement.[96]

Dulles, Eisenhower, and Anderson agreed that American hopes of persuading the Nasser regime to support a negotiated settlement of the Arab-Israeli conflict along the lines proposed by the Alpha Group rested on two key inducements: prevention of further Arab membership in the Baghdad Pact, and aid for the Aswan Dam. In discussing the former inducement, Dulles argued:

> I believe that Nasser would be willing to pay a considerable price to get the support of the United States in limiting the Baghdad Pact to its present Arab membership with concentration upon the peril from the North, with Egypt maintaining its hegemony of the Arab countries.[97]

Dulles felt that Western aid for the High Dam was a similarly valuable political lever. Eisenhower and Dulles stressed to Anderson, however, that linking the Alpha project to the Baghdad Pact and Aswan Dam issues would be an extremely delicate operation, given the need to placate both the British government, which was still interested in expanding the Pact (despite its disclaimers to Nasser), and the Egyptian government, which would fiercely resist any overt attempt to tie High Dam aid to an Arab-Israeli settlement.[98] As early as mid-November 1955, Nasser had confided to Tom Little that he suspected that the Eisenhower Administration would try to use aid for the Dam to extract concessions from Egypt on the Palestine issue.[99]

Eisenhower concluded the 11 January meeting by "expressing his great personal confidence" in Anderson, and by emphasizing that the former Deputy Secretary of Defense was empowered to commit the United States to "whatever [Nasser] wants in aid" to seal a Palestine agreement. "Eisenhower," Anderson said later, "just about gave me carte blanche." [100] On 14 January 1956, armed with a letter of introduction from President Eisenhower, and accompanied by Kermit Roosevelt, Anderson flew to Cairo.[101]

As soon as Anderson's plane touched down in Cairo, he and Roosevelt were whisked to a Cairo suburb for a clandestine midnight rendezvous with Nasser and Egyptian Minister of the Interior Zakaria Mohieddin. After a few minutes of small talk, Anderson launched into an enthusiastic presentation of the Alpha proposals in his strong Texas accent. Nasser appeared to be quite responsive to Anderson's arguments. Buoyed by Nasser's reaction, Anderson was driven back into Cairo to his hotel. At Nasser's request, Roosevelt remained behind for a moment after Anderson had departed. "What," Nasser asked Roosevelt, "was Mr. Anderson talking about? " It seemed that neither Nasser nor Mohieddin had been able to penetrate Anderson's Texas drawl. Roosevelt—who had little confidence either in Anderson's mission or in Anderson as missionary—replied: "I think he believes that you've agreed to meet with Ben Gurion to resolve all your differences." Genuinely shocked, Nasser told Roosevelt that any such meeting would be "suicidal," and emphasized that he could never agree to direct discussions with the Israeli government.[102]

Somewhat bemused by the whole affair, Roosevelt rushed back to Anderson's hotel and found the American envoy "in the midst of dictating a long and fulsome cable to Foster Dulles." Much to Anderson's chagrin, Roosevelt explained that Nasser had misunderstood him, and that the Egyptian leader adamantly refused to consider direct talks with the Israelis.[103] At a second meeting the following night, Roosevelt "interpreted" for Anderson and clarified the Alpha proposals for Nasser and Mohieddin. The two Egyptians derided the "converging triangles" scheme. Nasser considered the east-west Arab overpass a "gimmick" that he could not take seriously, exclaiming with tongue in cheek: "If an Arab on the upper level had to relieve himself and accidentally hit an Israeli, it would mean war!" Nasser insisted that the Israelis would have to make more substantial territorial concessions in the Negev than the American plan envisioned. In this and subsequent conversations with Nasser, Anderson hinted—but never declared explicitly—that the Eisenhower Administration would speed aid for the High Dam and move to limit membership of the Baghdad Pact if Nasser would modify his demands.[104]

On 23 January, Anderson made a secret trip to Tel Aviv, but found Ben Gurion uneager to make any territorial concessions in the Negev and insistent upon face-to-face talks with Nasser.[105] Still hopeful about the chances of narrowing Egyptian-Israeli differences through another series of "shuttles" between Cairo and Tel Aviv, but decidedly less optimistic than when he had set out on his mission, Anderson returned to Washington and reported the meager results of his discussions with Nasser and Ben Gurion to Eisenhower and Foster Dulles shortly before Eugene Black flew back from his talks in Cairo.[106]

High level enthusiasm for High Dam aid was evaporating by the time Black arrived in Washington. Herbert Hoover, Jr.— perhaps the most ardent proponent of Aswan assistance among senior Administration officials before its value as a political lever had been tested by the Anderson mission—"wanted out of Aswan as soon as he discovered he couldn't buy an Egyptian-Israeli peace with it."[107] Disappointed by the results of the Anderson mission, President Eisenhower and Secretary of State Dulles were certainly less excited about the prospect of providing financial backing for the Dam in early February 1956 than they had been in early January 1956. Black was distressed to find that he and Henry Byroade—who had initially had reservations about United States involvement in the Aswan project, but who now feared the repercussions of a cancellation of the Western offer of aid for the High Dam—"were the only people pushing for Aswan aid in Washington at the end of the winter of 1955–56." [108]

Eden's Second Thoughts About the Dam

Although the British government had been provided with only the vaguest of information about the Anderson mission,[109] its interest in Western aid for the Aswan Dam had also begun to wane at the beginning of 1956. The immediate cause of the Eden government's disenchantment with the idea of using High Dam aid to pacify Egypt was what it perceived to be Nasser's obstruction of British plans to bring Jordan into the Baghdad Pact.

Despite Eden's tacit agreement with Nasser to limit Arab membership of the Baghdad Pact to Iraq, the British Cabinet—particularly Harold Macmillan—remained eager to expand Arab participation in the Pact if the opportunity arose.[110] At a Pact meeting in Baghdad in mid-November 1955, Nuri Said and Turkish President Celal Bayar told Macmillan that King Hussein of Jordan was prepared to join the Pact if Britain would publicly support him. Macmillan was enthusiastic about bringing Jordan into the Pact. He would try to secure Eden's support for the scheme, he told Nuri, but in the meantime he urged the Iraqi Prime Minister to provide heavy subsidies to Hussein to convince him to sign the Baghdad treaty. In a memorable reply, Nuri told Macmillan that direct British pressure was necessary to convince Hussein to enter the Baghdad Pact, adding that "you can't buy Arabs. You can only rent them." [111]

Eden needed little prodding to agree to encourage Hussein to join the Pact in what Macmillan termed "a fresh attempt to draw the Arab world away from the growing ambitions of Nasser and the increasing temptations dangled before them by the Soviet government." [112] On 6 December 1955, General Sir Gerald Templer, Chief of the Imperial General Staff, was dispatched to Amman bearing gifts of ten jet fighters, £11 million in aid for the Arab Legion, and a similar amount in economic aid. While Templer tried to persuade Hussein to join the Baghdad Pact, Humphrey Trevelyan was instructed to assure Nasser in Cairo that the British government had no interest in enlisting Jordan in the Pact. Eden and Macmillan apparently hoped that Nasser's anger at being deceived would be assuaged by the High Dam offer of 16 December 1955.[113]

Templer's week long visit in Amman ignited widespread unrest in Jordan. In December 1955–January 1956, three successive Jordanian governments fell in the face of popular opposition to hints that Hussein was contemplating membership in the Baghdad Pact. Radio Cairo beamed Nasser's attacks on the Pact to a receptive audience in Jordan composed of Palestinians (who accounted for about 60 percent of the Jordanian population in 1955–56) and young Arab Legion officers (who idolized Nasser and the Free Officers). In early January 1956, Hussein publicly pledged that Jordan would not join the Baghdad Pact.[114]

Eden blamed Nasser for the Jordanian crisis, and for the damage to the Baghdad Pact and to British prestige in the Middle East caused by the crisis. In Eden's eyes, the unrest that had surrounded Hussein's flirtation with the Pact, coming as it did on the heels of the Western offer of aid for the High Dam, was evidence that economic assistance was not a particularly effective means of pacifying Nasser. By the end of January 1956, Eden, Macmillan (now Chancellor of the Exchequer), and Selwyn Lloyd (the new Foreign Secretary) all had begun to have second thoughts about Western financial backing for the Aswan Dam.[115]

Eden confided his doubts about the High Dam offer to Eisenhower and Foster Dulles during a three day summit meeting in Washington in late January-early February 1956.[116] With Robert Anderson's discouraging cables from Cairo fresh in their memories, Eisenhower and Dulles assured the British Prime Minister that they shared his sense of uncertainty about the Dam. In a discussion on the afternoon of 30 January 1956, Dulles told Eden that "it appeared that the Egyptians were dragging their feet" on the Alpha Project, adding that "we might soon know whether our whole attitude toward Nasser would have to be changed." [117] Buoyed by the Eisenhower Administration's responsiveness on the issue of Anglo-American policy toward Egypt in general, and toward High Dam aid in particular, Eden cabled the Foreign Office that no Western assistance for the Aswan project would be provided until Nasser had demonstrated a "willingness to cooperate" with Britain and America in the Arab world.[118]

"The Straw that Broke the Camel's Back": The Glubb Affair and the Collapse of British Support for High Dam Aid

One month after his return to London from the Washington talks, Eden's doubts about the Aswan project were transformed into firm opposition to High Dam aid by the Glubb affair. On 1 March 1956, King Hussein abruptly dismissed the British commander of the Arab Legion, General John Bagot Glubb. Hussein's action was evidently motivated by personal resentment of reports in the British and Arab press that Glubb was the "real ruler" of Jordan, and by a related desire to rebuild his popularity in Jordan after the Baghdad Pact fiasco by striking a blow against British "imperialism." Moreover, Glubb had been a natural target for Radio Cairo's attacks, and Hussein was anxious at this point to evade Egyptian criticism.[119]

Eden was outraged by Glubb's dismissal, which he considered a grave blow to British prestige in the Arab world. In a discussion of Glubb's sacking with Minister of State for Foreign Affairs Anthony Nutting on the night of 1 March, Eden "put all the blame on Nasser and brushed aside every argument that more personal considerations had in fact influenced Hussein's arbitrary decision."[120] Beset by mounting domestic criticism of his alleged "appeasement" of Egypt, the British Prime Minister decided in early March 1956 to punish Nasser by withholding aid for the Aswan project. For Eden, the Glubb affair was "the straw that broke the camel's back in his relations with the Nasser regime."[121]

Selwyn Lloyd shared Eden's conviction that Britain needed to take a hard line with the Egyptian government after Glubb's dismissal. Coincidentally, the British Foreign Secretary had been in Cairo conferring with Nasser when Glubb was sacked. Lloyd deeply resented what he perceived to be Nasser's "smug" reaction to Glubb's ouster, and was incensed by the Egyptian Prime Minister's barely concealed belief that "he had better cards in his hand . . . and could do more harm to us than we could do to him." Lloyd's anger was heightened a few days later when his motorcade was attacked in Bahrain by pro-Nasser demonstrators. Enroute back to London, Selwyn Lloyd cabled Eden that "we have to indicate our attitude to Egypt. I do not see how we can tolerate their behavior much longer. Must we go on with Dam? " [122]

Meanwhile, Eden's displeasure with Nasser was increasing. When Nutting proposed a revised British policy aimed at isolating Nasser in the Arab world in a memorandum in mid-March 1956, Eden responded furiously:

> What's all this nonsense about isolating Nasser or "neutralizing" him, as you call it? I want him destroyed, can't you understand? I want him removed, and if you and the Foreign Office don't agree, then you'd better come to the Cabinet and explain why.[123]

Still fuming at Nasser's perfidy, Eden called a Cabinet meeting on 21 March to plan a new anti-Nasser strategy. Selwyn Lloyd opened the discussion by reporting that Nasser was "unwilling to work with the Western powers in the task of securing peace in the Middle East." In the Foreign Secretary's view, the British government "could not establish a basis for friendly relations with an Egypt controlled by Nasser." Consequently, Lloyd argued, "we had to realign our policy in the Middle East. Instead of seeking to conciliate or support Nasser, we should do our utmost to counter him and uphold our true friends." Lloyd maintained that Britain should immediately seek American support for a revamped policy based on a strong and expanded Baghdad Pact. Suspension of financial aid for the Aswan Dam would be the first step in a concerted Anglo-American campaign to undermine the Nasser regime.[124]

Lloyd's recommendations were quickly approved by the Cabinet. Eden and Lloyd thereupon sent a message to Ambassador Makins in Washington "saying that our feeling was that we should not give Nasser the money for the dam unless he genuinely changed his attitude towards Western interests in the Middle East." [125] Eden had already written directly to President Eisenhower on 15 March to express his anxiety about Nasser's ambitions in the Arab world and to suggest that Britain and the United States ignore Nasser's *contre-mémoire* regarding the Western offer of aid for the Aswan project and let the issue of High Dam aid "wither on the vine." [126]

"Sniping at the Aswan Offer" : America's Allies and the Issue of High Dam Aid

The British were not alone in their attempts to pressure the Eisenhower Administration to withhold economic assistance from Egypt in the spring of 1956; as Fraser Wilkins, then chief of the State Department's Office of Near East Affairs, later recalled, "many of our allies began sniping at the Aswan offer from the moment it was announced." [127] On 20 December 1955, the Shah of Iran told the British ambassador in Tehran that he regarded the High Dam offer as "a reward for bad behavior." [128] Early in 1956, Nuri Said complained to the British and American governments that "the Egyptians had done better out of the West by bullying them than [we] had by cooperating." [129] At one time or another during the spring of 1956, the Pakistanis, Turks, and Filipinos echoed Nuri's complaint, noting that "you Americans seem to be falling over yourselves to do nice things for Nasser, after he made a military arrangement with Czechoslovakia" and contending that America's loyal allies were being shunted aside in the scramble to cultivate neutralists like Nasser.[130]

The French government, which had sought unsuccessfully in the fall of 1955 to participate in the Western offer of aid for the Aswan Dam, made a quick turnabout at the beginning of 1956 and began to lobby against economic assistance for the Nasser regime. Socialist Premier Guy Mollet, who had come to power in January 1956, distrusted Nasser, and was fond of making comparisons between the ambitions set out in Nasser's *Philosophy of the Revolution* and those expressed in Hitler's *Mein Kampf*. Moreover, it was widely believed in France that the Nasser regime's propagandizing and logistical support formed the backbone of Arab resistance to French rule in Algeria. For the French government, and for many of America's other allies, aid to Nasser had become anathema by the end of March 1956.[131]

Congressional Opposition to Aswan Aid

Foreign pressure on the Eisenhower Administration to suspend the Aswan offer was paralleled, in the first few months of 1956, by domestic pressure against involvement in the construction of the High Dam. Against a background of general Congressional hostility toward economic assistance to neutralist governments, both the Israel lobby and the cotton lobby labored to block appropriation of funds for the Aswan project.

Although the Eisenhower Administration could draw on the untargeted portion of the 1956 economic aid appropriation to meet its commitment to the first phase of the High Dam project, it lacked the authority at the beginning of 1956 to earmark funds for later phases of the project.[132] In his State of the Union message to Congress on 5 January 1956, President Eisenhower requested "limited authority to make longer term commitments to such projects, to be fulfilled from appropriations to be made in future fiscal years." [133] In subsequent Senate Appropriations Committee hearings on the "Financing of the Aswan High Dam in Egypt," Undersecretary of State Hoover argued that the Soviet challenge in the developing world "can only be met by our aiding those countries in long term projects. . . . Our help will largely fail in its appeal and effectiveness if it cannot be expressed in terms of major projects which can catch the imagination of the people." [134]

Congress did not seem particularly eager to grant the Eisenhower Administration the long term authority that it desired. In an election year, Congressional attitudes regarding the Aswan issue were especially susceptible to pressures from two powerful domestic interest groups, the Israel lobby and the Southern cotton growers' lobby. The Israel lobby conducted a subtle but effective anti-Dam campaign on Capitol Hill throughout the early part of 1956, contending that the U.S. government should not provide economic assistance to Egypt so long as Egypt refused to make peace with Israel.[135] In response to such arguments, the Administration maintained, first, that the Egyptians would turn to the Soviet Union for Aswan aid if the West withdrew its offer, a development which would be far more threatening to Israeli security than Western involvement in the High Dam project, and second, that construction of the Dam would absorb Egyptian resources and energies that might otherwise be directed against Israel. "The salient fact remains," Treasury Secretary George Humphrey dutifully testified in a closed session of the Senate Foreign Relations Committee in the first week of January 1956, "that . . . if the West does not do it . . . the Soviet bloc will." [136] Similarly, Herbert Hoover told the Senate Appropriations Committee later that month that "if [the Egyptians] do not do it with us they are going to do it with somebody else." Hoover added:

> To undertake this project, the Egyptians are having to furnish some $900 million over a period of twenty years, and it will require extreme austerity on the part of the Egyptians if they are to complete their end of the project. Obviously they are not going to be able to undertake a large arms race or a commitment of their resources toward war and at the same time carry on a project of this magnitude. [137]

While the Administration tried to fend off attacks from pro-Israel groups, it was beset by equally vigorous criticism of Aswan aid from Southern cotton interests. The cotton lobby feared that the construction of the High Dam and enlargement of Egypt's body of arable land would result in an expanded Egyptian output of superior quality, long staple cotton, which would in turn weaken America's already shaky grip on the European cotton market. In the 26 January Senate Appropriations Committee hearings on High Dam aid, Senator John Stennis (D-Miss.) emphasized to Undersecretary Hoover that "this is not only of deep concern to me but to all of these gentlemen representing cotton producing States." Senator Spessard Holland (D-Fla.) echoed Stennis, noting that it made little sense to subsidize the erosion of the Southern cotton industry. [138] Hoover responded that "there is a basic and fundamental fact that the Egyptians are desperately trying to get off a one crop economy," stressing that the Egyptian government had assured

the Eisenhower Administration informally that the land re-
claimed through the Aswan project would be used to grow
truck garden crops, not cotton. Assistant Secretary of State
Thruston B. Morton repeated Hoover's contention in a February
1956 letter to Appropriations Committee Chairman Carl Hayden
(D-Arizona).[139] In the absence of formal Egyptian commitments
regarding cotton production, however, the Southern bloc in
Congress remained skeptical of the desirability of providing
financial backing for the High Dam.

By the end of the winter of 1955–56, it was clear to
Eisenhower and Foster Dulles that obtaining Congressional
support for funds for the latter stages of the Aswan project
would be a difficult task. Sherman Adams later went so far as
to assert that "it was extremely doubtful if the President could
have obtained Congressional approval of the grants and loans
to the Egyptians at that point had he asked for them." [140] Less
pessimistic than Adams, Senator J. William Fulbright recalled
some twenty-five years after the Aswan debate on Capitol Hill
that "the Eisenhower Administration could have won Congressional approval of the Aswan aid package in the spring of
1956 if it had forced the issue. But Eisenhower would have
had to pay a substantial political price for this, and he and
Foster Dulles had already evidently begun to have doubts about
the Western offer of aid for the Dam. Congressional opposition
did not cause the Administration to abandon the Aswan offer,
but it certainly contributed to the Administration's growing
dissatisfaction with the idea of providing large-scale economic
assistance to Nasser." [141]

Cong. Pressure

The Second Anderson Mission

As foreign and domestic pressure against High Dam aid
built up, President Eisenhower and Secretary of State Dulles
sent Robert Anderson back to the Middle East in a final attempt
to stimulate Egyptian and Israeli interest in a negotiated settlement of the Palestine conflict. Although the results of the
first Anderson mission had been disappointing, it was clear
that Nasser had not yet closed the door to compromise on the

Arab-Israeli issue. On 6 February 1956, shortly after Anderson's return to Washington, Nasser wrote to Eisenhower:

> The establishment of Israel in Palestine was the gravest imagi-
> nable challenge to the peaceful preoccupation of the Egyptian
> and Arab people. But, despite the sense of injustice evoked by
> this development, in the interest of peace Egypt recognises the
> desirability of seeking to eliminate the tensions between the
> Arab States and Israel.[142]

On 29 February, Eisenhower replied eagerly that "I believe that the present time may offer the best opportunity to work out a settlement which will make it possible for the United States to give increasing assistance in achieving the aspirations of the Arab people." In the next paragraph of his letter to Nasser, Eisenhower wrote of his interest in "the negotiations on the construction of a High Dam at Aswan," noting that "the High Dam represents in finest form the policies of peaceful develop-ment for your people of which you wrote." Nasser could not have failed to notice the connection that Eisenhower was draw-ing between progress towards an Arab-Israeli settlement and American aid for the Aswan project, with High Dam aid being offered as an incentive to spur Egyptian concessions on the Palestine issue.[143]

During the first two weeks in March 1956, Anderson shut-tled back and forth between Cairo and Tel Aviv, struggling valiantly to narrow the differences between the Israeli govern-ment and the Nasser regime. Nasser seemed content to allow Anderson to continue to serve as an intermediary, carrying offers and counter-offers back and forth between Egypt and Israel, but Ben Gurion, as he had done in January, eventually insisted on face to face talks with the Egyptian Prime Minister. Nasser demurred. Anderson offered to arrange direct talks in deepest secrecy on board a U.S. aircraft carrier in the Medi-terranean, but Nasser—still fearful of the news leak that might prove fatal to his position in Egypt and in the Arab world—refused the offer. Dejected by his failure to bring Nasser and Ben Gurion together, Anderson flew back to Washington on 12 March.[144]

In a diary entry on 13 March, President Eisenhower reflected upon Anderson's report of his second mission to the Middle East. Eisenhower wrote:

> [Anderson] made no progress whatsoever in our basic purpose of arranging some kind of meeting between Egyptian officials and the Israelis. Nasser proved to be a complete stumbling block. He is apparently seeking to be acknowledged as the political leader of the Arab world.[145]

Eisenhower's frustration with Nasser was mirrored by disappointment with the Israeli government's intransigent attitude.

> On the other side, the Israeli officials are anxious to talk with Egypt, but they are completely adamant in their attitude of making no concessions whatsoever in order to obtain a peace. Their general strategem is "not one inch of ground," and their incessant demand is for arms.[146]

Noting that "to both Ben Gurion and Nasser, Anderson held out every pledge of assistance and association that the United States could logically make in return for a genuine effort on the part of both to obtain a peace," Eisenhower concluded sadly that "the chances for a peaceful settlement seem remote." "It is," added the President, "a very sorry situation." [147]

The Thickening Flow of Soviet-Bloc Arms to Egypt

By mid-March 1956, it seemed apparent in Washington that the policy of attempting to pacify Nasser with High Dam aid had not succeeded in limiting the Czech arms agreement to a "one shot deal." Rumors had begun to reach the American government that the Egyptians had supplemented their original barter arrangement with the Czechs to include more advanced Soviet bloc weaponry, notably the MIG–17 jet fighter.[148] On 16 March 1956, Israeli Prime Minister Ben Gurion argued in a letter to Eisenhower that Nasser was not genuinely interested in a settlement with Israel, but was simply stalling for time until his armed forces could absorb the accelerated flow of Soviet bloc military equipment.[149]

Eisenhower was greatly disturbed by Egypt's increasing dependence upon Soviet military aid. In his mind, one of the key restrictions on the Aswan offer had been that "Egypt could not simultaneously build up unwarranted defensive forces." [150] Like the failure of the Anderson missions, Egypt's continued reliance on Soviet bloc arms was seen by the Eisenhower Administration as a clear indication of Nasser's unwillingness to enter into the sort of political bargain that the American government expected in return for economic assistance.

The Demise of the Pacification Program

In the wake of the Czech arms deal, the Eisenhower Administration had hoped to use aid for the Aswan project as an inducement to discourage the Nasser regime from further involvement with the Soviet bloc and to encourage the Egyptians to seek a negotiated settlement of the Arab-Israeli conflict. Three months after the High Dam offer had been tendered to the Egyptian government, the chances of achieving the two chief objectives of American aid policy seemed more remote than ever. Eisenhower wrote in his diary on 8 March 1956:

> We have reached the point when it looks as if Egypt, under Nasser, is going to make no move whatsoever to meet the Israelis in an effort to settle outstanding differences. Moreover, the Arabs, absorbing major consignments of arms from the Soviets, are daily growing more arrogant and disregarding the interests of Western Europe and of the United States in the Middle East region.[151]

Similarly, the Eisenhower Administration had had little success in the pursuit of its broader aim of using High Dam aid to display its strength in the Cold War struggle for the allegiance of the developing world. Eisenhower and Dulles had hoped to use the Aswan offer to demonstrate that cooperation with the West brought economic favors that the Soviet bloc could not provide; to their dismay, Nasser had demonstrated in late

1955–early 1956 that it was possible to attract Western promises of aid while at the same time pursuing a foreign policy that was in many ways inimical to Western interests.

As in the earlier case of arms aid policy, there was a large gap between what the Eisenhower Administration expected to achieve with economic assistance in Egypt and the projected size of the aid program itself. Although Western support for the Aswan project was enormously important to the Nasser regime, that support evidently did not provide enough of an incentive to cause Nasser to risk his position in Egypt and in the Arab world by making public concessions on the Palestine issue and by severing his newly developed link to the Soviet bloc. Moreover, the vague Soviet offer of aid for the High Dam made originally to the Egyptian government in October 1955 and repeated in December 1955 seemed to give Nasser an attractive alternative to Western assistance.[152] The mere fact that the Soviets were prepared to bid for the right to underwrite the foreign exchange costs of the High Dam tended to undermine America's bargaining position.

The deep sensitivity of the Nasser regime to foreign encroachment made it acutely aware of the stylistic weaknesses of American economic aid policy. Nasser himself was always suspicious of American motives. Heikal reports that from the fall of 1955 "Nasser got the feeling that the Americans, through the size and expense of the [Aswan] project, thought that they could get a firm grip on Egypt and that the very duration of the project would give them time either to offset the growth of Soviet influence in Egypt or to topple him from power." [153] Given this innate sensitivity and suspiciousness, it is not surprising that the Egyptian government was antagonized by the conditions, restrictions, and uncertainties that were an unavoidable part of the process through which America's High Dam offer was made.

Having failed to pacify Nasser with promises of economic assistance, Eisenhower and Foster Dulles paused at the end of March 1956 to consider a major shift in tactics. If the Nasser regime seemed unresponsive to the lure of High Dam aid, thought Eisenhower and Dulles, then perhaps it would be more accomodating if the promise of High Dam aid were suspended and Egypt were ostracized by the West. "I am certain of one thing," wrote Eisenhower in his diary, "if Egypt finds herself thus isolated from the rest of the Arab world, and without an ally in sight except Soviet Russia, she would very quickly get sick of that prospect and would join us in the search for a just and decent peace in that region." [154]

CHAPTER THREE

Punishing Nasser:
The United States and the Aswan Dam, March 1956–July 1956

At the end of March 1956, the Eisenhower Administration began a major shift in its Aswan Dam aid policy. Disturbed by the Nasser regime's apparent unwillingness to cooperate with the American government, Eisenhower and Foster Dulles jettisoned the policy of using High Dam aid primarily as an inducement and set out to use the suspension of the Aswan offer as part of a general campaign to bring Nasser to heel. By attempting to isolate Egypt from the rest of the Arab world, the Eisenhower Administration hoped to contain the spread of Soviet influence in the Middle East, to temporarily defuse the Arab-Israeli issue, and, more broadly, to demonstrate that Nasser's tactic of playing off East against West did not pay.

Informal suspension of the Aswan offer, however, seemed to have no more effect on Egyptian behavior than the earlier policy of inducement had had. Beset by Congressional pressures, and convinced that the dangling High Dam offer had become more of a liability than an asset to American interests, Foster Dulles formally cancelled the U.S. government's proposal of aid for the High Dam on 19 July 1956. It is important to emphasize, first, that Dulles's cancellation of the Aswan offer was not the sudden decision that it is sometimes alleged to have been, but was rather a product of the gradual shift in American policy toward Egypt that had begun in late March 1956, and second, that the British government was not completely excluded from the deliberations which culminated in Dulles's cancellation of the Aswan offer, as has sometimes been suggested, but was rather kept fairly well informed about American thinking on the Aswan issue.

The immediate consequence of the Anglo-American withdrawal of the High Dam offer was Nasser's nationalization of the Suez Canal Company, and the subsequent Suez Crisis, which in turn had a powerful effect upon the course of international politics. Never before or since has America's use of economic aid as a political lever had quite the same impact that the cancellation of the Aswan offer had.

The Omega Memorandum

The failure of Robert Anderson's secret shuttle diplomacy and Egypt's continued reliance on Soviet bloc arms, coupled with pressures from the Eden government and from domestic opponents of High Dam aid, had seriously eroded President Eisenhower's interest in providing financial backing for the Aswan project by mid-March 1956. In a wide-ranging discussion of American strategy in the Middle East on 15 March, Eisenhower told the Joint Chiefs of Staff that "the time may be coming when we will have to serve some notice on certain of the Middle Eastern countries." The Nasser regime's behavior, Eisenhower suggested, had become a particularly annoying problem for the United States. As means of curbing Nasser, Eisenhower mentioned American entry into the Baghdad Pact, promotion of King Saud of Saudi Arabia as a rival to Nasser for leadership of the Arab world, and suspension of the Aswan offer.[1]

Secretary of State Dulles shared President Eisenhower's misgivings about providing aid for the High Dam. During a SEATO meeting in Karachi in the second week of March 1956, Dulles confided to Selwyn Lloyd—who was still seething with anger at Nasser over Egypt's presumed role in the Glubb affair—that he favored delaying conclusion of the High Dam negotiations with Egypt until the Nasser regime moderated its behavior.[2] Dulles subsequently sent a cable to Eisenhower outlining a new harder-line policy toward Egypt, based upon the strengthening of pro-Western Arab regimes, the provision of private security guarantees to the Israelis, and the gradual escalation of Western economic pressure against the Egyptian government. Eisenhower responded enthusiastically:

For some time now I have been talking to some of my friends
in a general and rather hazy sort of fashion along similar
lines. I tend to believe that if we could get Libya and Saudi
Arabia firmly in our camp, and do it at the same time that
we give Israel the necessary assurances, we would have the
possibility of trouble in that region very greatly minimized, if
not practically eliminated.[3]

On the morning of Saturday, 24 March 1956, shortly after
his return to the United States, Foster Dulles met at his home
in Washington with his brother Allen and a small group of
CIA and State Department advisers to conduct a comprehensive
reevaluation of American policy towards Egypt.[4] The result of
this discussion was the Secretary of State's four-page "Omega
Memorandum," presented to President Eisenhower at a meeting
at the White House on the afternoon of 28 March. In the
memorandum's introduction, Dulles wrote:

In view of the negative outcome of our efforts to bring Colonel Nasser to adopt a policy of conciliation toward Israel, we
should, I believe, now adjust certain of our Near Eastern policies, as indicated below. The primary purpose would be to let
Colonel Nasser realize that he cannot cooperate as he is doing
with the Soviet Union and at the same time enjoy most-fa-
vored nation treatment from the United States. We would
want for the time being to avoid any open break which
would throw Nasser irrevocably into a Soviet satellite status
and we would want to leave Nasser a bridge back to good
relations with the West if he so desires.[5]

Dulles then sketched a course of action which would aim,
first, to punish Egypt for its recalcitrance, and second, to bolster
the Western position in the rest of the Arab world. Under the
former heading, Dulles suggested that the United States and
Britain continue to block arms shipments to Egypt, "continue
to delay the conclusion of current negotiations on the High
Aswan Dam," and temporarily shelve plans to provide Egypt
with surplus American foodstuffs on concessional terms. At the
same time, the United States, in concert with Britain, would
endeavor to strengthen King Hussein in Jordan and King Idris
in Libya against pro-Nasser coups, would "give increased sup-

port to the Baghdad Pact without actually adhering to the Pact or announcing our intention of doing so," would shore up the pro-Western Lebanese government, and would provide military aid and political backing for King Saud. "In addition to the foregoing course of action," Dulles concluded, "planning should be undertaken at once with a view to possibly more drastic action in the event that the above courses of action do not have the desired effect." [6]

Eisenhower approved the shift in policy delineated in the Omega Memorandum, noting that:

> A fundamental factor in the problem is the growing ambition of Nasser, the sense of power he has gained out of his associations with the Soviets, his belief that he can emerge as a true leader of the entire Arab world—and because of these beliefs, his rejection of every proposition advanced as a measure of conciliation between the Arabs and Israel.[7]

President Eisenhower emphasized that "we should make sure we concert the overall plan with the British—i.e. with Eden and Lloyd." [8] One week before, on 21 March, the British Cabinet had approved a shift in policy toward Egypt that was considerably more far reaching than the proposals sketched in the Omega Memorandum.[9] The Eden government applauded the new hard line that the Eisenhower Administration had begun to take in its relations with the Nasser regime; moreover, it urged the Americans to begin contingency planning for a coup d'état against the Syrian government—which was rumored to have signed an arms agreement with the Soviet bloc—and for covert operations designed to subvert the Nasser regime. Foster Dulles and his brother Allen were intrigued by the idea of replacing the Baathist government in Damascus with a more pro-Western regime, but they considered the British interest in a plot to overthrow Nasser to be premature and unrealistic. To explore the possibility of staging a coup in Syria, to restrain the British in their plotting against Nasser, and generally to coordinate the shift in American and British policies in the Middle East, the Secretary of State set up a special interagency task force, code-named the "Omega Group," in early April 1956. Raymond Hare, then the Director General of the Foreign Service, was assigned to chair the group.[10]

Whatever their differences on the question of covert operations against Nasser, the Eisenhower Administration and the Eden government were in complete agreement in April 1956 on the need to shelve the Aswan offer until such time as the Egyptian government proved more cooperative on the issues of Palestine and regional defense.[11] The prospects for such a change in Egyptian behavior did not seem particularly bright at this point; in the early part of April, Radio Cairo had stepped up its anti-British campaign, and Egyptian-Israeli border clashes had increased markedly in frequency and intensity.[12] At a NATO meeting in Paris at the beginning of May, Foster Dulles and Selwyn Lloyd agreed to let the Aswan Dam project "wither on the vine"—the expression used by the Eden government to describe the policy of deliberate neglect of Nasser's *contre-mémoire* on High Dam aid, which had been gathering dust in Washington and London since January.[13]

Nasser Plays the China Card

Any chances that there might have been for reviving the Eisenhower Administration's interest in High Dam aid were smothered on 16 May 1956, when Egypt became the first nation to recognize the People's Republic of China since the Korean War. Although Nasser probably did not give much thought to what the U.S. reaction would be when he decided to extend formal recognition to Communist China, there were few things that he could have done in the spring of 1956 that would have antagonized the American government more than recognition of the PRC.[14]

The Nasser regime's decision to recognize the People's Republic seems to have been motivated by three important considerations. In the first place, Nasser hoped to use the PRC as an alternative source of arms in the event that the Soviet Union joined in a United Nations embargo of weapons shipments to the Middle East.[15] At a press conference in London on 27 April 1956, during a week long official visit to Britain, Khrushchev had expressed the Soviet government's willingness to take part in such an embargo.[16] Concerned about the reliability of the Soviets as arms suppliers, particularly at a time when Israel had accelerated its own military build up,[17] Nasser apparently thought that he could obtain substantial quantities of arms from the Peking regime. In fact, the Communist Chinese did not have a well-developed defense industry in this period. But as Yitzhak Schichor concludes, "all the evidence suggests Nasser really believed that in the event of an embargo, China could not only provide a transit channel for Soviet weapons, but could serve also as an independent source of supply of conventional weapons and eventually of nuclear weapons as well." [18] To underline his interest in Chinese arms, Nasser appointed General Hasan Ragab, the Deputy Minister of War in charge of armaments and military industries, as Egypt's first ambassador to the People's Republic.[19]

Secondly, Nasser hoped that recognition of the PRC would give a further boost to the already booming Sino-Egyptian trade relationship.[20] By the end of 1955, the People's Republic had become the largest foreign buyer of Egypt's cotton, and the Egyptian government had begun to make plans to barter more cotton for Chinese steel.[21] Finally, recognition of Communist China was an expression of Nasser's growing commitment to positive neutralism. In the thirteen months since the Bandung Conference, Sino-Egyptian political, economic, and cultural ties had grown apace with the deepening of Nasser's interest in the nonaligned movement. Disillusioned with the West and suspicious of the Soviets, Nasser saw recognition of the PRC— the self-proclaimed patron of the Afro-Asian bloc—as a natural step in the evolution of an independent foreign policy, free from superpower intrigue.[22]

In an era in which Red China was widely regarded in the United States as America's most intractable enemy, Egypt's recognition of the Peking regime was hardly calculated to boost Nasser's stock in Washington. Given the depth of its hostility to the People's Republic, however, the Eisenhower Administration's initial public reaction to Egypt's recognition was surprisingly mild. Foster Dulles conceded that Nasser's action was probably an "indication that the Egyptians do not feel confident that they can get arms indefinitely from the Russians," rather than a deliberate snub of the United States.[23] When questioned about Egypt's recognition of the PRC at a press conference on 22 May, the Secretary of State responded in tones which suggested not so much outrage as a general weariness with Nasser and his policies:

> This is an action we regret. I have indicated that we are sympathetic with whatever action he reasonably takes to emphasize the genuine independence of Egypt, and to the extent that he is a spokesman for Egyptian independence, we have sympathy with his point of view. . . . But to the extent that he takes action which seems to promote the interests of the Soviet Union and Communist China, we do not look with favor upon such action.[24]

At a press conference on 23 May, President Eisenhower echoed Dulles, noting simply that "we think that Egypt is mistaken." In its report on the President's press conference, the *New York Times* commented that Eisenhower did not seem to be greatly disturbed by Egypt's recognition of the PRC.[25]

In private, however, Dulles and Eisenhower were greatly disturbed by Nasser's action. Both men were alarmed by any move that brought the Peking regime into the mainstream of world affairs. Moreover, Dulles and Eisenhower realized that Egypt's recognition of Communist China would intensify opposition to the Nasser regime in the United States. The American press was uniformly critical of Nasser's decision to recognize the PRC. In an editorial entitled "Nasser's Nose Thumbing" on 18 May the *Washington Post* accused Nasser of "acting as a Soviet stalking horse against the West in the Middle East and Africa." [26] On 20 May the *New York Herald Tribune* urged Eisenhower to "take a tougher line" with Egypt.[27]

More importantly, from the point of view of the Eisenhower Administration, Nasser's recognition of the PRC hardened Congressional opposition to Egypt. Shortly after Egypt announced its recognition of the Peking regime, Senator William Knowland, a prominent Republican known as the "Senator from Formosa" because of his championship of the Chiang Kai-Shek government on Taiwan, told Foster Dulles bluntly that "it was going to be very difficult for him to get enough votes for the Aswan project." [28]

On 17 May, the day after recognition was announced, Secretary of State Dulles called Egyptian Ambassador Ahmed

Hussein into his office and expressed his extreme displeasure with the Egyptian government's ties to Communist China.[29] Later that day, Undersecretary of State Hoover reportedly told Hussein that Egypt would not receive High Dam aid from the United States unless it curbed its importation of Soviet bloc arms and became more responsive to the American government's proposals for an Arab-Israeli settlement.[30] On 18 May, Ambassador Hussein hurried back to Cairo to discuss the deteriorating U.S.-Egyptian relationship with Nasser.

Black Returns to Cairo

While Ahmed Hussein sought to convey the Eisenhower Administration's deep dissatisfaction with Egypt's recognition of the Communist Chinese to Nasser, Eugene Black flew into Cairo to see what could be done about resurrecting Western aid for the Aswan project. Black met with Nasser on 20 June, and found the Egyptian Prime Minister "rather surprised and hurt that he had gotten no answer to his suggested changes" in the terms of the Anglo-American aid offer. Black urged Nasser to scrap his *contre-mémoire* and accept the Anglo-American conditions, emphasizing that such conditions were an accepted feature of international loans and that neither the Eisenhower Administration nor the Eden government was likely to alter its terms. According to Black, Nasser said that he would give serious consideration to dropping the Egyptian *contre-mémoire*.[31]

Upon his return to Washington, Black met with Foster Dulles, Herbert Hoover, Jr., and Robert Murphy, the Undersecretary of State for Political Affairs, and reported that he was optimistic about the chances of Nasser accepting the terms of the Western offer of aid for the High Dam. Dulles told Black: "Well, you know, I've been thinking about this Aswan Dam project, and I just wonder if this isn't too much for the Egyptian government to undertake." Black replied that in the view of the World Bank the Egyptian economy was just as capable of bearing the financial burden of the High Dam in June 1956 as it had been when the Western offer was made in December 1955. Dulles persisted, concluding: "Well, I just don't know whether we should go through with this or not." Disturbed by Dulles's backsliding on the Aswan offer, Black warned the Secretary of State that "all hell might break loose" if the Western offer were cancelled.[32]

Shepilov and the Phantom Soviet High Dam Offer

The doubts that Foster Dulles expressed to Eugene Black about the strength of the Egyptian economy were less a product of a sudden conversion to Secretary of the Treasury Humphrey's line of thinking about the Aswan project than they were a convenient means of camouflaging the Secretary of State's mounting disenchantment with Nasser's ties to the Communist bloc. First Nasser recognized the People's Republic of China; then in June 1956, during newly appointed Soviet Foreign Secretary Dmitri Shepilov's official visit to Cairo, Nasser began to fan rumors that the Soviet Union had made an extremely generous offer of aid for the High Dam project. In an interview on 1 April 1956, Nasser casually mentioned to *New York Times* correspondent Osgood Caruthers that he was holding a Soviet offer of aid for the Dam, stressing almost too firmly that he did not want to use the Soviet proposal "as a threat or a bluff," and adding that the offer was "very general" and had not been studied closely by the Egyptian government.[33] When Shepilov arrived in Cairo in mid-June for the celebrations marking the final British evacuation from the Suez Canal Zone, Nasser and his subordinates deliberately leaked reports about a new and more detailed Soviet offer to the Western press.[34] On 18 June 1956, the *New York Times* claimed that Shepilov had offered Nasser a loan of $1.2 billion, repayable over twenty years at 2 percent interest.[35] The *Times* of London ran a similar story on 22 June, adding that the Soviet government had also agreed to purchase the total Egyptian cotton surplus in 1956–57 and pay for it in transferable sterling.[36]

Although Shepilov himself never expressly denied the existence of a firm Soviet offer of aid for the High Dam, the Soviet government began to back away discreetly from its alleged offer as soon as Shepilov returned to Moscow. On 29

June, a spokesman for the Soviet Embassy in Cairo denied any awareness of a definite Soviet offer of economic assistance.[37] In Moscow, the Soviet Foreign Office refused comment on rumors of a new High Dam aid proposal.[38] However eager it was to mine the public relations value of vague promises of aid, the Soviet government was evidently not yet prepared to commit itself to financial support for the Aswan project.

Foster Dulles suspected that Nasser had inflated Shepilov's very general offer of help in the construction of the High Dam in an effort to attract a more generous Western offer.[39] As the summer of 1956 wore on, Dulles became convinced that Nasser was repeating his tactic of the summer of 1955 and was attempting to ignite a Soviet-American bidding war for Egypt's favors. And in the summer of 1956 Dulles was even more determined than he had been in the summer of 1955 to avoid such a contest.

"Not One Cent for the Dam": Congressional Pressure and the Tactics of Dulles's Cancellation of the High Dam Offer

By the end of June 1956, Foster Dulles had concluded that the Nasser regime would never make the political concessions that the American government expected in return for High Dam aid. Informal suspension of the Aswan offer had not produced any marked change in Nasser's attitude. The Egyptian government continued to expand its ties to the Soviet bloc, and it continued to evade American pressure to seek a negotiated settlement of the Palestine problem. Dulles's hopes of using High Dam aid to demonstrate American strength in the Cold War struggle for influence in the Third World were disintegrating; the dangling Aswan offer now seemed to Dulles to be, if anything, a demonstration of the way in which opportunistic neutralists could manipulate Cold War rivalry for their own ends.

Cancellation of the Aswan offer was a logical extension of the course of action sketched in the Omega Memorandum. Foster Dulles and Selwyn Lloyd had agreed in early May 1956 that the preferred method of cancellation, assuming that Nasser's behavior did not change dramatically, was to let the Aswan offer "wither on the vine"—thus avoiding a politically damaging confrontation with Egypt. The United States and Britain would simply ignore Nasser's *contre-mémoire*, effectively withdrawing the Aswan offer but never formally rescinding it. In mid-July 1956, however, Dulles decided to scrap the "wither on the vine" policy and publicly repudiate the West's High Dam offer. Two considerations seem to have been uppermost in the Secretary of State's mind: first, he was anxious to avert a showdown with Congress over efforts on Capitol Hill to compel the Eisenhower Administration to abandon the Aswan offer; and, second, he wanted to cancel the offer in a fashion that would illustrate pointedly to Third World governments that the United States would not reward developing countries with aid if they refused to cooperate with the West and tried to use Cold War rivalry for their own ends.

internal pressures arg.

As pressure from the cotton lobby, the Israel lobby, and the China lobby mounted during the spring and summer of 1956, Congressional opposition to High Dam aid mushroomed.[40] At a closed House Appropriations Committee hearing in early June, committee chairman Clarence Cannon (D-Mo.) told Foster Dulles: "I want you to understand, Mr. Secretary, that we will not approve one cent for any dam in Egypt. So please bear that in mind."[41] The Senate Appropriations Committee was equally unsympathetic to the Aswan project. At a 19 June hearing on foreign aid appropriations for fiscal year 1957, Dulles was warned by several of the members of the Senate Appropriations Committee that the Administration would risk the loss of its entire foreign aid program if it persisted in its efforts to seek funds for the Aswan Dam. Dulles was warned specifically that he would not be able to obtain aid for Yugoslavia if he continued to press for economic assistance for the Nasser regime.[42] "The Senate was apparently willing to authorize aid for Yugoslavia, a Communist country leaning toward nonalignment," Fraser Wilkins said later, "but it was not prepared to authorize aid for both Yugoslavia and Egypt, a nonaligned country leaning toward the Communist bloc."[43] Eager to exploit a chink in the Soviet armor in Eastern Europe, Dulles attached great importance to the U.S. aid program in Yugoslavia. According to one source, "Dulles considered it imperative to salvage the Tito program."[44] If the price for passage of the

Yugoslavia over Egypt

Yugoslav aid appropriation was abandonment of Aswan aid, Dulles was not averse to paying it.

Dulles assured the Senate Appropriations Committee that "there is no commitment at the present time" to provide American financial backing for the High Dam, noting that plans had already been made to transfer the original $56 million allocation for the Aswan project to other aid projects when it lapsed on 30 June, at the end of fiscal year 1956.[45] "The situation," Dulles said, "is at present in abeyance." Unsatisfied by Dulles's assurances, Senator Spessard Holland (D-Fla.) sought a firm guarantee that the Eisenhower Administration would clear any future High Dam allocations with the Appropriations Committee. Holland told Dulles: "I think it is such a critical point that this committee ought to have a chance to see it and pass upon it before there is any commitment of any sort made by our government relative to the construction of the Aswan Dam. Do you agree with that?" The Secretary of State replied: "I think that is a reasonable suggestion, certainly, as far as it would involve consideration by this committee."[46] Dulles subsequently sent the Appropriations Committee a letter stating "that none of the funds which may be appropriated for fiscal year 1957 will be committed to finance the Aswan Dam without specific prior consultation with the committee."[47]

Still unsatisfied by Dulles's promises to consult with Congress before dipping into the untargeted portion of the 1957 foreign aid appropriation to provide financing for the High Dam, the Senate Appropriations Committee included the following passage in its report on the 1957 aid bill, released on 16 July 1956:

> The committee directs that none of the funds provided for in this act shall be used for assistance in connection with the construction of the Aswan Dam, nor shall any of the funds heretofore provided under the Mutual Security Act as amended be used on this dam without prior approval of the Committee on Appropriations.[48]

In a commentary on the Appropriations Committee's report on 17 July, the *New York Times* noted that the committee had "flatly ordered the Eisenhower Administration to spend no

mutual security money on the Aswan High Dam in Egypt."
The Committee's action was in many ways unprecedented,
implying the existence of a Congressional veto power over
White House use of untargeted aid funds.[49]

Foster Dulles was profoundly disturbed by the Senate Appropriations Committee's attempt to tie the hands of the Eisenhower Administration on the Aswan issue, fearing that such
a maneuver would set a dangerous precedent in Executive-
Legislative relations. Late on the afternoon of 16 July, Dulles
complained to one of his advisers that while he had indicated
that he would not commit funds to the High Dam without
consultation with the Senate Appropriations Committee, the
Committee report had "gone one step further and said without
approval." [50] On that same day, Dulles wrote a brief memorandum for President Eisenhower, which concluded:

> I believe that if the Executive branch does not at this time
> indicate its unwillingness to be bound by the language in the
> Senate report that we may later be estopped—from a stand-
> point of Congressional relations if not legally—from making
> any commitment to this project without the express approval
> of the Committee. I therefore believe it would be desirable for
> you to discuss this matter with the Senate leadership tomor-
> row morning and to make clear to them your unwillingness to
> consider yourself bound by the terms of this statement.[51]

The issue, as Dulles saw it on 16 July and as Eisenhower
explained it to the Senate leadership on the morning of 17
July, was not so much the need to preserve the option of
financing the Aswan Dam as the need to preserve Executive
freedom of action in foreign policy making.[52] In a telephone
conversation with Senator Knowland, the ranking Republican
on the Senate Appropriations Committee, on the afternoon of
17 July, Dulles said that he was "pretty sure we are not going
ahead [on High Dam aid] but think it is a grave constitutional
question as to the right of any committee to direct that nothing
should be done without approval of a committee." Knowland
replied that several Committee members felt so strongly about
blocking High Dam aid that they were contemplating writing
a prohibition on such aid into the foreign aid bill itself, thus

forcing the President to veto the entire bill if he wanted to preserve the Aswan option. Dulles told Knowland that he hoped that "they won't feel it necessary because we have just about made up our minds to tell the Egyptians we will not do it." Knowland noted that the Appropriations Committee wouldn't be considering the Aswan issue until Friday, 20 July. Dulles assured Knowland that "it might well be taken care of then, so action in the bill won't be necessary. It will be taken care of before I leave for Panama." [53]

"A Major Cold War Gambit": Global Objectives and the Tactics of Dulles's Cancellation of the High Dam Offer

Given Dulles's eagerness to avoid a confrontation on Capitol Hill that might make the already troublesome task of securing passage of the foreign aid bill even more difficult, and that might upset the Executive-Legislative power balance in foreign policy making, it is not surprising that the Secretary of State sought to preempt the Senate Appropriations Committee by withdrawing the Aswan offer before Congress could put precedent-setting legislative barriers in his path. If Congressional pressure thus constituted one important influence on the timing and style of Dulles's cancellation of the High Dam offer, Dulles's own interest in using the Aswan affair to teach a lesson to developing countries constituted a second major influence on American tactics. As one of Dulles's biographers put it:

> The choice was between letting him [Nasser] down easily, through protracted renegotiation that came to nothing, or letting him have it straight. Since the issue involved was more than simply denying Nasser money for a loan, a polite and concealed rebuff would fail to make the really important point. It had to be forthright, carrying its own built in moral for neutrals in a way that the formula of applied propaganda would not cheapen.[54]

Convinced that the rumored Soviet offer of aid for the High Dam was a bluff, Dulles resolved to expose both the hollowness of Soviet promises and the unprofitability of Nasser's strategy of trying to play East off against West to an audience of impressionable developing countries. "Dulles did not want to just quietly drop the Aswan offer in July 1956," Henry Byroade said later. "He wanted to kick Nasser in the teeth with a missionary twist, in order to set an example for other budding neutralists." [55]

On 13 July, Dulles drove out to President Eisenhower's Gettysburg, Pennsylvania farm to discuss the Aswan offer. Eisenhower was still recovering from intestinal surgery, and had not paid much attention to the Aswan affair since he had entered Walter Reed Hospital on 8 June. He readily deferred to Dulles's judgement on the High Dam issue, agreeing that cancellation of the Aswan offer would provide an object lesson to other Third World governments.[56] By mid-July 1956, the stage was set for what J.R. Beal later called a "truly major gambit in the Cold War." [57]

Byroade's Dissent and Descent

As the Eisenhower Administration's interest in High Dam aid disintegrated during the spring and summer of 1956, Henry Byroade expressed his increasing disenchantment with the drift of American policy. In a cable to Foster Dulles on 26 May, Byroade criticised the "punitive thinking" that underlay the State Department's approach to the Aswan issue. Byroade charged that Washington's "thinking on the High Dam had become . . . overly concentrated around political issues connected with East-West or Arab-Israel matters." As he had predicted in January, Byroade continued, the Eisenhower Administration had blamed Nasser for the failure of the Anderson mission and had quickly abandoned its commitment to High Dam aid. "Nasser and Egypt have done many things to displease us," Byroade argued, "but it seems to me that the real change in our attitude came about at the time that we concluded that no early miracle towards an [Arab-Israeli] settlement could be accomplished through Nasser. Our special stimulus for the High Dam was off." [58]

Byroade repeated his criticisms of American policy in a lengthy cable on 16 June. He noted the parallels between current U.S. procrastination on the Aswan issue and U.S. procrastination on the military aid issue in the summer of 1955, warning that the "Department should not (repeat not) be surprised if some day it reads in the press that a decision has been made to accept Russian assistance." Failure to fulfill the Western pledge to provide backing for the Aswan project would, Byroade concluded, "have consequences which in my opinion will make things really difficult here and I fear will extend again as in the case of the arms deal considerably beyond Egypt's own boundaries." [59]

In a pointed rebuke from Dulles, Byroade was treated to a detailed review of U.S.-Egyptian relations since 1952, which purported to "unveil the true nature of Egyptian policy as being one of maintaining U.S. expectations of future Egyptian cooperation while demanding U.S. assistance and in fact pursuing policies detrimental to U.S. objectives." Byroade's superiors closed their 9 July cable by stressing that "further moves in the direction of appeasement with nothing more than vague hope of still eliciting a positive Egyptian response would involve the abandonment of soundly conceived positions with the possibility of far-reaching adverse repercussions and result in further strengthening a regime the extent of whose activities against the U.S. and the West are becoming more apparent." [60]

Byroade responded sharply on 13 July that if the U.S. government continued to consider neutralists like Nasser "as being either in the enemy camp or as 'fellow travellers', I fear that before too long we will begin to appear in the eyes of these people as being the unreasonable member of the East-West struggle." Byroade added a reminder to Washington about the limited value of economic aid as a political lever.

Department knows that while economic assistance provides a very useful lubricator for foreign policy operations . . . assistance does not (repeat not) in itself establish basic common bonds between us and recipients and it does not (repeat not) buy repudiations of national objectives which may not (repeat not) coincide with our program and policies for containing the Soviet threat. For example, economic aid will never resolve our differences [with Egypt] over Israel.[61]

Byroade warned ag. US cancellation — "Egypt will go to Soviets." He was transferred.

92   Economic Aid and American Policy toward Egypt

In Washington, Byroade's criticism of American policy on the Aswan issue was attributed to "localitis," that mysterious disease that allegedly causes American diplomats at foreign posts to confuse promotion of the interests of their host governments with promotion of American interests.[62] The State Department's time-tested cure for localitis was immediate reassignment, a move which in Byroade's case was reinforced by Foster Dulles's desire to rearrange his advisers on Near Eastern affairs. In a major reshuffling of the Department's Near East experts, it was announced on 15 July that Byroade would be transferred to South Africa, Raymond Hare would replace him in Cairo, George Allen would take over the Athens Embassy, and his deputy, William Rountree, would replace him as Assistant Secretary of State. Although Byroade did not actually leave for South Africa until September 1956, the announcement of his departure was seen in Cairo as a sign of a new hard line in American policy toward Egypt.[63] Dulles wasted little time before confirming Egyptian suspicions.

The Dulles-Hussein Meeting

When the Egyptian government reversed its earlier position and announced its acceptance of the terms of the original Western offer of aid for the High Dam, Dulles was presented with an opportunity formally and publicly to cancel the American aid proposal. With the support of Foreign Minister Mahmoud Fawzi, Ahmed Hussein had badgered Nasser throughout June 1956 to accept the aides-mémoires attached to the Anglo-American High Dam offer. Hussein realized that the Eisenhower Administration and the Eden government were rapidly losing interest in the Aswan project, and he hoped that quick agreement to the conditions set out by the West in December 1956 would salvage Western High Dam aid.[64] Nasser was less sanguine than Hussein about the chances of the American and British governments fulfilling their pledges of assistance for the High Dam project. No matter how eager Egypt appeared to be to comply with the terms of the original Aswan offer, Nasser believed, Dulles and Eden would not provide financial backing for the Dam. As Nasser told Erskine Childers ten years after the Aswan affair, "I was sure that Mr. Dulles would not help us by financing the Aswan Dam." [65]

With an official visit to the Soviet Union scheduled for August 1956, however, Nasser felt compelled to clean the slate and force the Aswan issue with the Western governments, so that he could try to secure Soviet backing for the Dam during his talks in Moscow if the West, as expected, reneged on its offer.[66] During the second week in July 1956, Nasser informed Hussein that he could return to Washington and accept the Western offer unconditionally. Nasser added that he was "100 percent sure that there will be no [Western] financing." [67] On 17 July, Hussein arrived back in Washington and declared to the press that "Egypt has decided to take assistance from the West. It all depends on the United States and Britain now." [68]

On the morning of 18 July, Dulles indicated at a Cabinet meeting at the White House that he would probably rescind the Aswan offer when he met with Ahmed Hussein the next day. "Although the United States tried for a time to work with Nasser," Dulles said, "it became impossible to do so once Egypt accepted Russian arms in large quantity." [69]

Later that same day, Dulles summoned Herbert Hoover Jr., George Allen, William Rountree, Francis Russell, State Department Legal Adviser Herman Phleger, and Policy Planning Chief Robert Bowie to his office to discuss the approach that he should take with the Egyptian ambassador. "The consensus," recalled Bowie, "was that we should go ahead and cancel the offer, and that would take part of the weight of Congress off our necks and we'd have an easier job getting money for Yugoslavia." Bowie himself was apprehensive about a flat cancellation, fearing that such an action "would be a slap in the face and it will likely cause some kind of ruckus." Bowie argued that the United States and Britain should simply "negotiate the thing to death," but Dulles and the others present at the 18 July meeting overruled him and opted to turn Hussein down outright.[70]

Dulles then presented the group with a draft of a statement that he intended to hand to Hussein during their appointment on 19 July. The draft statement hinted strongly that the United States was withdrawing its offer because the Egyptian government had failed to make the political concessions that the

Americans expected in return for High Dam aid. The draft read in part:

> Such a gigantic undertaking could succeed only in an atmosphere of international tranquility and with close and understanding cooperation between the government and people of Egypt who provide the internal effort and those abroad who provide the foreign exchange portion of the effort. In the absence of such an atmosphere the project could generate ill will and success would be improbable.
>
> Last year the government of the United States hoped that such an atmosphere could be created and that indeed the launching of the first phase of the Aswan Dam project would assist in that respect. Since then, developments seem to put into question the basic premises referred to.
>
> Under the circumstances, the United States government has informed the Egyptian government through its Ambassador at Washington that the United States government is not now disposed to proceed with its part of the projected plan.[71]

Bowie objected to the language of Dulles's draft statement, considering it unnecessarily provocative. With the Secretary of State's permission, Bowie redrafted the cancellation statement, eliminating the vague references to political conditions and stressing the economic uncertainties of the Aswan project.[72]

Dulles met with Eisenhower shortly after the President arrived for work in the Oval Office on the morning of 19 July and secured his approval of the redrafted communiqué that the Secretary of State planned to present to the Egyptian ambassador that afternoon.[73] Hussein's appointment at the State Department was scheduled for 4:00 P.M. At 3:40 P.M. the Secretary of State called his brother Allen to discuss his plan of attack. Foster Dulles began the conversation by mentioning that Hussein had indicated in a telephone call to Eugene Black on 17 July that "it is certain that if we don't go ahead they [the Egyptians] will go ahead with the Soviets." Nevertheless, the Secretary of State said that he would tell Hussein at 4:00 that "we are not going ahead definitely." If he did not withdraw the Aswan offer, added the Secretary, "Congress will chop it off tomorrow and [I] would rather do it [myself]." The Secretary noted that even if the Soviets did step in to provide the foreign exchange for High Dam construction, "we can make a lot of use of it in propaganda within the satellite bloc," emphasizing to the people of Eastern Europe that "you don't get bread because you are being squeezed to build a dam [in Egypt]." Allen Dulles warned that cancellation might be hazardous, but was "inclined to think it wise in the long run." [74]

At 4:00 P.M. Ambassador Hussein was ushered into the Secretary of State's office, where Foster Dulles, Herbert Hoover Jr., George Allen, and William Rountree were waiting to greet him. After exchanging pleasantries, Dulles told Hussein that "he had reluctantly come to the conclusion that it was not possible at present for the United States to go forward with this undertaking." Dulles said that there were two reasons for his decision that "deserved special attention." The first was the "long range impact of the project upon relations with the Egyptian people and government." After the initial good feeling generated by Western High Dam aid had evaporated, Dulles maintained, the Egyptians would grow to resent the austerity measures imposed upon them by the Nasser regime and its Western creditors. The second element, said Dulles, "related to the impact upon our own people." The Secretary of State asserted that popular and Congressional suspicions of Nasser precluded the provision of Aswan aid for the foreseeable future. Dulles then presented the Egyptian ambassador with a copy of the cancellation statement that the State Department intended to release to the press later that day.

Hussein said that, "speaking entirely personally," he "sincerely hated to see the Russians take advantage of the present situation." Hussein claimed that the Soviets had made a "very generous" offer on the Dam, and noted that "the risk [of Nasser accepting the Soviet offer] would be very great if no deal [with the West] were concluded before [Nasser's] visit to Moscow." Dulles replied that "he realized the implications of what the Ambassador had said, and the decision to withhold American assistance had not been taken lightly." Hussein expressed his regret at Dulles's decision, and departed. The cancellation statement was then released to the press.[75]

The Secretary of State immediately informed the Congressional leadership that the Aswan issue had been disposed of. At 5:10 P.M. Dulles told Senator Knowland in a telephone conversation that he had "just had a talk with the Egyptian ambassador on the Aswan Dam project and had said that we were not in a position to go ahead with the Dam offer." Dulles added that "it would be interesting to see what happens." [76] At 5:30 P.M., the Secretary of State called his brother Allen and gave him a précis of what he had told Hussein, noting that the Egyptian ambassador "had handled himself surprisingly well and with dignity." [77] As he prepared to leave his office and return home, however, the Secretary of State apparently began to have second thoughts about withdrawal of the Aswan offer. William Macomber, one of Dulles's aides, recalls that Dulles slumped in a chair in his outer office on his way out to the elevator and said wearily: "Bill, I certainly hope we did the right thing." [78]

Anglo-American Consultation and the Withdrawal of the Aswan Offer

On 20 July, the day after the climactic Dulles-Hussein meeting, a British Foreign Office spokesman announced laconically that "we have concluded that in present circumstances it would not be feasible to participate in the [Aswan] project." [79] Although the Eden government would have preferred to have let the Western offer of aid for the High Dam "wither on the vine," it had clearly already decided to withdraw its Aswan offer, and was not surprised by Dulles's action.

It has often been asserted that the British government was given very little advance warning of, and no real opportunity to object to, Dulles's decision to drop the Aswan offer. Eden himself notes in his memoirs that "we were informed but not consulted and so had no prior opportunity for criticism or comment." [80] Selwyn Lloyd says that "Makins, the British ambassador, was informed one hour before the [Dulles-Hussein] meeting. I had had no idea that there was going to be this abrupt withdrawal." [81] Macmillan recalls that "it came as a shock to us when we heard of [the cancellation]." [82] On the American side, Winthrop Aldrich claims that "it [the withdrawal of the U.S. offer] came as a great shock to the British, they didn't have any idea that he was going to do this although they were partners in this whole arrangement." [83] Robert Murphy wrote in his memoirs that there was "regrettable lack of adequate notice to the partners in the consortium, especially Britain which was chiefly affected. The British ambassador in Washington, Sir Roger Makins, was notified of the American decision to cancel its offer to Egypt only an hour or so before Hussein called on Dulles." [84] Several historians have repeated this version of events. Richard Goold Adams, for example, maintains that Dulles cancelled the American offer of financial backing for the High Dam "without a single word of warning to his British colleagues." [85]

In fact, as Roger Makins later recalled, the Eden government "had about thirty-six hours advance warning of Dulles's decision, and chose not to object to the Eisenhower Administration's formal cancellation of the Aswan offer." [86] According to Makins, Dulles had told him on 17 July, after Ahmed Hussein had indicated Egypt's willingness to accept the original terms of the Western offer and after the Senate Appropriations Committee had insisted in its report on the foreign aid bill that the Eisenhower Administration obtain its approval before providing funds for the High Dam, that the United States government "would probably withdraw its Aswan offer." On the morning of 18 July Dulles called Makins and said that he intended to hand Hussein a statement cancelling the American offer at their meeting on the afternoon of 19 July. Dulles explained that he had no real alternative, given his desire to avoid a damaging confrontation over the Aswan issue on Capitol Hill. The Secretary of State promised to call Makins the next morning to confirm his decision to drop the American High Dam proposal.[87]

Makins immediately sent a cable to the Foreign Office describing his conversations with Dulles.[88] Makins's cable did not come as a shock to the Eden government; ten days earlier Anthony Nutting had reported after a talk with U.S. Ambassador Henry Cabot Lodge at the United Nations in New York that Dulles would probably abandon Aswan aid shortly because of Congressional pressure.[89] Makins was quite surprised when 18 July passed without a response from Eden and Lloyd. As he had promised, Foster Dulles telephoned Makins on the morning of 19 July and said that he would definitely cancel the American High Dam offer outright during his meeting with Ambassador Hussein. Makins replied that the British government "would have liked more time, but in view of the Congressional situation, it would support Dulles's decision." Shortly afterward, a cable from the Foreign Office finally arrived at the British Embassy, acknowledging Makins's cable of 18 July, and expressing general support for the American cancellation. Eden and Lloyd would have preferred that the Eisenhower Administration "play it long," they indicated to Makins, but they understood the nature of Eisenhower's difficulties with Congress and accepted his decision to withdraw American financial backing for the High Dam immediately.[90] During his conversation with his brother Allen just before Hussein arrived at the State Department, Foster Dulles noted that the Eden government had raised no objections to his decision to drop the Aswan offer, so he "guessed it was all right." [91]

In the immediate aftermath of the Dulles-Hussein meeting, the Eden government tried not so much to dissociate itself from the American renege as to emphasize that cancellation of the High Dam offer was a coordinated Anglo-American effort. The Foreign Office spokesman who announced Britain's withdrawal from the Aswan project on 20 July noted that there had been "continuous consultation" between London and Washington in the period before the Dulles-Hussein meeting.[92] On 25 July, Selwyn Lloyd responded to Parliamentary criticism that the British government had merely "followed the leader" in cancelling its Aswan offer by stressing that "we were in close consultation with the US government about this matter." [93] Moreover, it is doubtful that the Eden government would have announced the British cancellation three and one-half hours before officially informing the Egyptian embassy in London, as it did, if it had been as concerned about the impact of Dulles's decision on Egypt's sensibilities as it later claimed to have been.[94]

The most convincing explanation for the inaccuracy of the reminiscences of Eden, Lloyd, Macmillan, and Aldrich on the issue of Anglo-American consultation is that they allowed their recollection of events to become clouded by their bitter resentment of Foster Dulles's role in the subsequent Suez Crisis. The temptation to portray Dulles as the sole villain in the Aswan affair must have been very great, especially after Robert Murphy's account appeared and lent credence to British claims to have been wronged by Dulles. Murphy does not seem, however, to have played a key role in the deliberations which led to Dulles's withdrawal of the Aswan offer, and the testimony of Roger Makins and other former officials involved in the Aswan affair more intimately than Murphy offers substantial evidence that the Eden government had an opportunity to voice objections to the American cancellation of the Aswan offer, but chose not to.[95] It was not until after the Suez crisis had begun to break that Eden, Lloyd, and Macmillan discovered that they had been maltreated by Foster Dulles in the Aswan affair.

The Lull Before the Storm

Nasser was riding the crest of a wave of personal and national achievements when he learned of Dulles's cancellation of the American offer of aid for the High Dam: on 13 June the last British troops had left the Suez Canal zone; on 23 June Nasser had received 99.8 percent of the popular vote in Egypt's first presidential election; and on 12 July Nasser had flown to the Yugoslav island of Brioni for a summit meeting with Tito and Nehru, the other members of the neutralist "Big Three." [96] Nasser was still on Brioni when Ahmed Hussein's urgent cable describing Dulles's cancellation of Aswan aid reached him. The new Egyptian President, accompanied by Nehru, immediately flew back to Cairo, arriving early on the morning of 20 July.[97] Although not surprised by the American refusal itself, Nasser "was surprised by the insulting attitude with which the refusal was declared." He was especially annoyed by the slur on the Egyptian economy implicit in Dulles's cancellation statement.[98]

If Nasser was outraged by the collapse of Western financial backing for the Aswan project,[99] he could not help being discouraged by the Soviet government's none too nimble efforts to distance itself from High Dam aid. In response to a reporter's question on 21 July, Foreign Minister Shepilov said that "the Soviet Union is not considering aid to Egypt in the construction of the Aswan High Dam." [100] On 24 July, Soviet Ambassador to Egypt Kiselev told the Cairo press that Shepilov's earlier statement had been misinterpreted, and that the Soviet Union "stands ready to help finance the High Dam if Egypt requests help." [101] To complete the circle, the Soviet press attaché in

Cairo denied Kiselev's pledge later that same day.[102] In all the confusion surrounding Soviet policy on the High Dam, one thing was clear to Nasser: the Soviet government was not particularly eager to leap in and provide the foreign exchange needed for the first stage of the Aswan project. In his frustration, Nasser lashed out bitterly at the American government in a speech on 24 July:

> If an uproar in Washington creates false and misleading announcements, without shame and with disregard for the principles of international relations, implying that the Egyptian economy is unsound and casting shadows of doubts on Egypt's economy, then I look at Americans and say: May you choke to death on your fury.[103]

In a telephone call to Herbert Hoover, Jr., from Panama on 23 July, Foster Dulles had seemed surprised by the relative mildness of Egypt's reaction to the cancellation of the Western offer.[104] Buoyed both by the apparent tameness of Nasser's reaction and by the generally favorable reaction of the American and European press to the withdrawal of Aswan aid,[105] it was hard for the Eisenhower Administration to avoid a feeling of complacency as the first week after the Dulles-Hussein meeting drew to a close.[106] That incipient feeling of complacency was shattered on 26 July when Nasser announced in a dramatic two-hour-and-forty-minute speech in Alexandria that Egypt had nationalized the Suez Canal Company and would use the revenue earned from canal tolls to finance construction of the Aswan High Dam.[107]

26 July 1954   nationalization of Suez   the Suez...

For Anthony Eden, whose health and domestic political base were deteriorating and whose hatred of Nasser had grown apace with the decline of British power in the Middle East, and for his French counterparts, who were possessed of a rather exaggerated view of Nasser's role in the Algerian rebellion, nationalization of the Canal Company was an intolerable provocation. If the Suez Canal was no longer the lifeline of Britain's empire, it still held tremendous strategic importance for the British economy. In 1956, nearly one-fourth of Britain's imports passed through the Canal; one-third of the Canal's total traffic was of British registry; and, most importantly, Britain depended on the Canal for transportation of the bulk of its oil requirements.[108] Both the Eden government and the Mollet government, which was anxious to protect substantial French investment in the Canal Company and even more anxious to undercut Egyptian support for the Algerian nationalists, were determined to use any means necessary to force Nasser to relinquish control of the Canal Company in the short run and, in the long run, to topple Nasser or at least limit his ability to threaten Anglo-French interests in the Middle East. Eden made this clear to Eisenhower shortly after Nasser's 26 July speech:

> My colleagues and I are convinced that we must be ready, in the last resort, to use force to bring Nasser to his senses. For our part, we are prepared to do so. I have this morning instructed our Chief of Staff to prepare a military plan accordingly.[109]

As Gail Meyer observes, however, two important considerations prevented an immediate Anglo-French use of force.[110] The first obstacle was logistical. In 1956, the British could not simply sail up to Alexandria, let fly a few shells, land an expeditionary force, and rout the feckless Egyptians, as they had done in 1882; Anglo-French planners needed time to mount a joint invasion of the Canal zone. The second barrier was political: Eden and Mollet needed to secure at least the tacit approval of the Eisenhower Administration for military action against Nasser.

A detailed history of the Suez Crisis is well beyond the scope of this study, but the key developments in the crisis are worth recalling.[111] Throughout the late summer and early fall of 1956, while Britain and France prepared for military action against Nasser, the American government sought to avert an armed clash between its NATO allies and Egypt. The Eisenhower Administration's opposition to the use of force did not stem from any great sympathy for Nasser's position. At a meeting with Congressional leaders on 12 August, Foster Dulles said that Nasser had "Hitler-ite" tendencies, and was "an extremely dangerous fanatic," concluding that "if Nasser gets by with this action, the British and French are probably right in their appraisal of the consequences." President Eisenhower assured Senate Majority Leader Lyndon Johnson that the United States "wouldn't accept an inconclusive outcome leaving Nasser in control." [112] The Administration's opposition to the use of force by Britain and France stemmed instead from more practical considerations. The last thing that Dwight Eisenhower needed as the Presidential election of 1956 approached was a war in the Middle East waged in clear violation of international law by two NATO allies. The Republican Party platform laid great stress on the incumbent President's reputation as a peace-maker—as the man who had ended an unpopular war in Korea and who would keep American troops out of similar conflicts in the future—and Eisenhower was personally and politically committed to that ideal. Dulles and Eisenhower also feared that United States support for an Anglo-French attack on Nasser would badly tarnish the American image in the Third World and would enhance Nasser's international prestige as the heroic victim of strong-armed colonialist methods.[113]

Dulles and Eisenhower adopted a policy of prevarication in the Suez Crisis, attempting to calm tensions and tempers without appearing either to condone Egypt's action or to endorse the use of force by Britain and France.[114] To buy time, Dulles set in motion a series of negotiations designed to internationalize the Suez dispute, thus discouraging independent Anglo-French action against Egypt. Both the London Conference and the Suez Canal Users' Association attempted to foist international control of the operations of the Canal on Egypt; in both instances, Nasser balked, arguing that Egypt was obligated under the Constantinople Convention of 1888 only to ensure the "freedom and sovereignty of the Canal," not to submit to the dictates of the major users of the Canal.

While the Eisenhower Administration went to great lengths to avoid the impression that it was "ganging up" with Britain and France against Egypt, the Eden government managed to convince itself that Eisenhower would "lie doggo" (in Harold Macmillan's phrase) and refrain from active opposition in the event of an Anglo-French invasion of the Canal Zone. This was partly the result of wishful thinking on the part of the

1956

29 Oct. Israel attacks. UK) Fr. call for
cease fire
31 Oct. UK France attack.

Punishing Nasser 103

Eden government, and partly the result of deliberate ambiguity on the part of the American government. Although Eisenhower and Dulles, in their public statements during the Suez Crisis, periodically denounced resort to the use of force they were more equivocal in their private dealings with the British and the French. By carefully eschewing a clear and unequivocal stand against the use of force, the American leadership apparently hoped to retain the confidence of Britain and France, and to exert greater pressure on the Nasser regime to make concessions to America's allies.[115] In the first few weeks of the crisis, this overly artful tactic had apparently succeeded in averting military action, but in late October 1956, it came back to haunt the Eisenhower Administration.

By mid-October 1956, Britain and France had nearly completed preparations for a joint attack on Egypt. Meanwhile, the French government had coordinated Anglo-French plans for a campaign against Egypt with the Israeli government. For the Israelis, the Suez crisis provided an irresistible opportunity to smother Nasser before he could deploy his new Soviet weaponry along the Sinai frontier.[116] Between 22 and 24 October, French Foreign Minister Christian Pineau, Israeli Prime Minister Ben Gurion, and Selwyn Lloyd met at Sèvres, near Paris, and agreed that an Israeli strike across the Sinai would provide the pretext for Anglo-French intervention in the Canal Zone, ostensibly to safeguard the movement of shipping along the Canal. None of the plotters seemed certain of the ultimate objective of the tripartite attack, although they all clearly hoped that Nasser would be toppled from power once his armed forces were defeated in the Sinai and in the Canal Zone.[117]

Israel's invasion of the Sinai commenced on the evening of 29 October. The next day the British and French governments issued a joint ultimatum to Egypt and Israel to cease fighting and withdraw to positions ten miles from the Suez Canal within twelve hours.[118] On 31 October, citing the need to enforce the ultimatum and protect the Canal, Britain and France launched air attacks on Cairo and Ismailia, followed five days later by an amphibious assault on Port Said.

Although the CIA had alerted Eisenhower and Foster Dulles about the Anglo-French-Israeli military preparations, news of the actual event came as a "profound shock" to the President and the Secretary of State.[119] Declaring privately that he "wanted to establish the fact that we are not a colonial power," and that "in this struggle, they [Britain and France] are not our allies," Eisenhower made a nationwide television broadcast on 31 October, condemning the attack on Egypt, emphasizing that the United States had had no foreknowledge of the attack, and demanding the immediate withdrawal of British, French and Israeli forces from Egypt.[120] Eisenhower subsequently employed all the political and economic muscle at his disposal to dislodge the Anglo-French-Israeli invasion force.[121] Meanwhile, the Soviet government—although preoccupied with suppression of the Hungarian revolt—managed to find time to threaten to rain missiles down upon London, Paris, and Tel Aviv if hostilities did not cease.

The British and French governments argued that they had landed in Egypt only to safeguard the Canal until a United Nations peace-keeping force arrived to separate the Israelis and the Egyptians—a lame explanation reminiscent of that of bank robbers, caught in the act, who assure passersby that they intend to guard the vault until the police arrive—but finally succumbed to intense American pressure and accepted a cease-fire on 7 November, completing a phased withdrawal of their forces from the Canal Zone in December 1956. The Israelis—under similar American pressure—withdrew from the Sinai in March 1957.[122]

Hanson Baldwin noted in the *New York Times* on 10 November 1956 that "the consequences of this week's drama will spread for years to come, like ripples in a pond."[123] Britain's "moment in the Middle East" ended at Suez, as did Anthony Eden's brief moment at the pinacle of British politics. France, disturbed by her dependence upon the United States and Britain, edged towards a more independent policy based upon Continental European community. For both Britain and France, Suez marked the end of an era in international politics. As Harold Macmillan put it, "the fact that France and Britain, even acting together, could no longer impose their will was alarming. Never before in history had Western Europe proved so weak."[124]

Arab-Israeli enmity deepened. Nasser's prestige in the Arab world soared, and that of his conservative, pro-Western rivals crumbled. The Soviets emerged as the self-styled champions of Arab nationalism, even as Soviet tanks rumbled over Hungarian nationalism. With the collapse of Anglo-French influence, the United States became the chief guardian of Western interests in the Middle East and stepped in forcefully to counter the Soviet Union. In short, the Suez Crisis changed the political landscape of the Middle East, and of much of the rest of the world as well.

Aswan in Retrospect

More than a quarter century later, Foster Dulles's blunt withdrawal of American financial backing for the Aswan project seems to have been an immense political blunder. But given his anxiety about Congressional encroachment on the prerogatives of the Executive Branch in foreign policy making, his conviction that the Aswan offer was fast becoming a symbol of weakness in the East-West struggle for influence in the developing world, his inexperience in dealing with Third World nationalists, and his growing frustration with Nasser, Dulles's decision is readily comprehensible.

At the end of March 1956, Dulles had indicated in the Omega Memorandum that he doubted that Nasser would seek either to reduce his links with the Soviet bloc or to reach a negotiated settlement of the Arab-Israeli conflict, and that it was unlikely that Nasser would ever enter into the sort of political bargain that the Eisenhower Administration expected in return for High Dam aid. Subsequent events appeared to confirm Dulles's doubts: Nasser recognized the People's Republic of China; he continued to import substantial quantities of Soviet arms; and he continued to attack the West's allies in the Arab world. At the same time, Congressional pressure to withdraw the Aswan offer mounted. By mid-July 1956, maintenance of the fiction that the United States might provide funds for the Aswan project was becoming a serious drain on the Eisenhower Administration's political capital in Congress and threatened to erode the Executive Branch's foreign policy making authority. Seen against this background, Dulles's formal cancellation of the Aswan offer on 19 July is understandable, if not easily defensible.

It was the style of Dulles's withdrawal of the promise of Aswan aid, as much as anything else, that the Egyptian government found most aggravating. As Egyptian Minister of the Interior Zakaria Mohieddin put it at the time: "It is not so much the withdrawal of the money which we mind. We can find other ways of financing the High Dam. It is the way in which it was done." [125] Nasser echoed Mohieddin in a letter to President Kennedy a few years later. "There was no doubt," Nasser wrote, "that the way in which the offer was withdrawn carried with it a great deal that the Arab people in Egypt would not tolerate." [126]

Two aspects of the style of the American cancellation seemed to anger the Egyptian government most: Dulles's alleged brusqueness in his meeting with Ahmed Hussein, and the emphasis on Egypt's economic weakness in the cancellation statement released to the press. Although Dulles evidently took pains to convey the American decision to withdraw the High Dam offer to Hussein in a calm and diplomatic manner, a certain amount of Egyptian resentment of his conduct of the 19 July meeting was inevitable. However much Dulles had tried to soften the blow, his formal and unequivocal abrogation of the Aswan offer was bound to remind the Egyptians of their years of colonial subjugation, when Egyptian political leaders had been forced to go with hats in hand to seek funds from British colonial administrators. Similarly, the Nasser regime would no doubt have taken offense at whatever rationale the U.S. government offered for its abandonment of the Aswan project, but Dulles and Bowie hit a particularly raw nerve when they implied in their cancellation statement that the Egyptian economy was incapable of bearing the burden of construction of the High Dam. For a regime that prided itself on its commitment to economic modernization, the Eisenhower Administration's derogation of the Egyptian economy was a challenge that could not be ignored. "No one," Eugene Black said later, "likes being refused a loan by a bank, but people get very upset when they read in the paper the next day that they were refused because their credit wasn't any good." [127]

Far from moderating Nasser's behavior, the cancellation of Aswan aid drove the Egyptian leader to behavior which seemed in Washington to be more immoderate than ever. Moreover, the withdrawal of the Aswan offer greatly damaged America's reputation in the developing world, even as Eisenhower was straining to avoid being tarred by the neocolonialist brush during the Suez Crisis. For years afterward, the style with which Dulles abandoned the Aswan project was cited by Third World governments as evidence of American indifference to the psychological, as well as the material, needs of developing countries.

Instead of becoming an object lesson for Third World governments on the unprofitability of attempting to use Cold War rivalry for their own ends, the Aswan affair became an object lesson for the American government on the unprofitability of attempting to use economic aid too blatantly as a political lever in relations with developing countries. American governments, however, have a marvelous propensity for forgetting, ignoring, or simply misinterpreting historical lessons; within a decade, the threat of economic aid cut-offs would once again be brandished in U.S.-Egyptian relations.

CHAPTER FOUR

"Decent Interval":
Aid Policy in the Twilight Years
of the Eisenhower Era

There was, as Raymond Hare later put it, a "false glow" over U.S.-Egyptian relations in the wake of Suez.[1] The brief period of U.S.-Egyptian amity created by Eisenhower's opposition to the tripartite attack on Egypt was more apparent than it was real; far from seeking to build a better U.S.-Egyptian relationship on the foundation of Suez, the Eisenhower Administration set out at the beginning of 1957 to isolate Nasser and block the spread of his influence in the Arab world. The keystone of the Administration's effort was the Eisenhower Doctrine, a logical extension of the anti-Nasser campaign outlined in the Omega Memorandum. Another feature of the post-Suez drive to curb the Nasser regime was the suspension of America's modest program of technical and commodity aid. With the outbreak of hostilities in October 1956, the several dozen American technical advisers then working on Egyptian development projects were evacuated. At the same time, shipments of surplus wheat under a $19.2-million aid agreement reached early in 1956 were curtailed. Egypt received no economic aid from the United States during 1957.[2] When pressed about the chances for a revival of the aid program in Egypt, a State Department spokesman observed laconically in May 1958 that economic aid might be resumed after a "decent interval."[3]

That interval proved to be shorter than many people in Washington had anticipated. After the Iraqi revolution in July 1958 torpedoed the Baghdad Pact and revealed the bankruptcy of the Eisenhower Doctrine, the Eisenhower Administration launched a cautious effort to ease U.S.-Egyptian tensions. The chief ingredient of this new, more conciliatory approach was a revived economic aid program, consisting almost entirely of Public Law 480 food aid. A gradual improvement in U.S.-Egyptian relations and a gradual increase in PL480 shipments to Egypt went hand in hand in 1959–60. By the end of the Eisenhower era, the stage was set for the Kennedy Administration's dramatic effort to build a cordial U.S.-Egyptian relationship with American food aid.

The Rise and Fall of the Eisenhower Doctrine

Eisenhower's post-mortem view of the Suez Crisis was not that Britain and France had been wrong to attempt to check the growth of Nasser's influence in the Arab world, but that "the West had gotten into a lot of difficulty by selecting the wrong issue about which to be tough." [4] From Eisenhower's point of view, the "right" issue about which to be tough was the spread of Communist influence in the Middle East. To the extent that Nasser served as the Soviet Union's trailblazer in the region, Eisenhower believed, the Egyptian border deserved Western punishment. On 12 December 1956, Eisenhower cabled Foster Dulles, who was in Paris attending the first post-Suez meeting of NATO foreign ministers, that "I hope that our NATO friends will understand clearly that we have no intention of standing idly by to see the southern flank of NATO completely collapse through Communist penetration and success in the Middle East while we do nothing about it. I am sure that they know that we regard Nasser as an evil influence." [5]

To emphasize his point, Eisenhower appeared before a joint session of Congress on 5 January 1957 to seek legislative support for his argument that "the existing vacuum in the Middle East must be filled by the United States before it is filled by Russia." [6] On 30 January, the House of Representatives approved Eisenhower's request for prior authorization of the use of American military forces to assist "any nation or group of nations in the general area of the Middle East that requests such aid against overt armed aggression from a nation controlled by Communism," and for a $200 million appropriation for military and economic aid that the President could dispense at his discretion to thwart Soviet ambitions in the region. When the Senate followed suit on 9 March, the "Eisenhower Doctrine"—which the State Department had billed privately on Capitol Hill as a "Middle East version of the Truman Doctrine"—was born.[7]

Although not widely noted for his clairvoyant gifts, Khrushchev was right when he predicted that the Eisenhower Doctrine "would end up on the garbage heap of history."[8] The fatally flawed premise which underlay the Doctrine was that militant anti-Western nationalism was practically indistinguishable from "international Communism." The Eisenhower Doctrine set the United States squarely in the path of Nasser's brand of revolutionary Arab nationalism. Despite the euphemistic camouflage of the term "nation controlled by Communism," it was clear that the Doctrine aimed to isolate the Nasser regime and its Syrian allies and build an anti-Communist Arab alliance without them. As events were soon to demonstrate, it was a mistake to equate "Nasserism" with "international Communism" and an even greater mistake to suppose that anti-Communism was a potentially more powerful force in the Arab world than revolutionary Arab nationalism.[9]

With all the subtlety of temperance crusaders in a distillery, Eisenhower and Dulles set out in early 1957 to enlist the pro-Western Arab states in their anti-Nasser, anti-Soviet campaign. Less fearful of Communist take-overs than of Nasserist subversion of their regimes, Lebanese President Camille Chamoun publicly endorsed the Eisenhower Doctrine, King Saud tacitly subscribed to it, and a number of other Arab leaders voiced cautious enthusiasm for the American initiative.[10] In its first test in the Jordanian crisis of April 1957, the Doctrine scored an apparent success. Embroiled in a domestic conflict with pro-Nasser forces, King Hussein claimed that he was being threatened by "international Communist subversion" and invoked the Eisenhower Doctrine. The American government immediately responded by despatching the Sixth Fleet to the eastern Mediterranean and by providing $20 million in emergency aid to Hussein. With the support of his loyal Bedouin troops and the prompt assistance of the United States, Hussein quickly suppressed domestic opposition to his rule.[11]

The Eisenhower Administration's efforts to bridle the increasingly pro-Soviet Syrian government in the summer and fall of 1957 met with less success. In mid-August, Syria concluded an economic aid agreement with the Soviet Union and Czechoslovakia, and the new leftist chief of staff of the Syrian army, General Afif Bizri, began a purge of conservative elements in the armed forces. At the same time, the governments of Lebanon, Iraq and Jordan complained to the United States that the Syrians were plotting against them. In response, Eisenhower and Dulles reaffirmed America's commitments under the Eisenhower Doctrine; prepared airlifts of arms to Lebanon, Iraq and Jordan; again despatched the Sixth Fleet to the eastern Mediterranean; and encouraged the Turkish government to take a hard line with the Syrians over border differences. This last strategem backfired in the fall of 1957, as Turco-Syrian tensions rapidly escalated. When Turkey began to mass troops on the Syrian border in October, Nasser sprang to the Syrian regime's aid by sending Egyptian troops to Syria. Nasser also adroitly mobilized the rest of the Arab world—even Syria's antagonists in Lebanon, Iraq and Jordan—in a common Arab nationalist front against Turkey and, by inference, Turkey's American backers. Confronted by this show of strength, the Turks quietly scaled down their troop concentrations on the Syrian border.[12] The principal offshoot of the whole affair was a general strengthening of Nasser's influence in the Arab world, capped by the creation of the United Arab Republic, formally uniting Egypt and Syria, in February 1958.[13]

If there was a political "vacuum" to be filled in the Arab world in the aftermath of Suez, Nasser was determined that it be filled not with American influence, and not with Soviet influence, but with Egyptian influence. To this end, Nasser mounted an extremely effective campaign against the Eisenhower Doctrine in 1957–58, which seriously undermined popular support for several of Nasser's pro-Western Arab rivals. On 14 July 1958, the most implacable of those rivals, Nuri Said, was ousted from power in a brutal coup d'état in Baghdad. Fearful of a chain reaction, the Lebanese and Jordanian governments appealed to the West for support. Meanwhile the Israeli government hinted that it would be forced to intervene in Jordan if pro-Nasser forces overthrew King Hussein; then King Saud warned the Eisenhower Administration nervously that he "would go along with UAR foreign policy" if the West did not retaliate swiftly against Nasser, and he also stated that "if the United States and the United Kingdom do not do anything about Iraq and Jordan, they are finished as powers in the Middle East." [14]

At a meeting with Congressional leaders on the afternoon of 14 July, Foster Dulles concluded that "it is time to bring a halt to the deterioration of our position in the Middle East." [15] On 15 July, the first of 14,000 American troops landed in Lebanon, and British paratroopers landed in Jordan. The American intervention set the stage for a renewal of the national pact between Christians and Moslems in Lebanon, and the British intervention steadied Hussein's hand in Jordan, but neither intervention could reverse the outcome of the Iraqi revolution. The collapse of the Nuri Said regime—long the cornerstone of Western defense strategy in the Arab world— left Eisenhower and Dulles holding the pieces of the shattered Baghdad Pact/Eisenhower Doctrine policy of trying to organize an Arab defense against Soviet expansionism. The Lebanese intervention did enable the Eisenhower Administration to salvage something of American prestige from the wreckage, but it could not—nor was it intended to—revive America's moribund alliance-building strategy in the Arab world.

The "Icebox Approach" to U.S.-Egyptian Relations

The futility of a policy based upon sealing the rest of the Arab world off from Nasserism had become painfully apparent to the Eisenhower Administration by the fall of 1958. As they struggled to reconcile themselves to the fact that it made more sense to work with Nasser than to work against him, Eisenhower and Dulles were heartened by signs that the Egyptian leader was not quite the Communist stooge that they had sometimes presumed him to be in 1957.

After the Lebanese, Jordanian, and Iraqi crises of July 1958, Nasser's principal preoccupation was with the consolidation of the Syrian-Egyptian union. But as Nasser grappled with the problem of Syria in the fall of 1958, he was exposed to withering fire from a new antagonist in a familiar quarter. Nuri Said's violent downfall had been widely seen as a triumph for Nasserism, but Nuri's ambitious leftist successor, General Abdel Karim Kassem, soon demonstrated that he was determined to challenge Nasser for leadership of the Arab world.[16] In the ensuing Iraqi-Egyptian feud, the Soviet Union lent considerable moral and material support to Kassem, who had opened up his government to Iraqi Communists, and who seemed to many Kremlin strategists to be a potentially more reliable Arab ally than Nasser. There were, however, limits to the extent to which the Soviets were willing to provoke Nasser, in whom they had invested sizeable amounts of military and economic aid.[17] As the State Department's Office of Intelligence and Research noted in late October 1958, "while the Soviet government apparently is willing to add new strains to its relations with Nasser to achieve this goal (strengthening Communist influence in Iraq), it is not likely at present to pursue this aim to the point of a break in relations with Nasser." [18] Even as the Soviets supported Kassem in his propaganda war with Nasser, they agreed in December 1958 to provide $100 million for completion of the first stage of the Aswan High Dam.[19]

Similarly, Nasser attempted to keep his rift with the Soviets within manageable bounds. Although he launched a harsh campaign to repress Egyptian Communists in December 1958, he emphasized his desire to continue Soviet-Egyptian cooperation in the fields of economic and military development. Nevertheless, it was clear to foreign observers, among whom some of the most attentive were in Washington, that Nasser was by no means a Soviet pawn.[20]

It was partly with an eye toward balancing his deteriorating relationship with the Soviet Union with an improved relationship with the United States that Nasser instructed his new ambassador in Washington, Mustapha Kamel, in the fall of 1958 to "do anything you can to repair U.S.-Egyptian relations." [21] In extensive meetings with Assistant Secretary of State Rountree and his aides in October 1958, and in briefer meetings with Secretary Dulles and President Eisenhower in November 1958, Kamel outlined what he termed the "icebox approach" to U.S.-Egyptian relations. The Egyptian ambassador's plan was deceptively simple: The United States and Egypt would agree to "freeze" their differences, and then—with sources of friction safely stowed in the "icebox"—they could expand areas of common interest. Kamel cited the Palestine problem as the principal candidate for the U.S.-Egyptian icebox, arguing that "trying to improvise a solution to the problem is at this point worse than ignoring the problem." Kamel maintained, moreover, that U.S.-Egyptian cooperation in the modernization of the Egyptian economy would help repair the damage done to bilateral relations in 1957–58, and would offset whatever political influence the Soviets were able to glean from arms shipments and High Dam aid. Kamel specifically requested large-scale American food aid, which Egypt—suffering from soaring food import bills and dwindling foreign exchange reserves—desperately needed, and which only the United States was in a position to provide in substantial quantities.[22] Mohamed Heikal, one of Nasser's closest confidants, repeated Kamel's request for food aid to American Ambassador Raymond Hare in a conversation in Cairo in November 1958. "If you really want to improve relations," Heikal told Hare, "you should send us your surplus wheat." [23]

For an American government that had lost much of its interest in grappling with the Arab-Israeli conflict, that was anxious to reach some sort of accomodation with Nasser, and that had begun to recognize that Nasserism might be a more formidable barrier to the spread of Soviet influence in the Arab world that any Western-sponsored defense organization, Kamel's "icebox approach" had considerable appeal. At minimal cost, Eisenhower and Dulles reasoned, they could provide the Nasser regime with an incentive to keep its distance from the Soviet bloc, and they could reverse the downward drift in American prestige in the Middle East.[24]

Food for Peace

Food aid appeared to the Eisenhower Administration in late 1958 to be an ideal means of quietly easing U.S.-Egyptian tensions. Food aid was something that the Egyptian government genuinely needed, and it was something that the American government could provide with a minimum of effort and expense. Even more importantly, from the point of view of the Eisenhower Administration, food aid was relatively immune from the sorts of legislative attacks that bedevilled Executive Branch requests for capital or technical aid. To understand the reasons for this unusual popularity, it is necessary to digress

briefly and sketch the evolution of the Public Law 480, or Food
for Peace, program.

The PL480 program originated in 1954 as a means of
disposing of burdensome agricultural surpluses; belief in the
value of PL480 aid as a foreign policy instrument developed
very gradually in the late 1950s. Senator Hubert Humphrey
(D-Minn.) noted in 1959 that "the original Public Law 480 was
probably supported by more members of Congress who conceived of it as surplus disposal than by members who understood fully its constructive potentialities." [25]

Until World War II, the burgeoning U.S. population still
needed to import more food products than it exported, but
starting in the 1940s, American agriculture was revolutionized
by better technology, better seeds, and better use of chemical
fertilizers and pesticides. Stimulated by governmental price su-
ports, and by heavy wartime demand, U.S. grain production
increased by about 50 percent during the 1940s; domestic
consumption increased by only about 30 percent.[26] The price
support program was the legacy of Roosevelt's efforts to prop
up farm income during the depression by offering payments
to farmers who pledged to cut back individual production, and
by purchasing farm products that could not be sold on the
open market above a given price. By the late 1940s, the American government was locked into a system in which farmers
consistently produced more grain than the domestic market
could absorb, and got paid for it, while the outside world had
too little money to absorb the excess.[27]

The huge price-support inventories accumulated by the government's Commodity Credit Corporation (CCC) in the late
1940s and early 1950s were "a stone around the neck of every
President who came into office." [28] In the last few years of the
Truman Administration, the CCC's storage costs averaged more
than $1 million a day.[29] Yet both Truman and Eisenhower were
reluctant to abandon the price-support system and let market
forces depress American agriculture. One American in five still
lived on a farm in 1950,[30] and neither Truman nor Eisenhower
relished the thought of tangling with the politically powerful
farm lobby. Moreover, both Truman and Eisenhower realized
that the economic impact of an agricultural slump would be
felt not only by American farmers, but also by the far more
significant part of the population engaged in the agriculture-

related occupations of food-processing, packaging, and distribution.[31]

Given the durability of price-supports, the only solution to the surplus dilemma seemed to be development of larger overseas markets for American grain. The United States would have to induce people in other countries to adopt the American diet, converting rice-eaters into wheat-eaters, and introducing more grain-fed beef into foreign diets. In 1952, the national convention of the American Farm Bureau (AFB), the chief lobbying group for American farmers, proposed that poor countries be allowed to purchase American agricultural products with local currencies instead of dollars, thus maintaining the commercial price of American grain, while at the same time disposing of surpluses and building future markets in the developing world. In the summer of 1954, the Eighty-Third Congress translated the AFB's proposal into the Agricultural Trade Development and Assistance Act, which eventually became Public Law 480.

PL480 was in essence a rather businesslike attempt to ease storage costs by allowing "friendly" food-deficit nations with limited dollar supplies to purchase surplus American agricultural commodities with nonconvertible currencies. In the cryptic jargon of the Cold War, the act defined "friendly nation" as "any country other than the Soviet Union, or any nation or area dominated or controlled by the foreign government or foreign organization controlling the World Communist Movement." [32]

The concessional sales program operated under "Title I" of Public Law 480. Title I transactions enabled poor countries to conserve precious foreign exchange reserves, which could be used to import nonfood items necessary for economic development. A small portion of the local currency accumulated by the U.S. government was used to meet the operational costs of the American diplomatic mission in the recipient country; most of the accumulated soft currency was channelled back into the local economy in the form of long-term loans at very low rates of interest to support specific development projects.[33]

PL480 also included a "Title II" provision for the donation of surplus American food to volunteer relief agencies (notably CARE, Catholic Relief Services, and Church World Services) for distribution in poor countries, and a "Title III" provision for the barter of surplus agricultural commodities for strategic materials (zinc, bauxite, lead, and beryllium among others). In response to the serious balance of payments difficulties experienced by the American economy in the late 1950s, a fourth title was added to PL480 in 1959, providing for long-term credit sales for dollars. The terms of Title IV required dollar repayment over a ten-year period, with a two-year grace period.[34]

Faced with mounting agricultural surpluses, Congress rapidly expanded the PL480 program betwen 1954 and 1960. In that period, PL480 exports were valued at roughly $6 billion, accounting for about 25 percent of total United States agricultural exports.[35] Concessional sales under Title I quickly became the workhorse for PL480, accounting for over 60 percent of total PL480 exports in the late 1950s.[36]

Few American policymakers had seemed especially excited about PL480's potential as a political lever in developing countries when the program was conceived, despite the fact that food aid had played a significant role in U.S. foreign policy in the twentieth century.[37] The Department of Agriculture—which was charged with emptying CCC surplus stocks—was concerned primarily with expansion of overseas markets for American products, and paid scant attention to the foreign policy uses of the food aid program.[38] The State Department—which negotiated PL480 agreements with needy countries—seemed initially less interested in the political utility of food aid than in PL480's negative impact on U.S. relations with other major agricultural exporters, who resented the "dumping" of American foodstuffs at concessional rates in Third World markets. In the mid and late 1950s, the governments of Canada, Australia, New Zealand, Argentina and Brazil all lodged complaints with the State Department, protesting U.S. surplus-disposal practices.[39]

As the food aid program expanded, however, and as its value to Third World governments became apparent, more and more legislators and Executive Branch officials perceived that food aid could be a powerful political instrument. In February 1958, Senator Hubert Humphrey submitted a report to the Senate Agriculture Committee, alliteratively entitled "Food and Fibre as a Force for Freedom," that called for multiyear appropriations for PL480, rapid expansion of PL480 shipments to key Third World countries, and appointment of a fulltime "Food for Peace" administrator to the White House staff to coordinate the activities of the Agriculture and State Depart-ments.[40] The Eisenhower Administration had by this point begun to realize than PL480's domestic political popularity made it a very valuable part of the economic aid program. Although PL480 was widely advertised as an aid program for foreign countries, it was above all a boon to American farmers—disposing of huge CCC inventories that caused too many embarassing questions about the cost of subsidizing American agriculture. The support of the farm lobby—principally the AFB, the Grange, and the National Council of Farmer Cooperatives (NCFC)—gave PL480 a status on Capitol Hill that capital and technical aid programs lacked.[41] Well aware of the significance of PL480's relative immunity from Congressional parsimony, President Eisenhower preempted Senator Humphrey's move to legislate changes in the scope of the PL480 program in the spring of 1959 by renaming PL480 the "Food for Peace" program, and by appointing Don Paarlberg, an aide to Secretary of Agriculture Ezra Taft Benson, as the White House's first Food-for-Peace Coordinator.[42]

"Burying the Hatchet": Food Aid and United States-Egyptian Relations, 1959–60

PL480 proved in 1959–60 to be a far more reliable means of improving U.S.-Egyptian relations than the politically more problematical capital and technical aid programs of 1952–56. Despite intermittent and generally ineffectual sniping from the Israel lobby,[43] the Eisenhower Administration quietly signed a series of Title I agreements with Egypt in 1959–60 that provided $153 million in food aid to the Nasser regime.[44] These Title I shipments were supplemented by $17 million in Title II aid, most of which was distributed by CARE, and by $3 million in technical aid.[45] "The revival of our economic aid program, and the increased reliance on PL480", Raymond Hare later observed, "helped greatly to restore some degree of cordiality to U.S.-Egyptian relations after the disastrous chain of events in 1956–58. We could at least begin to try to bury the hatchet underneath all of this American grain." [46]

Although many bilateral strains persisted, Kamel's "icebox" approach met with much success in the last two years of

Eisenhower's Presidency.[47] Concluding that "the short-term as well as the long-term outlook for improvement in UAR-Israeli relations is bleak," State Department analysts nonetheless noted in the spring of 1960 that Egyptian-Israeli border clashes had begun to diminish, and that Nasser's rhetorical denunciations of Israel had lost some of their former bellicosity.[48] Meanwhile, Soviet-Egyptian bickering continued, despite further Soviet assurances of support for the High Dam.[49] The Iraqi-Egyptian rift widened, particularly after Kassem brutally suppressed a coup attempt by pro-Nasser forces in the spring of 1959. Preoccupied with his quarrel with Kassem, Nasser tempered his attacks on America's conservative Arab allies.[50]

With PL480 shipments supplying 24 percent of Egyptian grain imports in 1959, and 66 percent in 1960, the Nasser regime was able to plug the drain on its foreign exchange reserves.[51] In the fall of 1959, Nasser unveiled an extremely ambitious ten-year development plan, which aimed to double Egyptian national income by 1970. It was clear that one of the key determinants of the success or failure of the Ten Year Plan would be the Nasser regime's ability to attract American food aid in the 1960s.[52]

The gradual reduction of U.S.-Egyptian tensions in 1959–60 and the Nasser regime's commitment to a long-term program of economic modernization that would depend to a considerable extent on American aid, and hence to some extent on a reasonably cordial relationship with the American government, gave rise to much optimism in Washington. The State Department's Office of Intelligence and Research maintained in March 1960 that "while UAR and U.S. views will never be apt to coincide extensively, the UAR is showing willingness to develop the areas of mutual interest." [53] Nasser himself seemed to share the view that U.S.-Egyptian relations would continue their slow improvement, commenting obliquely to Wilton Wynn of the Associated Press and Harry Ellis of the *Christian Science Monitor* in October 1959 that "in the sphere of international relations, it is not possible for bad relations to turn into good relations by a stroke of the pen. However, what is certain is that with the disappearance of pressure, matters return gradually to normal." [54] In September 1960, Nasser made his only trip to the United States, flying to New York for the opening of the fifteenth United Nations General Assembly session. On 26

September, Nasser met briefly with President Eisenhower and Secretary of State Christian Herter. Although little of substance was discussed at this encounter, it symbolized a mutual commitment to continue to try to repair the damage done to U.S.-Egyptian relations in the period 1956–58.[55]

Much changed in U.S.-Egyptian relations between Foster Dulles's meeting with Nasser in May 1953 and Eisenhower's brief encounter with the Egyptian leader in September 1960. From a peak in the first year or two after the Egyptian revolution, when the Free Officers seemed to be a potential bulwark for Western interests in the Middle East, U.S.-Egyptian relations descended rapidly into a valley marked by differences over Western defense plans, Soviet designs in the Middle East, and the Palestine problem. American aid—or the lack of it—was a key issue in U.S.-Egyptian relations throughout the 1950s, most dramatically during the Aswan affair of 1955–56. In the slow climb out of the valley of mutual differences in 1959–60, American food aid served as a crucial bilateral bond. In the ambitious plans of Eisenhower's successor, food aid was to play an even more crucial role.

Kennedy's "Great Unseen Weapon": Food Aid and American Policy Toward Egypt, 1961–63

"Food for Peace was the great unseen
weapon of Kennedy's Third World policy."

Arthur Schlesinger, Jr. 1965.[1]

Encouraged by the gradual improvement of U.S.-Egyptian relations in 1959–60, John F. Kennedy and the "best and the brightest" who accompanied him to Washington in 1961 made a major effort to build a friendly relationship with the Nasser regime on a foundation of American food aid shipments. By 1963, Egypt had become the world's largest per capita consumer of American food aid.[2]

The central objectives of Kennedy's aid policy were variations on the familiar themes of the Eisenhower era: the Kennedy Administration sought to keep the Arab-Israeli conflict "in the icebox"; to limit Soviet influence in Egypt; and to restrain Nasser from attacking Western interests in the Arab world and in the rest of the developing world. In addition to these immediate security concerns, Kennedy and his advisers placed new emphasis on the importance of promoting Egyptian economic development, which they believed would result eventually in a durable, amicable U.S.-Egyptian relationship.

The initial aid tactic favored by the Kennedy Administration was a continuation of the Eisenhower Administration's practice in 1959–60 of offering incremental inducements to the Nasser regime, usually in six month installments. Lucius Battle, who served as U.S. Ambassador to Egypt between 1964 and 1967, later referred to this approach as the tactic of "continuous negotiation," suggesting that the constant negotiating process necessitated by short-term aid agreements was the best way to keep Egyptian attention focused on the need to maintain good relations with the United States.[3] Buoyed by the apparent success of its efforts to moderate Nasser's behavior in 1961–62, the Kennedy Administration concluded a large, three-year PL480 agreement with the Egyptian government in October 1962, in hopes that such a commitment would reinforce the Nasser regime's interest in cooperating with the United States. Unfortunately, U.S.-Egyptian friction stemming from Egypt's involvement in the Yemeni civil war and its rapid military build-up caused a steady deterioration in bilateral relations in 1963, even as the American government poured unprecedented quantities of food aid into Egypt. By the time of Kennedy's death in November 1963, much of the early promise of the Kennedy-Nasser relationship had evaporated, as had much of the New Frontiersmen's confidence in their "great unseen weapon."

The United States and Egypt: The View From the New Frontier

The Kennedy Administration came to power convinced that its predecessor had demonstrated an appalling lack of imagination in its attitude toward Third World nationalists like Gamal Abdel Nasser. Seen from the perspective of the New Frontier, the Eisenhower Administration's reluctance to accept nonalignment in the Cold War had created widespread opportunities for the spread of Soviet influence in the developing world. Two weeks before Kennedy took office, Khrushchev had publicly endorsed "wars of national liberation" in the Third World;[4] to many observers, it seemed that the Soviets, by exploiting American inflexibility and by shrewdly distributing military and economic aid and political support to Third World nationalists, had secured a commanding position on what had become "the critical battleground between Communism and democracy." [5]

As Kennedy saw it, the seepage of Soviet influence into the nooks and crannies of the developing world had been in large part the result of the Eisenhower Administration's rigid and unimaginative reliance on containment doctrines derived

from the immediate postwar experience in Europe. The time
had come, thought Kennedy and his advisers, to dispose of
anachronistic notions about formal alliance-building in the developing world. In Kennedy's eyes, neutralism was not some
Trojan Horse concealing Soviet expansionism, but the foundation of a future barrier against the spread of Communism:

> We support the independence of those newer or weaker states
> whose history, geography, economy, or lack of power impels
> them to remain outside "entangling alliances"—as we did for
> more than a century. For the independence of nations is a bar
> to the Communist "grand design"—it is the basis of our
> own.[6]

To demonstrate his interest in working with neutralist governments, Kennedy set out early in his term of office to cultivate
several prominent Third World leaders. As Dean Rusk, Kennedy's Secretary of State, later put it: "When the Kennedy
Administration took office, we made a major effort to improve
relations with certain key leaders of the so-called nonaligned
world. We wanted to overcome the impression left by my friend
John Foster Dulles that neutralism was 'immoral'." [7] Kennedy
and Rusk decided that Nkrumah of Ghana, Sukarno of Indonesia, Ben Bella of Algeria, and Nasser of Egypt deserved
special American attention.[8] Kennedy was particularly intrigued
by the idea of restoring good relations with Nasser, whose
alienation from the United States he traced to the Eisenhower-
Dulles preoccupation with the Soviet-American conflict. Kennedy argued:

> We tended to deal with [this area] exclusively in the context
> of the East-West struggle. Their own issues of nationalism, of
> economic development and local political squabbles, have been
> discussed by our policy-makers as being of secondary impor-
> tance. . . . We have given our support to regimes instead of
> to people. . . . The question is not whether we should recog-
> nize the form of Arab nationalism, but how we can help to
> channel it along constructive lines.[9]

Forsaking the Microphone for the Bulldozer

The Kennedy Administration was confident that it could use economic aid to solve the problem of channeling Nasserism "along constructive lines." As Kennedy and many of his senior advisers saw it, the key feature of the process of modernization in Egypt and in the rest of the Arab world was the creation of "new men"—a class of educated, skilled, pragmatic individuals who were intent upon the destruction of the old social and political order and who were committed to economic, social, and political development.[10] By underwriting much of the cost of the Egyptian development program without putting alliance-building pressures on Nasser, Kennedy believed, the United States could win the confidence of the "new men" and lay the basis for a solid U.S.-Egyptian relationship. As William Polk, the Middle East expert on the State Department's Policy Planning Staff from 1961 to 1964, put it: "Since a prime cause of Arab unrest and hostility over the last generation has been their feeling of inferiority, weakness and humiliation, I believe that a mellowing process will accompany development. The Arabs believe that the weak cannot afford to be generous or considerate." Promotion of Egyptian economic development, said Polk, would enable the United States to "moderate Nasser's positions so that they remain below the threshold of real danger to our interests." [11] Chester Bowles, initially Kennedy's Undersecretary of State but later "Special Representative of the President for African, Asian, and Latin American Affairs," put this line of thinking in somewhat more colorful terms when he wrote in 1962 that "if Nasser can gradually be led to forsake the microphone for the bulldozer, he may assume a key role in bringing the Middle East peacefully into our modern world." [12]

The Kennedy Administration's appreciation of the political value of promoting Egyptian economic development reflected a general American belief in the political desirability of encouraging economic progress in the Third World. In the early 1960s, economic backwardness was usually seen in Washington as a breeding ground for political instability, violence, and Communism. As late as 1965, Robert McNamara, then Secretary of Defense and until recently President of the World Bank, argued that a clear relationship existed between economic underdevelopment and the incidence of civil and international violence.[13] According to Robert Packenham, most American policy-makers in this era supposed that "poverty had a positive and linear relationship to Communism: i.e., that as poverty decreases, Communism decreases."[14]

Coupled with this belief in the political benefits of economic progress was an equally strong belief in the effectiveness of economic aid as a means of promoting economic development. Perhaps the most forceful exponents of this latter belief in the late 1950s were Max F. Millikan and Walt W. Rostow of the Massachusetts Institute of Technology Center for International Studies.[15] The essence of the Millikan-Rostow thesis was that the political value of economic aid lay not so much in its usefulness as a short-run means of moderating the behavior of Third World governments as in its effectiveness as a means of enabling poor countries to reach the "take-off-point" for self-sustained economic development. In the idealized view of Millikan and Rostow, American aid policy should concern itself less with immediate security interests—enlisting recipients in defense associations, obtaining military base rights, molding Cold War sympathies—and more with the economic needs of those developing countries that demonstrated a genuine commitment to modernization. In the long-run, economic aid would deepen the bonds between such Third World countries and the United States, whatever the level of short-run political friction between donor and recipient.[16]

With this long-run goal in mind, Kennedy and his advisers were prepared to tolerate—within the limits of Congressional patience—a far higher level of short-run U.S.-Egyptian friction than their predecessors had been willing to. So long as the Nasser regime remained practically committed to a sound economic development program, American aid remained, in the eyes of the Kennedy White House, a political good in itself. Moreover, by paving the way to modernization of the Egyptian economy, the Kennedy Administration hoped to reinforce Nasser's interest in the development effort, to divert his attention from foreign adventures, and gradually to reduce short-run U.S.-Egyptian differences. By subtly persuading Nasser to "forsake the microphone for the bulldozer," Kennedy hoped to have more success in moderating Egyptian behavior than Eisenhower and Dulles—employing far more blatant forms of pressure—had had.

"Continuous Negotiation" and U.S.-Egyptian Relations, 1961–62

As the chosen instrument of American economic aid policy toward Egypt, food aid had enormous appeal within the Kennedy White House. Don Paarlberg's successor as Director of Food for Peace, George McGovern, later recalled that the food aid program was "something that excited" President Kennedy, who was "anxious to put the public spotlight on this great asset." [17] McGovern himself believed that food aid was "a far better weapon than a bomber in our competition with the Communists for influence in the developing world." [18] The logic behind Kennedy's emphasis on Food for Peace was actually quite straightforward: the Kennedy Administration had inherited the largest wheat and feedgrain surplus in American history; Food for Peace fit neatly into the dynamic, innovative, empathetic image that Kennedy sought to project in the Third World; Food for Peace was relatively immune from Congressional attacks; thus it made good sense to make greater use of food aid as a tool of American foreign policy.[19]

Between January 1961 and February 1962, the Kennedy Administration signed three Title I Food for Peace agreements with the Egyptian government, committing the United States to provide about $170 million worth of surplus commodities to Egypt.[20] These Title I commitments were supplemented by agreements to provide $24 million worth of Title II aid and $43 million worth of Title III aid.[21] In 1961, PL480 shipments accounted for 77 percent of Egyptian wheat imports, and 38 percent of Egypt's net supply of wheat and wheat flour; in 1962, the corresponding figures were 99 percent of wheat imports and 53 percent of net supply.[22] By enabling the Nasser regime to transfer foreign exchange that it would normally have had to use to pay food import bills to investment in development projects, Food-for-Peace shipments made it possible for the Egyptian government to sustain its ambitious Five Year Development Plan.[23]

As John Badeau, Kennedy's ambassador to Egypt, later explained, "we attempted to expand the size and duration of our food aid agreements with Egypt very gradually at first, so that Nasser would be made to appreciate the link between his behavior and Congressional support for our aid program." [24] Through the tactic of "continuous negotiation," the Kennedy Administration hoped both to test the soundness of Egypt's development program and to impress Nasser with the fact that there was "some relationship between UAR policies and attitudes toward the United States and continuation of such assistance in the future." [25] In Dean Rusk's words, "we did not expect Nasser to grovel in gratitude for this assistance, but we did expect him to work for a step by step improvement in U.S.-Egyptian relations." [26]

[handwritten margin note: purp. of continuous negotiations]

Badeau and Rusk were pleasantly surprised not only by the Nasser regime's appreciation of the connection between its policies and American aid, but also by its apparent readiness in 1961–62 to adjust its attitudes to ensure the continued flow of food aid from the United States. Badeau later cited an experience at the Nonaligned Nations Economic Conference in Cairo in the summer of 1962 as evidence of the Egyptian government's awareness of the linkage between its behavior and PL480 aid. Badeau feared at the time that U.S.-Egyptian relations would suffer "if Egypt allowed itself to be used as a sounding board [at the conference] for violent anti-American propaganda," and made his apprehension clear to the Egyptian government. Much to Badeau's relief, the tone of the conference was "exceedingly moderate"—due in no small measure to Egyptian restraint. Badeau recalls:

> It was a good, constructive conference and I think I got the clue of it. When it was over, I went to see Ali Sabri and congratulated him on conducting a constructive, useful conference without dragging in side issues and a conference that didn't hurt our relationships. And he looked at me and said rather quietly, "I presume you noticed, as I did, while we were having this conference, that the Congress of the United States was debating the foreign aid bill." Now, I think that was it. I think they had enough sense to recognize that there was a connection between these things.[27]

Friction Fades

Badeau and his superiors in Washington were further encouraged by the disappearance in 1961–62 of much of the
acrimony that had previously characterized U.S.-Egyptian exchanges on the Palestine problem, on the issue of Soviet influence in Egypt, and on the question of Egyptian policy in
the Arab world and in the rest of the Third World. With
remarkable political skill, President Kennedy succeeded in 1961
in gaining simultaneously the confidence of both Israeli and
Egyptian leaders. Kennedy's outspoken support for Israel during
the 1960 election campaign had made a favorable impression
upon the Israeli government and its backers in the United
States, as had Kennedy's efforts to maintain close links between
his White House staff and the American Jewish community.[28]
At the same time, however, Nasser had been favorably impressed by Kennedy's public declarations of support for the
Algerian nationalists, by the sympathy for Arab problems that
he had expressed in private meetings with Egyptian officials,
and by his youthful vigor and appealing personality.[29] When
Kennedy wrote to Nasser in May 1961 to express his interest
in progress toward a mutually acceptable settlement of the
Arab-Israeli dispute, the Egyptian President sent back a long
and unexpectedly positive reply. Nasser began by recounting
in considerable detail the familiar litany of Arab grievances
against the United States, but concluded by emphasizing to
Kennedy that he "did not link the possibilities of understanding
between us with the necessity of our views on the [Palestine]
problem meeting on an identical basis."[30] Although Kennedy
was not particularly gratified by the long denunciation of Israel
in Nasser's letter, he was encouraged by Nasser's evident willingness to "agree to disagree" with the United States on the
Palestine question. Despite the failure of an American-sponsored
attempt to resolve the Palestine refugee problem in 1961,[31] the
Kennedy Administration was on the whole pleased with the
cordial tone of private U.S.-Egyptian exchanges on the Arab-
Israeli issue, with the less bellicose tone of Nasser's public
comments on the issue, and with the Nasser regime's readiness
to keep the Palestine question securely "in the icebox".[32]

Meanwhile, Kennedy and his advisers were encouraged by the persistence of the Soviet-Egyptian rift that had begun in 1958–59. In December 1960, the *World Marxist Review* publicly condemned Nasser's "reign of terror" against Egyptian Communists. In April 1961, Khrushchev delivered a blistering lecture to a visiting Egyptian parliamentary delegation led by Anwar Sadat, warning the Egyptians "not to cut down the tree that gives you shade." [33] Although Soviet support for the High Dam project and for the Egyptian military continued to be of crucial importance to the Nasser regime, there was much popular resentment of the Soviet presence in Egypt.[34] From the point of view of the Kennedy Administration in 1961–62, it seemed clear that Nasser was determined to keep his distance from the Soviets, whatever the degree of his dependence upon Moscow for economic aid and military equipment.

Nasser's anti-Western campaign in the Arab world faltered in 1961–62, largely because of the collapse of the Syrian-Egyptian union in September 1961. The union had never been particularly popular in either Egypt or Syria; when the Syrians withdrew from the United Arab Republic, complaining of Egyptian heavy handedness, many Egyptian officials were glad to be rid of the administrative burden of governing their fractious Arab brethren. As John Badeau later observed, "the general mood in Egypt even among very senior government officials was on the whole one of relief. There was a good deal of resentment that the bride had run off at the altar, but not very much love lost." [35]

Nasser blamed the break-up of the UAR on the Syrian bourgeoisie, which had been one of the groups which had most fiercely resisted Egyptian attempts to dominate Syrian political and economic life. In the immediate aftermath of the UAR break up, Nasser set out to crush the Egyptian bourgeoisie as a political force, so as to prevent a domestic repetition of the Syrian challenge to his authority. Although Nasser eventually translated his efforts to subdue the forces of "reaction" in Egypt into a general campaign against conservative Arab governments, in late 1961–early 1962 the Egyptian President preoccupied himself with the task of completing the socialization of the Egyptian economy and consolidating his grip on power in Egypt.[36] For some time after the dissolution of the UAR, it appeared to many observers in Washington that Nasser's capacity for, and interest in, undermining the Western position in the Arab world had been dramatically reduced. The Kennedy Administration, for its part, forbore the temptation to orchestrate an anti-Nasser movement in the Arab world in the wake of the Syrian-Egyptian split. Nasser apparently appreciated Kennedy's restraint. Ambassador Badeau later noted that "we did not try to exploit the break-up; had Dulles been there we probably would have tried to exploit it, and I think Nasser was conscious of this fact." [37]

The Nasser regime also seemed to demonstrate growing consideration for American interests in the rest of the developing world in 1961–62. Nasser's predilection for supporting revolutionary movements and generally "keeping the pot boiling" in the Third World had become legendary in Washington by 1961. The Egyptian leader's reputation as a troublemaker provided the foundation for a joke that circulated in the State Department in the early 1960s. It seemed that one of Nasser's favorite forms of relaxation was watching movies. On one of his trips abroad, Nasser brought along a number of films, among which was *Mutiny on the Bounty*. After a long day of diplomatic discussions, Nasser sat down wearily to view *Bounty*. In the middle of the picture, Nasser suddenly summoned one of his aides and ordered him to send a cable to the Egyptian Foreign Ministry, saying "Contact the mutineers on the *Bounty* immediately. Tell them we support their cause and any attack on them will be considered an attack on the United Arab Republic." [38]

Nasser's role in the Congolese civil war in 1961 belied, to some extent, his reputation in Washington as an incorrigible miscreant. The Belgians had once dubbed the Congo the "happy colony," but the Congo seemed anything but "happy" in 1961. Vicious internecine conflict had followed on the heels of the Belgian withdrawal from the Congo in 1960. By the winter of 1960–61, the United States and Egypt found themselves supporting different factions in the Congolese civil war—with the Americans backing the centrist government of Joseph Kasavubu, and the Egyptians supporting the ill-fated leftist Patrice Lumumba. Nasser had come to regard the African continent as a sort of Egyptian eminent domain and had sought in the late 1950s to ensure that as the African territories achieved independence, they would look to Cairo for political leadership and would exert their influence to further Arab causes. By 1961, at least thirteen African liberation and dissident movements had established their headquarters in Cairo.[39]

When it was alleged that the CIA had arranged the assassination of Lumumba early in 1961, the Nasser regime reacted with characteristic vociferousness. Cairo's Voice of the Arabs, never prone to understatement, maintained that "the whole water of all the oceans, if used, would not remove the blood dyeing the hands of the U.S. authorities." [40]

In his personal correspondence with President Kennedy, however, Nasser pursued a much more conciliatory line. In a letter dated 20 February 1961, Nasser pledged to support United Nations efforts to reach a compromise settlement of the Congolese conflict.[41] Advised by Chester Bowles to try to "strengthen Nasser's desire to pursue an uncommitted, as opposed to a wholly pro-Soviet, policy on the Congo," Kennedy replied to Nasser on 1 March in a long letter which stressed the "area of general agreement between our two governments on key points of policy towards the Congo problem." [42] Egypt eventually cosponsored a United Nations Security Council resolution which called for a compromise solution in the Congo, a resolution for which the United States voted and on which the Soviet Union abstained. For the Kennedy Administration, Nasser's relatively moderate stance on the Congolese conflict in 1961 seemed to provide additional evidence of the Egyptian government's interest in cooperating with the United States.

1961 imp. to moderate Egyphan stand on congo. issue

Assessing the Egyptian Development Program

While short-run U.S.-Egyptian differences eased in 1961–62, the Kennedy Administration noted with satisfaction that the Nasser regime appeared to be firmly committed to a fairly sound economic development program. In February 1962, President Kennedy sent Chester Bowles to Cairo to assess the Egyptian development program, and "to indicate . . . the urgency and sincerity of the U.S. interest in moving further along the path of mutual cooperation." It was hoped in Washington that Bowles could obtain a "frank statement from Nasser on how he envisions the evolution of the U.S.-UAR relationship over the years ahead." [43]

After two long meetings with Nasser, Bowles reported that "whatever their defects I am certain that the Egyptian leaders are sincerely dedicated to the improvement of the conditions of the Egyptian people." According to Bowles, it was also "clear that the UAR government has made a decision to improve its relations with the United States." [44]

Bowles was followed into Cairo at the beginning of March 1962 by Dr. Edward S. Mason, a Harvard economist sent by Kennedy to "appraise the development potential of the UAR." In his subsequent report to the President, Mason expressed skepticism about Nasser's chances of reaching his ambitious goal of doubling national income by 1970, noting that "a serious contradiction exists between President Nasser's statement of the development targets he expects to attain and the measures he is prepared to adopt." Mason observed that the only way to double Egyptian national income over a ten year period would be to clamp down heavily on consumer spending and curb government spending on social services and the military, in order to raise the level of savings and channel investment into development programs. Mason could see no evidence that Nasser was willing to pay the short-term political and economic price demanded by his extravagant long-term ambitions.

But Mason noted that "whether or not the Plan is attainable, however, seems to me irrelevant to any significant U.S. interest." In Mason's view, there was "positive evidence" that the Egyptian government took the development of the Egyptian economy seriously and was willing to take the steps necessary to bring about a rate of growth of national income substantially in excess of the rate of population growth—that is to say, a growth rate in national income of 4 to 6 percent per annum. Mason considered this rate of growth "satisfactory," and advised Kennedy that the Nasser regime seemed to have made a solid commitment to economic development. [45]

The Three Year Agreement

With the gradual reduction of short-run U.S.-Egyptian tensions and the apparent deepening of the Nasser regime's commitment to economic development in 1961–62, support began to grow in Washington for a rapid expansion of the PL480 program in Egypt. In the summer of 1961, Ambassador Kamel had asked President Kennedy to consider a multiyear Title I sales program to ease the task of long term development planning in Egypt. "I emphasized to the President," Kamel recalls, "that a single three year food aid commitment would produce far greater economic dividends for Egypt, and far greater political dividends for the United States, than all these six-month agreements." Kennedy expressed general agreement with Kamel's line of reasoning.[46]

In succeeding months, the State Department bolstered Kennedy's enthusiasm for a dramatic enlargement of the size and scope of the food aid program in Egypt. Although some officers at the American Embassy in Cairo disparaged PL480 shipments as a "glorified means of garbage disposal," and doubted that they had much political usefulness, Ambassador Badeau and his political counselor, Donald Bergus, believed that food aid, particularly if channeled through a three-year agreement, could reinforce the Nasser regime's interest in internal modernization and could diminish its interest in short-run political conflict with the United States. Badeau and Bergus argued that a long term PL480 commitment would be a very constructive way of reassuring the Egyptian government about the sincerity of the Kennedy Administration's interest in building a mutually satisfactory U.S.-Egyptian relationship.[47] Echoing Badeau and Bergus, Assistant Secretary of State for Near Eastern Affairs Phillips Talbot informed McGeorge Bundy, Kennedy's National Security Adviser, in late February 1962 that "a plateau seems to have been reached in overall [U.S.-Egyptian] relations. Under present arrangements, it has no doubt appeared to the UAR that the U.S. doles out aid the UAR sorely needs, such as wheat, while remaining ready at any time to withhold further deliveries." Talbot added that it might be worthwhile to consider "whether a less cautious posture could lead to greater mutual confidence in U.S.-UAR relations and facilitate achievement of our broader objectives in the area."[48]

Egyptian Finance Minister Kaissouny spent several weeks in Washington in April–May 1962 lobbying for a three-year food aid commitment,[49] but it was not until the fall of 1962 that President Kennedy finally decided that the potential political rewards of a long term pledge to the Nasser regime were worth the domestic political risks that such an agreement would entail.[50] On 8 October 1962, in what Kamel recalls as "the greatest triumph of my nine years in Washington," the Kennedy Administration announced that it had agreed to provide Egypt with $431.8 million worth of food aid for fiscal years 1963, 1964, and 1965.[51]

The Kennedy Administration and "Nasser's Vietnam"

The ink was not yet dry on the 8 October agreement when U.S.-Egyptian differences arising out of Egyptian involvement in the Yemeni civil war and the Nasser government's rapid military buildup began to undermine the optimistic expectations of Kennedy and Kamel. Nasser made it quite clear to Kennedy and his advisers in 1963 that economic development was not the only, or even the most important, goal of his regime, and that Egypt's interest in ensuring the continued flow of food aid through cordial relations with the United States was a far less crucial concern in Cairo than Egypt's interest in protecting and advancing its prestige in the Arab world.

Yemen provided an unlikely setting for "the first major crisis that the Kennedy Administration faced in its relations with Egypt."[52] Situated on 75,000 square miles of desert and rugged mountains at the southwestern tip of the Arabian peninsula, and populated by four million tribesmen whose lifestyle had not changed appreciably since the Middle Ages, Yemen hardly seemed at first glance to be the sort of place that would attract much attention from either Egypt or the United States. Yet no issue during the early 1960s was more damaging to the U.S.-Egyptian relationship, or had more impact upon the direction of American food aid policy, than that of Egypt's military intervention in Yemen, eventually referred to in Cairo and in Washington as "Nasser's Vietnam."[53]

On 26 September 1962, the Imam Badr, who had just succeeded his father as ruler of Yemen, was overthrown by a small group of Yemeni officers. Badr fled to Saudi Arabia and, with Saudi financial assistance, began to organize a royalist counter-revolt. The Yemeni revolutionaries, led by Brigadier General Abdullah al-Sallal, announced the establishment of the Yemen Arab Republic and appealed to Nasser for assistance.

Nasser's attitude toward the Yemeni civil war was shaped less by any great fascination with Yemeni affairs or any great affinity for Sallal and his "Free Officers" than by a powerful desire to repair the damage done to Egyptian prestige in the Arab world by the breakup of the United Arab Republic. When Sallal made his request for Egyptian aid, Nasser could have spurned it only at the risk of destroying his reputation as the leader of the Arab nationalist movement, and of further reinforcing the position of his conservative Arab antagonists in Saudi Arabia and Jordan. Moreover, it no doubt appeared to Nasser and his advisers that establishment of an Egyptian puppet government in Yemen might prove to be a springboard for revolutionary action against the Saudi royal family and against the British and British-backed rulers of Aden and the Gulf Sheikhdoms.[54]

The alacrity with which Nasser responded to Sallal's appeal surprised even the most diehard of his supporters within the new Yemeni regime; by early November, 1962, it was estimated that there were at least 10,000 Egyptian troops in Yemen.[55] With the support of the Egyptian army, Sallal seized control of Yemen's principal towns and launched an offensive against royalist forces in the mountains north and east of the Yemeni capital, Sana. The Egyptian air force bombed Badr's supply depots inside Saudi Arabia, much to the dismay of King Saud, who was by this point, the CIA reported, "in a psychopathic state of suspicion and worry over the Yemenis."[56]

The Yemeni civil war provided the Kennedy Administration with an opportunity to test the strength of its relationship with Nasser.[57] Priding themselves on their sophisticated understanding of the forces at work in the Arab world, Kennedy and many of his close advisers were sympathetic to the Yemeni republicans, but the Kennedy Administration could not help being concerned about the catalytic effect that Yemeni unrest might have on Western interests in Saudi Arabia and in Aden and the Persian Gulf.[58] The Kennedy Administration's central aim in the Yemen crisis in the fall of 1962 was to pry Nasser out of Yemen gracefully, and to restore stability to the Arabian peninsula—preferably through the establishment of a moderate republican regime in Sana.

Badeau reported from Cairo that the Egyptians were eager to extricate themselves from what had quickly become a costly and unpopular endeavor in Yemen.[59] The crack Egyptian units sent to Yemen, trained for desert warfare, did not fare well in the Yemeni mountains; as Egyptian casualties mounted—and as reports of mutilations by the barbarous Yemeni tribesmen increased—Egyptian morale plummeted.[60] United States Chargé d'Affaires Robert Stookey reported from Sana that the Sallal regime could survive without Egyptian support if Saudi and Jordanian assistance to the royalists was cut-off.[61]

The reports of Badeau and Stookey suggested to top level policy-makers in Washington that it might be possible to use United States recognition of the Yemen Arab Republic (YAR) as a lever to pry Egypt out of Yemen and restore some measure of stability to the Arabian peninsula. The Kennedy Administration's line of reasoning was as follows: American recognition would be followed by that of most other countries, including Great Britain, whose interests in Aden and in the Gulf were threatened; American recognition of the YAR would cause both the Saudis and the Jordanians to falter in their support of Badr; Sallal would gain the upper hand over the unaided royalists and consolidate the power of the republican regime in Yemen; with the foreign intervention in Yemen ended, and the royalists defeated, Sallal could be induced with offers of American aid to concentrate upon internal development and refrain from external adventures.[62]

The Administration's scenario had a certain persuasive logic to it, despite the fact that the British government had been pressuring the Kennedy Administration to take a stronger stand against Nasser and seemed disinclined to recognize the Yemeni republicans.[63] Moreover, Kennedy was fearful that the Soviets—who had recognized the YAR on 29 September—would preempt the Americans and develop a position of influence in Yemen.[64] In the heady aftermath of the Cuban Missile Crisis, Kennedy and his advisers were confident that the United States could "manage" the Yemeni crisis and restore stability to the southwest corner of the Arabian peninsula. On 19 December 1962, Kennedy recognized the Yemen Arab Republic.[65]

Unfortunately, the scenario constructed by the Kennedy Administration failed to unveil itself after the YAR was recognized. Although the United Nations seated a republican delegation in place of the Imam's representatives on 20 December, and more than fifty countries followed the American lead and recognized the YAR, the British government refused to recognize the Sallal regime.[66] Badr did not seem at all eager to fade meekly away, and the Saudi government—now under the competent direction of Crown Prince Feisal—was unwilling to sever its ties to the Imam and concede Yemen to one of Nasser's protégés. Nasser—who had agreed to withdraw his troops from Yemen if the Saudis cut off their aid to the royalists[67]—was left in the middle of the Yemeni quagmire, unenthusiastic about expanding Egyptian military support for Sallal, but unwilling to evacuate in the face of Saudi and British pressure. "The Kennedy Administration," Donald Bergus recalled, "was left holding the bag, having failed to reap any political reward from its endorsement of a republican regime which appeared on close inspection to be much flimsier than we had originally believed." [68]

Nasser chose to increase his commitment to Sallal in a very visible way—by bombing the Saudi cities of Jizan and Najran on 30 December 1962 and 1 January 1963. Kennedy responded by renewing the U.S. commitment to defend Saudi Arabia against unprovoked aggression, and by despatching an American jet fighter squadron to Riyadh.[69] In a letter to Nasser on 19 January 1963, Kennedy explained that the U.S. government was seeking actively to persuade Feisal to disengage in Yemen, but that "each time we have felt we were making some progress toward disengagement, such actions as the Najran bombings have set us back." [70]

The Kennedy Administration stepped up its diplomatic efforts in Cairo and Riyadh in the spring of 1963. Ellsworth Bunker, a State Department official with extensive experience as an international mediator, was assigned the task of negotiating an agreement for simultaneous disengagement between Nasser and Prince Feisal. The United Nations had meanwhile been brought into the mediation effort and undertook to furnish military observers to enforce termination of outside aid to the royalists and to supervise a phased Egyptian evacuation.[71]

By this time, both Nasser and Feisal desired to end hostilities in Yemen, but neither had the slightest confidence in the other's good faith. Bunker, described by Badeau as "an absolutely superb negotiator," managed nonetheless to hammer out a disengagement agreement in a flurry of shuttle diplomacy in March–April 1963.[72] Under the terms of the agreement negotiated by Bunker, the Saudi government agreed to cease all aid to Badr, as well as to prohibit the use of Saudi territory as a sanctuary or staging post for the royalists. Nasser agreed to begin a phased withdrawal of the 25,000 Egyptian troops in Yemen, and to refrain from punitive attacks on the royalists. Nasser and Feisal also agreed to underwrite the costs of a team of United Nations observers stationed throughout Yemen to monitor compliance with the disengagement agreement.[73]

Unfortunately, the two-hundred-man United Nations Yemen Observation Mission did not begin its operations until 4 July 1963, by which time the fragile Saudi-Egyptian rapprochement had begun to crumble. Exasperated by what he perceived to be U.N. Secretary General U Thant's dithering in May–June 1963, Badeau had urged that a team of American observers be assembled from the U.S. military missions in Iran and Turkey and despatched to Yemen to monitor the Bunker agreement until the U.N. force arrived. Badeau later contended that "we could have put one hundred observers in there . . . within a week's time; had that been done, it is possible that this agreement would have taken place."[74] As it happened, Badeau's superiors were uneager to deepen American involvement in the Yemeni affair; Badeau's proposal was vetoed, although Secretary of State Rusk did appeal to U Thant in late May to despatch the U.N. observer team to Yemen "promptly."[75]

The tiny U.N. observation mission, when it finally did arrive in Yemen, proved incapable of policing the Bunker agreement. Although the Saudis did begin to curtail their assistance to the Imam, Nasser—despite repeated assurances to the American Embassy in Cairo—gradually increased the number of Egyptian troops in Yemen. It had become apparent to the Egyptian government that the republican regime could not survive without massive Egyptian support, and Nasser was not under any circumstances prepared to permit Sallal's downfall. Under the pressure of a royalist offensive in the summer and autumn of 1963, the republicans foundered; Nasser responded by stepping up Egyptian air strikes against royalist enclaves in northern Yemen, sometimes using poison gas bombs against Badr's tribesmen.[76]

As his term of office neared its end, Kennedy became increasingly frustrated by Nasser's intransigence in Yemen. In October, 1963, Kennedy wrote to Nasser to express "his personal concern over the United Arab Republic's failure to date to carry out its part of the Yemen disengagement agreement." The Saudis, said Kennedy, were "carrying out their end of the bargain"; the Egyptians, on the other hand, were not making "phased withdrawals to a scale consistent with our understanding of the spirit of the agreement." [77] To Kennedy's dismay, his expressions of concern seemed to have little effect upon Nasser.

By the fall of 1963, the Egyptian intervention in Yemen had revived much of the hostility to Nasser that had lain more or less dormant in Washington since the Eisenhower Doctrine period. Opposition to Egyptian involvement in the Yemeni civil war created some strange bedfellows in the American capital. Like a lover scorned, the CIA turned against the Nasser regime in 1962–63 with the same intensity that it had demonstrated in its courtship of Nasser and the Free Officers in 1952–53.[78] The politically influential oil lobby—anxious to prop up the Saudi royal family—sought to persuade the Kennedy Administration to take a hard line on Egyptian meddling in the Arabian Peninsula.[79] The Israel lobby, unsurprisingly, threw its considerable weight on Capitol Hill behind efforts to curb Nasser. This imposing correlation of forces made it increasingly difficult for the Kennedy White House to continue its relatively conciliatory policy toward the Nasser regime. "It was ironic," Raymond Hare later observed, "that at the moment the Kennedy Administration put the capstone on its conciliatory policy toward Egypt and signed the three year PL480 agreement, the seeds of future discord had already been sown in Yemen." [80]

The Kennedy Administration and Nasser's Military Buildup

A second source of U.S.-Egyptian friction in 1962–63 was the rapid rise of Egyptian defense expenditures, which increased from 7 percent of GNP in 1960–61 to 11 percent of GNP in 1963–64.[81] This upsurge was caused partly by the expense of the intervention in Yemen, which had reached $1 million a day by the end of 1962[82], and partly by a costly guided missile program, which was designed both to counter the much more sophisticated Israeli rocket program and to demonstrate Egypt's commitment to the Arab struggle in Palestine. Nasser's relatively moderate approach to the Palestine question in 1961 had elicited a constant stream of abuse from the rest of the Arab world; the most vocal of Nasser's critics, the Syrians, alleged after the breakup of the UAR that Egypt "had sold out on Palestine for a few bushels of American wheat." [83] Extraordinarily sensitive to accusations that he was playing Esau to Kennedy's Jacob and was mortgaging the Arab cause in Palestine in return for American food aid, Nasser set out in 1962 to do a little sabre-rattling.

In July 1962, Nasser announced with great fanfare that Egypt—with the help of several hundred imported West German technicians—had successfully launched several test rockets, which were essentially slightly modernized versions of the World War II German V-2 missile. Nasser claimed that the missiles were already in "large-scale production." When questioned by reporters about the range of his missiles, Nasser replied enigmatically that they could reach targets "a little south of Beirut." [84]

Egypt's rockets—few in number and equipped with erratic guidance systems—did not in fact pose much of a military threat to Israel.[85] Kennedy and his advisers were not particularly disturbed by the immediate military problem created by the primitive Egyptian missile program, but they were profoundly disturbed by its long-run implications. An expensive missile program could cripple the Egyptian development effort; moreover, an intensive Egyptian–Israeli missile race would shatter American hopes for regional stability.

To add to Kennedy's difficulties, the former political affiliation of many of Nasser's German advisers reinforced Congressional hostility to Nasser. In the summer of 1962, stories about ex-Nazi scientists in Nasser's employ began to appear regularly in the American press; such stories did not do much to boost Nasser's popularity amongst legislators still recoiling from the horrors of the Holocaust. Congressmen never noted for their

[Handwritten margin note: Why would weapons be built (missiles) to combat accusations of softness by Arab/Israel? by other Arab States.]

sympathy towards Egypt became even more intemperate in their denunciations of Nasser. Congressman Seymour Halpern of New York suggested that Nasser's German employees were "building missiles for another try at that final solution of the Jewish problem that Adolf Hitler sought in the Warsaw Ghetto and the crematorium camps of Nazi Germany."[86]

Anxious to deflect criticism from the Israel lobby during the run-up to the 1962 midterm elections, the Kennedy Administration decided in August 1962 to supply HAWK surface to air missiles to the Israelis.[87] Realizing that this departure from the long-standing American practice of avoiding direct involvement in arms sales to the combatants in the Arab-Israeli conflict would upset Nasser, Kennedy secretly sent Robert Strong, chief of the State Department's Office of Near East Affairs, to Cairo to cushion the blow. Strong emphasized the defensive nature of the HAWK system to Nasser, and was somewhat surprised when the Egyptian leader "seemed unperturbed by the military implications of the sale." Nasser, Strong reported, "dwelt chiefly on the political repercussions of the missile sale. In particular he noted that the Israeli issue is now the hottest theme of intra-Arab propaganda warfare and is being used . . . as a weapon to attack the UAR with the accusation that the American price for continuing its substantial UAR aid program is Nasser's acquiescence to a softer line on Israel."[88] The timing of the public announcement of the HAWK sale—on 27 September, ten days before the announcement of the three year food aid agreement with the Egyptian government—did little to disprove Arab allegations that Nasser was being bought off by the Kennedy Administration.[89] Despite an initially mild Egyptian reaction to the HAWK sale, which Badeau attributed to Nasser's appreciation of Kennedy's efforts to keep him informed of changes in American policy, the Egyptian government gradually stepped up its missile program and its propaganda attacks on Israel in 1963.[90]

By the summer of 1963, the Kennedy Administration's concern about the spiralling Arab–Israeli arms race—which the HAWK sale had aggravated—had deepened. In June 1963, Egypt concluded a very large arms agreement with the Soviet Union, whose relations with the Nasser regime had improved as Nasser had become more and more bogged down in Yemen, and hence more and more dependent upon Soviet military

[handwritten margin note: '63 Soviet arms sale to Egypt]

support. Under the terms of the 1963 agreement, which Jon Glassman describes as "clearly the most significant of the pre-Six-Day-War period," the Soviets provided the Egyptians with a variety of first-line military equipment, including the T-54 tank and the MIG-21 aircraft.[91]

Kennedy and his advisers continued to consider the Israeli and Egyptian missile programs to be the most disturbing elements in the Arab-Israeli arms race. Secretary of State Rusk revealed to the Senate Foreign Relations Committee in a closed session in early June that "we are trying to, and this . . . should not be mentioned in any way whatsoever, we are trying privately to work out a qualitative arms limitation in the Near East . . . We think maybe in the next month or so we may have some indication whether this is possible." [92] In late June, John J. McCloy, a veteran diplomatic troubleshooter and a prominent member of the American foreign policy "establishment," flew to the Middle East at President Kennedy's behest for secret talks with Egyptian and Israeli leaders. McCloy was accompanied by Hermann F. Eilts, a State Department Middle East specialist.[93]

[handwritten margin note: '63 attempt to stop arms race fails.]

In essence, McCloy was charged with persuading the Egyptian and Israeli governments to dismantle simultaneously their missile programs. For the Israelis, whose nuclear test facility at Dimona was a source of great anxiety in Washington, the incentives for cessation of their efforts to develop the capability to produce nuclear missiles were increased economic aid and an Egyptian pledge to halt its much more primitive rocket program. To sweeten the pot for the Egyptians, McCloy was to offer—in exchange for renunciation of the rocket program—American assistance in the development of a civilian nuclear energy program in Egypt.[94]

On 27 June, McCloy met privately with Nasser and explained Kennedy's concern about the Egyptian-Israeli missile competition.

> I stated that the President was deeply interested in the stability of the Middle East so that economic progress could continue there free of the diversions which an arms race involved. An intensive arms race particularly in the field of nuclear and missile development was contrary to the interests of both the U.S. and the whole Middle East area. I stated that

the President felt that in this respect there was a clear common interest which could serve as a basis for a sound program from which both the UAR and Israel could benefit.

Nasser was, however, unenthusiastic about McCloy's proposal, citing the pressure that he was under from the rest of the Arab world to maintain an aggressive stance on the Palestine issue.[95] At a second meeting on 29 June, also attended by Eilts and Badeau, McCloy remarked to Nasser that he "sensed a little suspicion on your part that we were too favorably disposed to Israel and that we were too subject to its pressure." Nasser smiled and replied that he had "a little more than a little suspicion." McCloy subsequently reported to President Kennedy that he had "gained the impression that the main motivation of Nasser's attitude toward our proposal was based on political sensitivities as he sensed them both in Egypt and in the Arab countries." [96]

The failure of the McCloy mission added to Kennedy's mounting frustration with the Nasser regime's military buildup. "Egyptian military spending," Edward Mason reported after a return visit to Cairo in July 1963, "has become an anchor on the Egyptian development effort." [97] More ominously, Egypt's arms acquisitions from the Soviet Union and its missile program helped heighten Arab-Israeli tensions, and dramatically increased the chances of a preemptive Israeli strike against Egypt. Kennedy and his advisers understood that Nasser's sabre-rattling was at least partly a response to pressures from the rest of the Arab world, but it appeared in Washington by the fall of 1963 that Nasser was only too eager to take the Palestine problem out of the "icebox" to disprove his Arab critics.

The Congressional Drive to Restrict Food Aid Shipments to Nasser

Dean Rusk recalls that "Nasser's conduct in Yemen in 1963 and his arms program appeared to make it unwise to let him believe that we were quietly condoning many of the things that he was doing by continuing our aid program at existing levels." [98] Although the Kennedy Administration thought that any attempt to renege on the three-year agreement would have little benefit for the United States and would needlessly provoke Nasser, Kennedy and his advisers had decided by November 1963 to shelve Egyptian requests for supplementary PL480 shipments and to consider a slowdown in deliveries of grain under the October 1962 accord.[99]

Kennedy was, however, under great pressure in this period both at home and abroad to employ more severe coercive measures. The Saudi government argued that American food aid enabled Nasser to divert Egyptian resources in order to buy arms and to support an expensive venture in Yemen, maintaining that he would be forced to curtail both his arms buildup and his intervention in Yemen if PL480 shipments were cut off.[100] Similarly, the British government—deeply concerned about Nasser's efforts to push Yemeni unrest across the border into Aden—lobbied in Washington for a reduction of U.S. aid to Egypt.[101]

Of far more immediate concern to the Kennedy Administration were Congressional efforts to legislate a suspension of food aid to Egypt. In April 1963, Senator Ernest Gruening (D-Alaska) concluded a lengthy report to the Senate Committee on Government Operations by recommending that continuance of the PL480 program be conditioned upon "Egypt's prompt compliance with the terms of the United Nations settlement of the Yemen dispute" and "Egypt's reversal of policy so as to cease production of missiles, warplanes, submarines, and other implements of war clearly designed for aggressive purposes." [102] Gruening's recommendation was amplified by Bushrod Howard, Jr., a lobbyist for the Yemeni royalists, in testimony to the Senate Foreign Relations Committee in June 1963. Howard maintained that no PL480 aid should be provided to Egypt after October 1963, "unless the President determines that the United Arab Republic has complied with the agreement entered into by the United Arab Republic, Saudi Arabia, and the Secretary General of the United Nations on 8 April 1963." [103]

The Kennedy Administration's opposition to such tactics was twofold: first, Kennedy and most of his top-level advisers doubted that threats to cut off aid, or actual suspensions of existing agreements, would moderate Nasser's behavior; and second, the Kennedy White House, like its predecessor, was anxious to avoid legislative restraints on its conduct of foreign policy. In a letter to Senator Gruening on 25 July 1963, Assistant Secretary of State for Congressional Relations Fred Dutton stressed that "it had been amply demonstrated in the Near East that the use of an assistance program in this area as a bludgeon to force solutions will not work where deep-seated beliefs and long-standing grievances are held." [104] In private conversations with key legislators, Dutton and his staff emphasized that President Kennedy shared the general Congressional dissatisfaction with the Nasser regime, but that the White House did not want to "have its hands tied" on the issue of aid to Egypt.[105]

Dutton's arguments fell on deaf ears in Congress. For politicians weaned on the belief that good political bargains bring immediate, tangible returns, the U.S. food aid program in Egypt seemed in the fall of 1963 to be a classic example of bad politics and poor bargaining. On 7 November 1963, the Senate voted 65–13 to approve an amendment to section 620 of the Foreign Assistance Act offered by Senator Gruening. The Gruening Amendment, which was identical to an amendment that had been passed by the House of Representatives, forbad aid to "any country which the President determines is engaging in or preparing for aggressive military efforts directed against (1) the United States; (2) any country receiving assistance under this or any other Act; or (3) any country to which sales are made under the Agricultural Trade Development and Assistance Act of 1954. . . ." Although the amendment was couched in general terms, the floor debate on the Gruening proposal made it clear that the legislation was aimed at Nasser and his involvement in Yemen.[106]

The Kennedy Administration was not bound by the Gruening Amendment to condition continued food aid to Egypt on Nasser's withdrawal from Yemen—the legislation contained an "escape clause" that allowed the President to judge the aggressive intent of aid recipients—but Kennedy and his chief advisers were disturbed by the growing strength of the Congressional drive to limit the Administration's ability to make food aid policy toward Egypt. When questioned about the Administration's reaction to the Gruening Amendment at a news conference on 8 November, Secretary of State Rusk noted that he was "concerned about the loss of flexibility, the loss of any ability to move to protect and forward the interests of the

United States wherever they might be engaged anywhere in the world." [107]

Nasser was greatly displeased by the Gruening Amendment. At a meeting with West Berlin Mayor Willy Brandt in Cairo on the afternoon of 8 November, Nasser "spoke bitterly and at length about the American tactics of using aid to pressure him." Nasser reportedly told Brandt that "the UAR had emerged from the 1956 experience convinced that it could not depend on the Western World but that recent American policy had made him hope that this judgment could be revised." Nasser concluded by telling Brandt that "it now seemed clear that he must go back to 1957." [108]

Nasser's reaction to the Gruening Amendment seemed to underscore the Kennedy Administration's contention that aid could not profitably be used as a "bludgeon" in U.S.-Egyptian relations. "The despatches from Cairo make it clear," National Security Advisor McGeorge Bundy wrote to Senator J. W. Fulbright on 11 November, "that the Gruening Amendment has had a strong impact there, but unfortunately the effect is the opposite of what supporters of the Amendment must have intended. On the evidence so far, there seems to be no alternative to the conclusion that we make people more, and not less, nationalistic by actions which seem to them to be 'neocolonial pressure'." [109]

The End of an Era

"The passage of the Gruening Amendment and President Kennedy's death in November 1963," recalls Donald Bergus, "marked the end of an era in our food aid policy toward Egypt and in U.S.-Egyptian relations generally." [110] Full of confidence in its "great unseen weapon," the Kennedy Administration had hoped in 1961 to use food aid to induce the Nasser regime to respect America's immediate security interests in the Middle East and in the rest of the Third World, to strengthen Nasser's commitment to Egypt's economic development program, and more broadly to demonstrate the New Frontiersmen's willingness to assist neutralist developing countries. Encouraged by Egyptian behavior in 1961–62, Kennedy had gradually expanded food-aid shipments under the tactic of "continuous negotiation," and then, in October 1962, had concluded an unprecedented three-year PL480 agreement with the Nasser government. But—contrary to American expectations—U.S.-Egyptian relations deteriorated as a result of the Egyptian intervention in Yemen and the Egyptian military buildup. As U.S. concern over Egyptian attacks on short-run American political interests mounted, the Egyptian development program began to falter, and the food aid program in Egypt began to seem less a symbol of the Kennedy Administration's skill in taming difficult Third World nationalists than a symbol of the Nasser regime's continued ability to accept aid from the Americans with one hand while stirring up trouble for them with the other. Disillusionment with Nasser produced a familiar reaction in Washington: Congress began to agitate for a much more restrictive American aid policy, and the Administration tried to fend off Congressional encroachment on Executive Branch foreign policy-making powers while at the same time employing more coercive tactics in its aid policy toward Egypt.

As important as PL480 aid had become for the Egyptian economy in 1963, it was not important enough to Nasser to cause him to put what he saw to be his vital political interests in jeopardy. Nasser's prestige in Egypt and in the Arab world in the early 1960s was largely a product of his successful defiance of Western attempts to pressure him in the mid-1950s. To sustain his heroic image, Nasser was prepared to lash out at the American government—even if the price for such attacks might be suspension of American aid and economic dislocation in Egypt—if criticism of his relationship with the United States began to build up in the Arab world. Arab accusations that Nasser had softened his policies in return for American aid in 1961–62 severely diminished the Egyptian leader's willingness to compromise with the United States over the issues of Yemen, defense spending, and Israel. Nasser was in a sense victimized by his spectacular success in the mid-1950s: having built up an enormous store of prestige through extreme anti-imperialist positions, he could not moderate his stance without risking the loss of much of his prestige in the Arab world.

Kennedy's personal style helped ease some of Nasser's doubts about cooperating with the United States in the early 1960s; as Mustapha Kamel later put it, "Nasser appreciated

Kennedy's efforts to treat him as an equal and as an important world leader, just as he had resented Eisenhower and Dulles's efforts to treat him like some sort of pawn in the big chess game with the Russians." [111] But no amount of personal rapport could erase the basic fact that, in 1963, in Nasser's eyes, the political costs of satisfying American desires on the issues of Egyptian policy toward Israel, Egyptian policy in Yemen, and Egyptian defense spending far outweighed the political and economic benefits of American food aid.

CHAPTER SIX

Johnson's "Short Leash": Food Aid and American Policy Toward Egypt, 1964-67

If ye be willing and obedient, ye shall eat the good of the land: But if ye refuse and rebel, ye shall be devoured with the sword: for the mouth of the Lord hath spoken.

Isaiah 1:19.20.

For Lyndon Johnson, diplomacy was essentially an extension of the game of national politics. As an instrument of diplomacy, food aid was bound—in the Johnsonian scheme of things—by the cardinal rule of national politics: never do something for nothing. Johnson shared many of Kennedy's convictions about the long-run political benefits for the United States of economic development in poor countries, but he had far less patience than his predecessor had had with recipients of American largesse who created short-run difficulties for the American government, and for Lyndon Johnson. Economic development was a slow and uncertain process, and in the meantime Johnson wanted something to show for his efforts. As Philip Geyelin put it, "Lyndon Johnson was for doing favors to those who showed themselves to be appreciative . . . in what they did for themselves . . . and what they did, or did not do, that might run counter to the larger interests of the benefactor." [1] Johnson wasted little time in making his philosophy clear to aid recipients. Three days after Kennedy's death, for example, he warned the Pakistani Foreign Minister that "continued sympathy for Communist Chinese causes and antipathy toward those of the West could produce a discontinuance of American aid in Pakistan." [2] Johnson, one AID official later commented, "wanted to put those so-and-so's in the Third World on a short leash." [3]

Distressed by Nasser's role in the Arab-Israeli conflict, by his growing economic and military dependence on the Soviet Union, and by his increasing attacks on Western interests in the Arab world and in Africa, Johnson grew more and more frustrated in 1964 with the three-year American commitment to provide food aid to Egypt. In a year in which PL480 aid accounted for 92 percent of Egyptian wheat imports and 53 percent of Egypt's net supply of wheat,[4] Johnson thought it incredible that Egypt could show such disregard for American interests. Finally, after the United States Information Service Library in Cairo was burned to the ground in November 1964, after Nasser denounced the Johnson Administration and its aid programs in a particularly vituperative speech in December 1964, and after intense pressure had begun to build on Capitol Hill for abrogation of the three-year agreement, Johnson stepped in and shortened Nasser's leash, suspending delivery of the last installment of aid under the October 1962 accord.[5] After a period of more restrained Egyptian behavior in the spring and summer of 1965, the Johnson Administration resumed food aid shipments to the Nasser regime, completing the 1962 agreement and then, at the end of 1965, negotiating a new, six-month PL480 agreement. But when U.S.-Egyptian relations again began to deteriorate in 1966—at a time when the American agricultural surplus had diminished considerably—Johnson again turned off the spigot of PL480 aid. From the points of view of both the Johnson Administration and the Nasser regime at the beginning of 1967, continuation of the PL480 program in Egypt cost more in domestic and regional political terms than it was worth. By May–June 1967, any political leverage that economic aid had once produced for the United States in Egypt had long since dissipated.

Johnson Versus Nasser

The personal rapport that Kennedy had managed to establish with Nasser in 1961–62 eluded Lyndon Johnson. Although Johnson wrote to Nasser shortly after Kennedy's death and expressed his desire to "continue the frank and friendly dialogue that has already contributed to understanding between our two governments," [6] Nasser distrusted the new American President from the start. This distrust seemed to stem from both a vague aversion to Johnson's unsophisticated approach to international affairs and a belief that Johnson was far more sympathetic to Israel than he was to its Arab antagonists. In the caricatured view of most high-ranking Egyptian government officials and most influential Egyptian journalists in the mid-1960s, Johnson was a crude, unschooled, manipulative Texan, interested in U.S.-Egyptian relations only insofar as they affected his domestic political fortunes. In Mustapha Kamel's opinion, "Egypt lost a great deal with the death of Kennedy. Johnson was a disaster for Egypt. He didn't know very much or care very much about Egypt. He was interested only in winning the next election." [7] Heikal later wrote that Nasser had "an instinctive dislike for President Lyndon Baines Johnson. He did not like what he had heard about this Texas politician, the party man, the wheeler-dealer." Among other things, Nasser thought that Johnson lacked "stature" in international affairs; for the fastidious Nasser, exhibiting scars from a gallbladder operation to photographers was not the mark of a statesman. [8]

This aversion to Johnson was reinforced by a strong suspicion that the American President's attitude toward the Arab-Israeli conflict was nearly identical to that of the Israel lobby. Johnson's impressive record of support for Israel during his years in the Senate was well known in Cairo. When Johnson chose to make his first major policy statement on the Middle East to a pro-Israeli audience at the Weizmann Institute in New York on 6 February 1964, the Nasser regime immediately concluded that Kennedy's attempts at "evenhandedness" in the Arab-Israeli dispute had been abandoned. [9] Radio Cairo contended that Johnson's speech meant that "the United States has finally chosen Israel and that the so-called Arab-American friendship does not go beyond words and sympathies." [10]

Johnson reciprocated Nasser's suspicion and hostility. To some extent, it was true that his antipathy for Nasser was the result of a predisposition to favor Israel in the Arab-Israeli dispute. Johnson had built up close contacts with the American Jewish community during his Senate career, and had been generally supportive of the goals of the Israel lobby. After

Johnson had championed Israel's futile effort to retain control of the Sinai in late 1956–early 1957, one Jewish lobbyist described him as the "most sincere supporter of Zionism in the American government." [11] Shortly after President Kennedy's assassination, Johnson reportedly told an Israeli diplomat: "You have lost a good friend of Israel. But you have gained an even better one." [12]

Of equal importance as an explanation for Johnson's suspiciousness was his inability to understand Nasser's persistent refusal to abide by the rules of the Johnsonian game of politics. "Johnson treated Third World leaders like Senators," McGeorge Bundy later observed. "He presumed that they were all reasonable men who could be persuaded to compromise on almost any issue if the right combination of threats and incentives was employed." [13] But Nasser confounded Johnson, displaying a stubbornness and an unwillingness to compromise that the American President had not encountered in his political career. When Nasser's seeming unreasonableness began to create domestic political problems for the Johnson Administration, Johnson's suspiciousness was transformed into a deep personal animosity toward the Egyptian leader.

U.S.-Egyptian Differences Mount

The personal friction that developed between Johnson and Nasser did little to slow the rise of U.S.-Egyptian differences in 1964 over the Arab-Israeli dispute, the Soviet-Egyptian relationship, and Egyptian policy in the Arab world and in Africa. To the chagrin of Mustapha Kamel and John Badeau, it proved impossible to push the Palestine problem back into the "icebox" in 1964. Early in 1964, the Israeli government began to divert the waters of the Jordan River as part of an ambitious national irrigation project. Deeply disturbed by the potential threat to their water supplies posed by the Jordan waters off-take, and humiliated by their inability to prevent the unilateral Israeli action, the Syrian and Jordanian governments pressured Nasser to retaliate against Israel. Unprepared to launch an attack against the militarily superior Israelis, Nasser convened an Arab summit meeting in Cairo in mid-January 1964 to organize an Arab response to the Jordan River diversion that would appease the bellicose Syrians without producing a third round of Arab-Israeli hostilities. Prodded adroitly by Nasser, the Arabs agreed, first, to build engineering works on Arab territory to redirect some of the headwaters of the Jordan and thus reduce the flow of water into Israel, and, second, to coordinate Arab military planning under an Egyptian-led Arab High Command, head-quartered in Cairo, and supported by Arab oil revenues. By the end of January, Nasser had managed to avoid being dragged into a conflict for which Egypt was not prepared and yet at the same time had solidified his claim to undisputed leadership of the Arab world.[14]

[handwritten margin note: Jordan River problem]

[handwritten margin note: Egypt consolidates power as Arab leader]

Ambassador Badeau attributed Nasser's avoidance of attacks on the United States at the Cairo Summit not to "disembodied goodwill toward the United States of America", but to "his need for a good American connection and his anxiety that this be preserved." Citing Egyptian behavior at the Cairo Summit as evidence of the political value of the food aid program, Badeau cabled Washington that "within the limits of aid legislation I urge that we continue to make those contributions to the U.A.R. economy which will give us maximum diplomatic leverage."[15] Johnson and Rusk, however, saw Nasser's role in the Jordan River controversy less as evidence of his moderation than of his willingness to exploit the Palestinian problem to promote his own extravagant ambitions in the Arab world. Moreover, Arab attacks on Israel provided ammunition for the Israel lobby to use against the Johnson Administration's links to Egypt. Johnson held Nasser responsible for such criticism, which was an unwelcome addition to the President's 1964 election campaign.[16]

Nasser, for his part, remained convinced that Johnson had discarded Kennedy's "even-handed" approach to the Arab-Israeli dispute. In late February 1964, the Egyptian President told Assistant Secretary of State Talbot in Cairo that "he could not accept the American contention that U.S. Middle East policy had not changed since the death of President Kennedy." Talbot subsequently reported that Johnson's record of sympathy for Israel had "given rise to an unshakeable Arab belief that the enlightened Kennedy policies had given way to Truman-like pro-Israel policies."[17]

[handwritten note: Nasser believes US is now pro-Israel.]

Egypt's increasingly cordial relationship with the Soviet Union in 1964 placed further strains on its relations with the United States. In May 1964, Khrushchev paid an official visit to Egypt to celebrate the completion of the first stage of the Aswan High Dam, the great symbol of Soviet-Egyptian co-operation.[18] With the shadowy image of John Foster Dulles's 1956 default in the background, both Khrushchev and Nasser used the Aswan ceremonies to extol the virtues of Soviet-Egyptian collaboration and to denigrate "neocolonialist" Western attempts to use aid as a political lever.[19] Khrushchev promised to provide Egypt with a further $277 million in economic assistance, and made a more ambiguous pledge to meet Egyptian arms requests.[20] The Egyptian government was gratified by this renewed Soviet commitment to Egyptian economic and military development, particularly since it came "at a time when there was much talk in the West about reducing aid and 'getting tough' with the Nasser regime."[21]

Nasser's growing dependence on the Soviet Union was a source of considerable anxiety in Washington, as were his continued attacks on Western interests in the Arab world and in Africa. U.S.-Egyptian differences in the Arab world in 1964 stemmed not only from the deepening Egyptian involvement in Yemen, but also from Nasser's campaign to expel the US Air Force from Wheelus Air Base in Libya. Wheelus, the largest American air force installation outside the continental United States, was used primarily as a gunnery and training site by units attached to NATO. Under the terms of a 1954 treaty with the Libyans, the United States government agreed to train the Libyan air force in return for the lease of Wheelus. Although the base treaty was not due to expire until 1970, Nasser began to pressure Libya's King Idris to abrogate the treaty and eject the Americans early in 1964. Claiming that foreign military bases on Arab soil were "a derogation of sovereignty and a threat to the independence and integrity of the U.A.R. and the other Arab states," Nasser castigated Idris in a speech in Cairo on 22 February 1964 for permitting the United States to operate the Wheelus base.[22] Fearing that Nasser intended to "overthrow the monarchy and annex Libya, thereby bringing oil revenues to relieve his own serious economic problems and providing additional land to relieve overpopulation," Idris hastily announced on 26 February that Libya would not renew the

Wheelus agreement when it expired in 1970.[23] Not surprisingly, the Wheelus affair deepened the Johnson Administration's displeasure with Nasser. In what he later described as "one of the stormiest meetings I ever had with Nasser," Ambassador Badeau subsequently warned the Egyptian leader not to meddle in a matter that the American government considered to be "solely the concern of the Libyans and ourselves." [24]

To add to the Johnson Administration's frustrations, the Nasser regime resumed its involvement in the Congolese civil war in the spring of 1964, sending shipments of small arms overland to leftist guerillas. Nasser's gun-running—which was no doubt partly motivated by a desire to establish his influence in Black Africa before the July 1964 summit meeting of African leaders in Cairo and the October 1964 Nonaligned Summit in Cairo—hampered United Nations efforts to promote a negotiated settlement of the bloody conflict.[25]

"Removing the Serpent's Fangs": The 1964 Congressional Campaign to Suspend Aid to Egypt

Nasser's behavior in the spring and summer of 1964 provoked a powerful reaction on Capitol Hill. With his usual penchant for hyperbole, Senator Gruening declared on 12 May 1964 that Egypt's attacks on American interests were evidence that "Khrushchev has pulled the strings—and Nasser has moved. With the help of the appeasers in our own State Department, Russia is about to succeed in its centuries-old drive to control the nations of the Middle East." [26] Gruening added cryptically on 18 May that "now President Nasser is showing his true colors—and they are red." [27] Gruening's prescription for dealing with Nasser was very simple. The Senator from Alaska argued that "we could stop Egypt's involvement in the Yemen very easily. All we would have to do would be to tell Nasser to pull his troops back into Egypt or he would not receive any of our food aid." [28] Representative Samuel Stratton (D-N.Y.) echoed Gruening in the House.

> The elimination of aid to Mr. Nasser would help us ensure the peace in the Middle East . . . let us not be deceived, as

we were with Hitler's *Mein Kampf* . . . let us once and for all remove the fangs of this serpent.[29]

On 10 June 1964, Stratton offered an amendment to section 620(i) of the Foreign Assistance Act that would ban aid to Egypt:

> Unless the President determines that Egypt is not engaging in, preparing for, promoting or stimulating aggressive military efforts against Israel or any other country in the eastern Mediterranean, and unless the President also determines that the furnishing of such assistance is essential to the national interest of the United States.[30]

By forcing President Johnson, in effect, to put his imprimatur on Nasser's foreign policy before sending aid to Egypt, Stratton sought to raise a domestic political barrier in the path of PL480 shipments to Egypt that Johnson would find it difficult to circumvent. Although Johnson was certainly sympathetic to Congressional efforts to curtail aid to Nasser, he, like his predecessors, disliked legislation which restricted his conduct of American foreign policy. Basing its case on the need for Executive flexibility, the Johnson Administration mobilized sufficient strength in the House to defeat the Stratton Amendment narrowly in a roll-call vote.[31]

But the defeat of the Stratton Amendment did not end Congressional efforts to suspend aid to Egypt in 1964. With the approach of the November elections, many legislators were eager to record their support for Israel and their opposition to aid to Nasser for the benefit of their constituents. On 2 September, Representative Oliver Bolton (D-Ohio) offered an amendment to Public Law 480 that would declare Egypt an "unfriendly nation" and thus exclude it from the pool of countries eligible for American food aid.[32] In his defense of the Bolton Amendment, Representative Leonard Farbstein (D-N.Y.) revealed a misunderstanding of the political usefulness of food aid and of the psychology of Third World nationalism that was widespread in Congress:

This man Nasser is an adventurer; this man is another Hitler; this man has made statements which no one believes but, like Hitler, will come to pass if we are not careful.
We feed about half of Egypt's people through Public Law 480. Without Public Law 480 he would have to buy food. If he did not do so they would starve and the people might revolt. Perhaps that is what should happen to him. We enable this man to save the money that he would have to spend to buy food with which to feed his people; we enable him to use his cotton in exchange with the Soviet Union for arms.
The best way to stop Nasser is to agree to this amendment.[33]

Like the Stratton Amendment, the Bolton Amendment foundered on the reefs of opposition from the Majority leadership in the House and the Johnson Administration.[34] Nasser's unpopularity on Capitol Hill persisted, however. On 6 October, Senator Kenneth Keating (D-N.Y.) proposed that Nasser be served with an ultimatum: "all U.S. aid to Egypt would be cut off on 1 January 1965, unless Nasser's troops were pulled out of Yemen and unless his military forces were scaled down to domestic needs." Although Keating did not attempt to embody his ultimatum in legislation, his proposal reflected a continuing Congressional antipathy for the American aid program in Egypt.[35]

Lucius Battle's "Little Horrors"

Distressed both by Nasser's recalcitrance and by the depth of Congressional support for the "foolhardy view that Egypt could be brought to heel on any specific issue by the threat—or fact—of total aid withdrawal," [36] John Badeau resigned his post in Cairo and returned to the United States to take up a position at Columbia University at the end of the summer of 1964. The reception that Badeau's successor, Lucius Battle, received in his first few months in Egypt strengthened the hand of Nasser's enemies on Capitol Hill and provided the extra incentive that Lyndon Johnson needed to shorten the Egyptian leader's leash and suspend delivery of American grain to Egypt. Battle recalls that "I went out to Cairo and immediately had several rather devastating experiences. I arrived in September and presented my credentials in mid-September of 1964; and then a series of little horrors occurred that caused considerable difficulty." [37]

On Thanksgiving Day in November 1964, a mob of African students, protesting American policy in the Congo, burned down the United States Information Service Library in Cairo. Hedrick Smith, then the *New York Times* bureau chief in Cairo, recalls that "the police assigned to control the protesting students were apparently surprised when the Embassy library was set afire. Nasser's embarrassment about the incompetence of his police made him very reluctant to apologize to Battle." [38] Mohamed Heikal adds that "in order to disguise the fact that the police had lost control, Nasser was prepared to accept responsibility for the attack and even be truculent about it." [39] Battle was upset by the Nasser regime's failure to provide the prompt apology required by normal diplomatic practice, and by the lethargy with which the Egyptian government moved on the question of compensation. [40] The Thanksgiving Day fire—captured dramatically in a series of photographs which appeared in the American press—did little to reassure a hostile Congress about Nasser's interest in good relations with the United States; on a day when gratitude was supposed to be the watchword, Nasser's actions were remarkable for their ingratitude. In Washington, President Johnson summoned Ambassador Kamel and asked him bitterly, "How can I ask Congress for wheat for you when you burn down our library? " [41]

Johnson's frustration with Nasser mounted when the Egyptian Air Force shot down an unarmed private plane near Alexandria on 18 December, which was owned by one of the President's friends, Texas oilman John Mecom. The plane had allegedly strayed from the civil air corridor between Cairo and Alexandria, overflown a restricted military zone in the Western Desert, and ignored instructions to land at Cairo airport. The American pilot of the Mecom plane and his Swedish copilot were killed. [42]

With a very poor sense of timing, Egyptian Minister of Supply Ramsey Stino called Battle to his office to discuss the food aid program a few hours after the American ambassador had returned from viewing the wreckage of the oil company plane. Stino was worried about diminishing Egyptian wheat supplies, and wanted to obtain an additional $35 million worth of PL480 wheat before the end of 1964.[43] In what Battle later described as a "very brief and very tense meeting," he told Stino that he was "unwilling to discuss a supplementary food aid shipment under the circumstances that exist today." [44]

Stino—now more anxious than ever about the American wheat connection—reported his conversation with Battle to Ali Sabri, who was then serving as Nasser's Prime Minister. Sabri, whose hostility toward the United States had grown steadily since his humiliating 1952 trip to Washington, apparently relayed an embellished version of Stino's story to Nasser while on board a train to Port Said to celebrate the anniversary of the 1956 Anglo-French withdrawal. According to Sabri, Battle had threatened to cut off American food aid if Egypt did not moderate its behavior.[45]

Nasser was enraged by Battle's alleged threat. Moreover, he was in this period eager to reinforce his ties to the Soviets. Khrushchev had fallen from power in October 1964; Nasser feared that the new Soviet leadership would be less friendly to Egypt than Khrushchev had been. After learning of Khrushchev's demise, Nasser reportedly exclaimed: "Oh my God, now we have got to start all over again." [46]

Nasser's anger at Battle and his concern about the Soviet-Egyptian relationship proved to be a highly combustible combination. In his Victory Day speech at Port Said on 23 December before an audience that included Alexander Shelepin, the Soviet Deputy Premier, Nasser launched what the CIA termed "Egypt's bitterest attack on the United States since 1956." [47]

> The American Ambassador says that our behavior is not acceptable. Well, let us tell them that those who do not accept our behavior can go and drink from the sea.
> What I want to say to President Johnson is that I am not prepared to sell Egyptian independence for thirty million pounds or fifty million pounds. We are not ready to discuss our behavior with anybody. We will cut the tongues of anybody who talks badly about us.
> If we are now drinking tea seven days a week, we can make do with it on only five days. If we are drinking coffee five days, we can make do with four. If we are eating for four days, we make do with three. We can tighten our belts.

I want to say that we have troubles. We don't mind troubles. But we are not going to accept pressure.
We are not going to accept gangsterism by cowboys.[48]

Nasser 1964

The Suspension of Aid to Nasser

Nasser told a CIA informant early in January 1965 that "the USA is afraid to cut off aid to Egypt because the US knows that Egypt will react by sabotaging all American efforts in the area." [49] It was true, as Nasser observed, that there was much apprehension within the State Department at the beginning of 1965 about the dangers of provoking Egypt by cutting off PL480 assistance. But if Nasser assumed that this anxiety would prevent a suspension of aid to Egypt, he was profoundly mistaken. In the aftermath of the Port Said speech, fear of the political repercussions of cancelling aid to Egypt was overwhelmed, on Capitol Hill, by anger at Nasser's ingratitude and by the conviction that Nasser would eventually be forced by the loss of American assistance to moderate his behavior. Johnson himself was furious with Nasser, and ordered a temporary cessation of food shipments to Egypt in the first week of January 1965, pending the outcome of the Congressional debate on the Egyptian aid program.[50]

Nasser's Port Said speech was not, to say the least, well received on Capitol Hill. Dean Rusk later commented that "when Nasser came before those huge crowds in Cairo and elsewhere, he would let his rhetoric get the best of him. He would shout such things as 'Throw your aid into the Red Sea.' Repeated performances of that sort of thing simply persuaded the Congress to accommodate him." [51] On 26 January 1965, the House of Representatives voted 204–177 to approve a rider to a routine appropriations bill offered by Representative Robert Michel (R-Ill.) that would prevent shipment of the $37 million worth of foodstuffs remaining under the 1962 PL480 agreement. "It makes no sense," argued Michel, "to supply aid to a man who has abused and vilified Americans, has operated as a Soviet agent and has served as an instrument of Soviet foreign policy." Michel added:

I think that we now have an excellent opportunity to demonstrate to both Colonel Nasser and others like him that the American people and their elected representatives will not sit idly by while we have our property destroyed and our motives misjudged. . . . Nasser has indicated clearly that he does not consider our aid necessary. . . . I therefore find little reason for continuing to give him any aid.[52]

Representative Silvio Conte (D-Mass.) capsulized the thinking of many of his colleagues on the political value of cutting off aid to Egypt when he concluded:

It is my strong belief that the only way that we can control this man is by stopping our aid through PL480. If we maintain this firm policy, it will be only a matter of time before Nasser can be contained.[53]

Much as it sympathized with the Congressional drive to block aid shipments to the Nasser regime, the Johnson Administration was determined to retain control of aid policy toward Egypt. When the Senate began consideration of the Michel Rider, Johnson and his advisers launched a major effort to modify the House legislation so that it would register Congress's disapproval of continued aid to Nasser but would leave the actual decision to suspend aid to the President's discretion. Appearing before a closed session of the Senate Foreign Relations Committee on 27 January 1965, Secretary of State Rusk expressed disappointment at the House action on the Michel Rider, although he noted that he was personally appalled by Nasser's behavior. Rusk appealed to the Committee to amend the Michel Rider to give the Administration an "escape clause" like the one included in the Gruening Amendment in 1963. The Secretary of State insisted that "we need this card. It is one of the few cards we have in our relations with Nasser at the present time." Rusk assured the Committee that the Administration intended to "shorten the string on Nasser" after the 1962 agreement was completed.[54]

The members of the Foreign Relations Committee did not seem particularly enthusiastic about altering the language of the Michel Rider. Senator Bourke Hickenlooper (R-Ind.) contended that "Nasser's obnoxious attitude is a stimulus to every other little postage stamp country . . . to insult the United States and say 'we'll get more out of it if we insult them'." Senator John Pastore (D.-R.I.) complained to Rusk about the domestic political liabilities of voting for continued aid to Nasser's Egypt, noting in exasperation that "every time you vote out here you go home and have to answer for all this." [55]

Undersecretary of State George Ball had more luck in his lobbying efforts at the Senate Appropriations Committee. In testimony to the Appropriations Committee on 1 February, Ball conceded that "relations between Cairo and Washington in the last few weeks have been anything but satisfactory," but argued that "the President should have the power to complete the 1962 agreement if he decides it is to the advantage of the United States." Ball assured the Committee that he was "not saying the President is necessarily going to carry it out." [56] At the Undersecretary of State's urging, the Appropriations Committee voted 17–6 later that same day to amend the House ban to permit completion of the three-year agreement "if the President determines that the financing of such exports is in the national interest." [57] On 3 February the Senate voted 44–38 to adopt the Michel Rider as amended by the Appropriations Committee. [58]

At a press conference on 4 February, President Johnson said that he was pleased by the Senate's version of the Michel Rider, and hoped that the House would reconsider its position and endorse the Senate language:

> I judge it of the highest importance that the flexibility provided the President by the Senate version be sustained by the Congress. I hope the House of Representatives will accept the improvements made by the Senate Committee and voted by the Senate.
> It is of course obvious that the relations between the United States and the United Arab Republic must be improved . . . if we are to have any degree of success in this sensitive relationship the President must have some freedom of action. [59]

Uneager to disturb a President who had just been elected by an enormous margin, the House reversed its earlier vote and adopted the Senate version of the Michel Rider on 8 February. [60]

1965 – last shipment of PL480 aid indefinitely postponed.

Having established the primacy of the Executive Branch in the making of aid policy toward Egypt, Johnson had no intention of immediately exercising the "escape clause" provided in the final rendering of the Michel Rider. Citing the strength of Congressional opposition to the resumption of aid, the Johnson Administration informed the Egyptian government in February 1965 that delivery of the final installment of the 1962 agreement would be delayed indefinitely, and that consideration of Egyptian requests for a multi-year extension of that agreement would be postponed, also indefinitely. The State Department hinted strongly to Ambassador Kamel that restoration of PL480 aid would depend upon the degree to which Egypt respected American interests in the Middle East and in Africa.[61]

Nasser's Response to Johnson's Short Leash

The suspension of aid to the Nasser regime in the spring of 1965 seemed to the Johnson Administration to have a salutary effect upon Egyptian behavior. Despite U.S.-Egyptian differences over the American decision to supply Israel with M–48 Patton tanks in late February 1965, and despite Nasser's continued public denunciations of the American decision to delay completion of the 1962 PL480 agreement, there were signs that the Nasser regime was prepared to modify some of its positions to ensure the resumption of U.S. food deliveries.

To balance the Soviet shipment of T–54 tanks to Egypt in 1963, the Johnson Administration had authorized West Germany, which since the early 1960s had been quietly providing Israel with limited quantities of arms under the Israeli-West German reparations agreement, to ship American-produced M–48 tanks to Israel. The West German-Israeli tank accord, reached secretly in October 1964, was discovered by the Egyptians in January 1965. Under the threat of Arab punitive action, the West German government abrogated the M–48 agreement with Israel. At the end of February 1965, the Johnson Administration announced that it would fill the breach left by the West German default and supply tanks directly to the Israelis.[62] In a letter to Nasser on 18 March 1965, Johnson defended the sale in much the same way that Kennedy had defended the

[margin note: Arms race continues]

1962 HAWK missile transaction, arguing that the provision of arms to Israel was intended to balance the rapid Egyptian military buildup.[63] Predictably, Nasser reacted angrily to the U.S.-Israeli tank deal.[64]

At the same time, Nasser continued to voice sharp criticism of the Johnson Administration's decision to postpone completion of the 1962 food aid agreement. Recalling Dulles's efforts to influence Egyptian behavior during the Aswan affair, Nasser told a Cairo crowd on 1 May 1965 that "we are facing a stage of economic pressure similar to the one we faced in 1956." [65]

Nevertheless, Johnson and his advisers perceived a definite improvement in Egyptian attitudes toward American interests in the spring of 1965. The Nasser regime apologized privately to Ambassador Battle for the burning of the Embassy library, and agreed to pay $500,000 toward rebuilding costs.[66] Egyptian arms shipments to the Congo were halted. The Egyptian government resumed negotiations with the Saudis to bring about an end to the Yemeni civil war. Battle recalls:

[margin note: Spring '65 Nasser mollifies]

> It was clear to us in the Cairo Embassy that Nasser was making an effort in the spring of 1965 to tone down his anti-American behavior. Nasser's more moderate actions were not due entirely to his interest in preserving the PL480 program—his meddling in the Congo, for example, was getting him nowhere anyway—but his need for American aid certainly contributed to his avoidance of an open break with the United States.[67]

On 31 May 1965, Battle advised the Administration to resume deliveries under the 1962 PL480 accord, noting that the Nasser regime had only a three-week reserve of grain remaining, and that "we are nearing major difficulties here as concern over food shortages increases." [68] Hoping to reinforce the positive trend in Egyptian behavior, Johnson authorized shipment of the last $37 million of foodstuffs under the 1962 agreement on 21 June 1965.[69] Battle was instructed to warn the Nasser regime that "untoward developments" would "limit Executive Branch capability to deal with Congressional critics" and would jeopardize future aid shipments.[70]

The Six-Month Agreement

The Johnson Administration was generally pleased with Nasser's conduct in the summer and fall of 1965. The Egyptian government had not, to be sure, expressed much public appreciation for the resumption of deliveries under the 1962 PL480 agreement. The stony silence with which American aid shipments were greeted in Cairo in the summer of 1965 contrasted markedly with the enthusiastic reception accorded emergency grain shipments from the Soviet Union, which had responded to Nasser's appeal for help in June 1965 by diverting Soviet ships laden with Australian and Canadian wheat to Alexandria.[71] Radio Cairo used the arrival of the first Soviet grain ships as an excuse to blast "pro-Zionist American Congressmen who clamor for stopping the export of wheat and foodstuffs to Egypt so that its sons may starve and succumb to American policy." [72]

On the whole, however, Johnson and his advisers were satisfied with Egyptian behavior. Dean Rusk told the Senate Foreign Relations Committee in a closed session on 13 October 1965 that "we do believe that there has been substantial improvement in Nasser's attitude toward our interests." Rusk continued:

> I think if we were to make a list of the principal items in which we feel our interests are engaged and a list of the things we would want Nasser to do, that on the whole over the last six months he has moved very well from the point of view of American interests. One can't guarantee that there won't be another Suez speech or something of the sort, in which case these things would be opened up again. But in terms of using the leverage, I think we have used it in a pretty powerful way here over the last six months.[73]

Rusk cited the Saudi-Egyptian agreement to end outside involvement in the Yemeni civil war, reached at Jidda in August 1965, and Nasser's appointment of Zakaria Mohieddin (a noted proponent of economic retrenchment and accommodation with the West) as Prime Minister in September 1965, as evidence of Egyptian moderation.[74] In view of these promising developments, Rusk informed the Committee that "we are giving . . . some thought to another PL480 agreement [with Egypt]." [75]

One week before Rusk's testimony, the Johnson Administration had reopened negotiations for a PL480 agreement to succeed the 1962 arrangement with an Egyptian delegation led by the Minister of Finance, Dr. Kaissouny. Kaissouny estimated that Egypt would need to import about $300 million worth of foreign grain in 1966, and expressed his hope that the American government would provide the bulk of it through a new one or two-year food aid agreement. The Johnson Administration, however, made it clear to Kaissouny that it was not prepared to remove the "short leash" that it had placed on American aid policy.[76] President Johnson, Secretary of State Rusk, and Ambassador Battle were all certain that short-term PL480 agreements offered the best hope for exercising effective leverage over Nasser's behavior. As Battle put it at the time:

> I am convinced as I have said almost since arrival here that our aid must be based on more quid pro quo. . . . I do not favor, even if it were possible, a new long-term PL480 agreement . . . if the future permits, I would like to be in almost continual negotiation with the UAR . . . so that the value of our cooperation is not forgotten and a constant requirement is before the Egyptians to contribute to the climate that makes cooperation possible.[77]

The most attractive offer that the Johnson Administration was prepared to make to the Egyptians at the end of 1965 was a half-year Title I accord worth about $55 million. Increasingly frustrated by Johnson's short leash, but nonetheless eager to secure its American food aid connection, the Egyptian government accepted the modest six-month American offer on 3 January 1966.[78]

Nasser Snaps the Short Leash

The Nasser regime tried throughout the winter and spring of 1966 to persuade the American government to expand the size and duration of the January 1966 PL480 agreement. In

February, Egyptian Vice President Anwar Sadat visited Washington to lobby for increased food aid,[79] and in April Ambassador Kamel presented a formal request for a one-year, $150 million extension of the six-month accord to the State Department.[80] But at the same time, Nasser seemed to observers in Washington to be reviving his anti-American campaign of 1964. While Sadat was in the United States, Nasser made a series of bitterly anti-American speeches in Cairo.[81] During the late winter and early spring of 1966, the Nasser regime used the much-publicized trial of Mustapha Amin, a prominent Egyptian journalist accused of collaborating with the Cairo CIA station, as a forum for denouncing the Johnson Administration's policies in the Middle East.[82] Shortly after Amin's conviction, Nasser permitted the Vietnamese National Liberation Front to open an office in Cairo—an action which had much the same effect in Washington that Nasser's recognition of the People's Republic of China had had ten years before.[83] When Soviet Premier Alexei Kosygin visited Cairo and Aswan in May 1966, the Egyptian press fired a barrage of attacks at the United States for its "horrible aggression" in Vietnam.[84]

Johnson and his advisers were perplexed and irritated by Nasser's habit of appealing privately for American aid and then suddenly launching fierce public attacks on the United States. Richard Parker, who had succeeded Donald Bergus as Battle's political counselor in the summer of 1965, recalls that "there seemed to be an element of schizophrenia in Nasser's behavior toward us in 1966. He wanted our aid, but as soon as we seemed on the verge of improving relations and increasing PL480 aid, he would exhibit this fateful compulsion to lash out at American interests."[85] In an article in the *New York Times* in late February 1966, Hedrick Smith compared Nasser's conduct to that of the scorpion in the Egyptian folk tale of the frog and the scorpion. It seemed that the scorpion, unable to swim, asked the frog to carry it across a stream. The frog refused, fearing that the scorpion would inflict a fatal wound in midstream. The scorpion pleaded with the frog, promising not to sting it. Reluctantly, the frog acquiesced, put the scorpion on its back, and proceeded across the stream. Halfway across the stream, the scorpion suddenly stung its benefactor. As both frog and scorpion began to drown, the frog asked in confusion "Why did you do that? " "I couldn't help it," was the scorpion's plaintive reply.[86]

Nasser's attacks on the United States in 1966—a year in which Egyptian cereal and grain imports rose by 19 percent, creating a deeper need for American aid[87]—seem to have had several roots. In the first place, Nasser was convinced that the CIA was actively plotting to topple him. Despite Ambassador Battle's efforts to dissuade him, Nasser firmly believed that the U.S. government had begun a major counter-offensive in the Third World in 1965, aimed at replacing neutralist leaders with pro-Western puppets. The overthrows of Ben Bella in Algeria in 1965, and Nkrumah in Ghana and Sukarno in Indonesia in 1966, were seen by Nasser as straws in the wind; the Egyptian President feared that he was the Johnson Administration's next target.[88] Coupled with this anxiety was a desire to use anti-American rhetoric to divert popular attention from the fact that the Egyptian economy lay in a shambles.[89] And underlying both of these factors was the basic anti-imperialist psychology of the Nasser regime. No matter how important American aid was to the Egyptian economy, maintenance of the PL480 connection was secondary, in Nasser's eyes, to the central task of ridding Egypt of all forms of foreign dominance, from military occupation to the manipulation of an aid relationship. Whenever the American government publicly implied—as it did in the negotiation of the six-month agreement—that U.S. food aid was contingent upon what it considered to be acceptable Egyptian behavior, Nasser felt compelled to fire a broadside at American interests in order to demonstrate Egypt's independence. Nasser was enormously sensitive to charges, levelled by domestic and foreign critics of his regime, that he had modified his policies in return for American grain shipments; in Nasser's view, such allegations were a far more serious threat to his position in Egypt, in the Arab world, and in the rest of the Third World than were domestic economic troubles.

Whatever the source of Nasser's truculence, the Johnson Administration never developed much interest in extending the January 1966 PL480 accord. Preoccupied with the war in Vietnam, President Johnson and his top-level advisers had little patience with the Nasser regime. During a meeting with Ambassador Kamel in the summer of 1966, the usually imper-

Nasser believed CIA was out to topple him.

turbable Dean Rusk reportedly lost his temper and exclaimed: "We've got a war in Asia—we've got no time for this Arab thing!" [90] Moreover, American agricultural surpluses had begun to diminish by 1966, and the PL480 program was entering into a period of retrenchment.[91] The contraction of the PL480 program forced the Administration to be more selective in its food-aid policy. One symptom of this new selectivity was Johnson's decree, at the beginning of 1966, that every PL480 agreement was to be cleared with him personally.[92] After Indian farmers suffered disastrous harvests in 1965 and 1966, Johnson directed that 20 percent of the 1966 U.S. wheat crop be shipped to aid the Indian government in its relief efforts.[93] In the face of rising opportunity costs, and in the face of continued Congressional hostility to the Nasser regime, the Johnson Administration rapidly lost its interest in maintaining its PL480 connection to Egypt.

Johnson's unwillingness to respond to Nasser's April 1966 request for a renewal of the six-month agreement reinforced Nasser's determination to establish his independence from American pressure. On 22 July, on the eve of the fourteenth anniversary of the Egyptian revolution, Nasser told a Cairo audience:

> It was reported in newspapers and by news agencies that we had not been behaving well and therefore America was not going to give us wheat till we behaved better. But we are not prepared to yield or surrender. We shall continue to voice our opinion frankly and we shall defend our freedom with blood. The freedom we have bought with our blood shall not be sold for wheat, rice, maize, or anything else.[94]

By the end of 1966, U.S.-Egyptian relations had sunk to their lowest point since the Eisenhower Doctrine era. In August 1966, Nasser had dismissed Zakaria Mohieddin as Prime Minister and had abandoned many of Mohieddin's economic reforms.[95] Throughout the fall of 1966, Nasser had stepped up his criticism of Saudi efforts to establish an "Islamic alliance" with the Shah of Iran, seeing this as part of the broader CIA-sponsored anti-neutralist drive in the Third World.[96]

Increasingly exasperated by the American refusal to reply one way or the other to the request for a new PL480 accord—

a tactic which Lucius Battle later attributed partly to the Johnson Administration's anxiety that "an outright refusal would provoke another Suez" [97]—Nasser finally told Battle during the American ambassador's farewell call in late February 1967 that Egypt was no longer interested in American food aid. "We have been very patient with all the pressure you have applied to us with your aid program," Nasser reportedly concluded, "but our patience has run out." [98] Mohamed Heikal revealed Nasser's withdrawal of his request in one of a much-publicized series of articles on U.S.-Egyptian relations in *Al-Ahram* in the spring of 1967, stressing that the Egyptian government preferred to pay the economic costs of doing without American aid than to submit to United States manipulation of the aid relationship.[99] In his May Day speech, Nasser roundly denounced American attempts to use economic aid as a political lever, declaring that "I am not prepared to sell one grain of sand from this country to anyone even for $100 million." [100]

Having effectively burnt his bridges to the United States, Nasser had little incentive to heed American requests for restraint in the run-up to the 1967 Arab-Israeli War.[101] Soon after Battle's departure, Chargé d'Affaires David G. Nes warned the State Department that a major conflict in the Middle East was imminent, predicting that Nasser's economic troubles, his determination to retain leadership of an increasingly fractious Arab world, and his frustration with U.S. policy would lead him either to escalate the Egyptian campaign in Yemen or to instigate a war with Israel.[102] With the fulfillment of the latter of these prophecies in the first week of June 1967, Egypt broke diplomatic relations with the United States and expelled the few remaining American technical advisers working on Egyptian development projects—the last vestiges of an economic aid program that had played a central role in U.S.-Egyptian relations for more than a decade.

Relearning Old Lessons

"Ten years after the Aswan affair," Donald Bergus later commented, "the Johnson Administration was relearning the old lessons about the limited political value of economic aid." [103]

Johnson had quickly concluded in 1964 that the three-year PL480 commitment that his predecessor had made to the Nasser regime was more of a political liability than a political asset. Three of the key premises of the strategy behind the 1962 accord—that long term aid would reinforce Egypt's interest in reducing short-term political differences with the United States, that it would accelerate Egyptian economic development, and that it would build a store of popular goodwill for the United States in Egypt—seemed to President Johnson by the end of his first year in office to be seriously flawed. The flaw in the first premise appeared to Johnson and his advisers to stem from the Egyptian government's tendency, over the three-year period covered by the 1962 agreement, to lose sight of the fact that some degree of Egyptian respect for American interests was a prerequisite for continued aid. As the Cairo AID mission put it in its July 1967 post mortem on the PL480 program in Egypt:

> A massive, long term untied PL480 sales program is unlikely to achieve any of its major purposes. Far from creating the impression of US interest and goodwill, the three-year 1962 agreement came to be taken for granted and even to be regarded by some Egyptian officials as advantageous to the US in relieving it of its surplus commodities. Far from encouraging the UAR along lines of greater international political and domestic economic responsibility, it may well have given the Egyptian leadership the false assurance to pursue whatever courses of action suited their political and economic expediency.[104]

Similarly, it seemed to the Johnson White House that the economic security afforded by the three-year accord gave the Nasser regime an irresistible opportunity to divert scarce economic resources to defense spending and foreign adventures, not an incentive to devote more attention to the distinctly secondary goal of promoting internal modernization. And finally, it had become apparent by the end of 1964 that it was unlikely that the United States would ever stockpile much popular goodwill in Egypt as a result of its food aid shipments. Embarrassed by its dependence on American largesse, the Nasser government gave very little publicity to the PL480 program.[105] After a brief trip to Egypt in the fall of 1964, Con-

gressman Thomas Stafford (R-Vt.) concluded that "it was my
very strong impression that the citizens of that country, except
for those in the seaport where some of our aid comes in, have
no idea that the wheat being distributed there comes from the
United States. They believe that Mr. Nasser raises it himself." [106]
On the few occasions when Nasser did draw public attention
to the U.S. aid program, he invariably stressed the political
motives behind PL480 shipments, decrying American economic
assistance as a neocolonialist device designed to constrain Egyptian
freedom of action.

At the beginning of 1965, Johnson had imposed his "short
leash" on Nasser, suspending PL480 shipments after a series
of anti-American actions on Nasser's part in November–December
1964. Johnson was determined to avoid long
term aid commitments to the Nasser regime, thinking that short-term
arrangements tied more explicitly to Egyptian behavior
would compel Nasser to pay more attention to the desirability
of maintaining good relations with the United States. Despite
some early success in restraining Nasser, which led to the
conclusion of a six-month PL480 agreement in January 1966,
Johnson eventually discovered that the short leash did not have
much more effect on Egyptian behavior than Kennedy's long-term
commitment had had.

In much the same way that the rapport between Kennedy
and Nasser had helped to ease Egyptian anxiety about the
U.S.-Egyptian aid relationship, the tension between Johnson
and Nasser aggravated Egyptian fears of being exploited through
political manipulation of food shipments. At the core of the
difficulties encountered by the Johnson Administration in its
efforts to use economic aid as a political lever in Egypt, however,
was a lesson first learned by John Foster Dulles in 1956; despite
a clear need for American economic assistance, the Nasser
regime was psychologically and politically unprepared to make
the sorts of concessions that the American government expected
in return for its aid. No amount of food aid could induce
Nasser to make peace with Israel, abandon his hegemonic
ambitions in the Arab world, or sever his ties with the Soviet
Union in the mid-1960s, just as no amount of capital aid would
have brought a Palestine settlement, ended Egyptian attacks
on Western interests in the Arab world, or caused Nasser to
abandon his relationship with the Soviet bloc in the mid-1950s.

There was, in short, nothing particularly original in the Cairo AID mission's conclusion in July 1967 that it had been "unrealistic to expect that President Nasser would abandon or significantly modify political actions which he determined to be in his own and Egypt's best interests in consideration of continued American wheat imports." [107]

Unlike Eisenhower after the Suez War, Lyndon Johnson was in no hurry to restore the status quo ante after the Six Day War. He believed that the sight of a militarily superior Israel sitting astride the West Bank, the Gaza Strip, and the Golan Heights would eventually compel the Arab States to trade peace for territory, as envisioned in United Nations Security Council Resolution 242. The Johnson Administration's relations with Nasser in the late 1960s were icy; there could be no thought of restoring aid to Egypt so long as Johnson and Nasser remained in power.

No longer the gallant young hero of Bandung and Suez, Nasser remained a tragic figure during the last three years of his life.[108] The crushing Arab defeat in June 1967 came as a profound shock to Egyptians and to other Arabs weaned on a decade of swaggering Nasserist rhetoric. As the 1968 riots in Egypt and the violent clashes between Palestinians and Jordanians two years later painfully illustrated, both his own countrymen and the Arab masses that he had once enthralled had grown restive after the enormity of the 1967 defeat had stripped away the illusions that Nasser had helped create. All of this took a physical toll on Nasser. His death in September 1970, at the age of fifty-two, was mourned by millions in Cairo and in other Arab capitals, but it paved the way for a rehabilitation of Egyptian fortunes which Nasser himself, chained as he was to the images of the past, probably could not have achieved.

CHAPTER SEVEN

Sadat's Peace Dividend

If Gamal Abdel Nasser survives in the American memory as a dimly recollected villain, Anwar Sadat is remembered by the American public he captivated in the 1970s as a great historic figure. Neither image is entirely accurate. Just as Nasser's villainous image belies the complicated nature of his relationship with the United States, Sadat's heroic image is in some ways a distortion of reality and an oversimplification of the impact that his achievements and his failures have had on Egypt and on American interests in the Middle East.

Few foreign leaders have ever captured the imagination of Americans as completely as did Anwar Sadat in the years after the October War of 1973. Henry Kissinger, in a moment of humility rare for a man who fancied himself the heir to the great European diplomatists of the nineteenth century, described Sadat in 1979 as "the greatest [statesman] since Bismarck." [1] Kissinger's praise was echoed by his colleagues in the Nixon and Ford Administrations, by his successors in the Carter and Reagan Administrations, by the American news media, and by legislators on Capitol Hill who embraced Sadat as they had rebuffed Nasser.

One tangible sign of the popularity of Sadat and his policies in the United States was the rapid resumption of American economic aid to Egypt after the October War, on a scale unparalleled since the Marshall Plan era in Western Europe. This multi-billion-dollar assistance program, at heart an act of faith in Sadat himself, was designed to help make the political risks the post-1973 peace process entailed for Egypt worth taking. Sadat promised his compatriots that his commitment to a diplomatic resolution of Egypt's differences with Israel and his close association with the United States would produce a "peace dividend," in the form of social and material progress for all Egyptians. The American government realized early on that failure to underwrite Sadat's pledge would jeopardize its evolving special relationship with Egypt, and, as a consequence, its hopes for a general Middle East peace settlement. Perceiving an historic opportunity to establish a strong American position in Egypt and to bring an end to the Arab-Israeli conflict, the Nixon Administration and its successors plunged enthusiastically into the task of bolstering the Egyptian economy.

Sadat's soaring rhetoric, coupled with the rapid growth of the U.S. economic aid program, created dangerously inflated expectations in Egypt about the nature and extent of the benefits which the Egyptian populace would derive from U.S. largesse. When collaboration with the United States failed to produce the quick economic solutions that many Egyptians had come to expect, some of the old frustrations and resentments that had dominated the Egyptian view of the American government in the Nasser era began to resurface. To be sure, the U.S.-Egyptian relationship was on far firmer political footing in the late 1970s and early 1980s than had ever been the case in the Nasser years; nevertheless, it had become clear by the time of Sadat's death in October 1981 that American economic assistance was not the political panacea that some Americans and Egyptians had thought it to be in the first heady days of the post-1973 U.S.-Egyptian rapprochement.

Sadat and the United States, 1970–73

Amidst all the euphoria and exhilaration which accompanied the spectacular improvement of U.S.-Egyptian relations in the mid-1970s, it was easy to forget how singularly inauspicious the beginnings of President Sadat's relationship with the American government had been. When Sadat took office after the death of Gamal Abdel Nasser in September 1970, he was generally dismissed by experts in the State Department and the White House as a political lightweight whose days as chief of state were already numbered. "Sadat," Kissinger admitted in his memoirs, "was little known and vastly underestimated." [2] Coupled with this unprepossessing personal image, Sadat had to contend in his relations with the Nixon Administration with the legacy of weakness and anti-American posturing bequeathed to him by Nasser.

Sadat inherited an economy on the verge of complete collapse. In the wake of Egypt's devastating defeat in 1967, Nasser had done his best to avoid making the hard choices between guns and butter that Egypt's terrible economic predicament demanded. Sadat could no longer enjoy the luxury of such procrastination in the fall of 1970. Deprived of tourist revenue, Suez Canal tolls, and income from Sinai oil production, the Egyptian economy was seriously short of hard currency. Military spending consumed about one-third of the national income. Rapid population growth strained urban infrastructures and overburdened Egypt's food producers, creating a deeper dependence on imported foodstuffs. Although subsidies from Egypt's oil-rich Arab allies helped stave off imminent disaster, the Egyptian economic outlook was decidedly bleak.

While he wrestled with these internal problems, Sadat was determined to attempt to redeem both the land and the honor that Egypt had lost in 1967. It soon became clear to him, however, that continuation of the state of "no war, no peace" that had prevailed since the June War would not bring about the return of the Sinai, would not cure the profound psychological malaise that had gripped the Egyptian public since the overwhelming Israeli victory, would not cure Egypt's economic difficulties, and would serve only to tighten the Soviet embrace around the Egyptian government. Although Sadat realized that he could not contemplate any sort of military action against Israel without Soviet help, he was deeply suspicious of Soviet motives and was also worried about the spread of Soviet influence in the Egyptian military and economic establishments. His suspicions were not much eased in May 1971 when he discovered and suppressed a plot to topple him, engineered by Ali Sabri, his colleague in the Revolutionary Command Council and a long-time supporter of close ties with the Soviet Union.

Even as he kept up the appearance of Soviet-Egyptian amity and sought to use Soviet assistance to rebuild Egypt's armed forces, Sadat decided in 1970–71 that the United States would somehow have to be enlisted in his efforts to recover Egyptian territory and pride and to modernize the Egyptian economy. His conventional anti-American diatribes notwithstanding, Sadat was an admirer of American society. He had been much impressed with what he saw during a 1966 visit to the United States, prompting Nasser to kid Lucius Battle that "that friend of yours, Anwar Sadat, is downright pro-American! " [3] Whatever his personal feelings about Americans, Sadat evidently concluded early on that United States involvement in the pursuit of his internal and external goals was a practical necessity. As he was later fond of saying, he believed that the American government held "99 percent of the cards" in the Arab-Israeli conflict. The trick, as he began to discover, was to attract American interest in Egypt's predicament and to persuade the U.S. government to play the cards that it held.

Active involvement in the Middle East had little appeal for the American Administration in the early 1970s. President Nixon was preoccupied with the war in Indo-China and major foreign policy initiatives in Moscow and Peking, and was convinced that the combination of Israeli military superiority and Arab political intransigence argued against any new American diplomatic efforts. Although both the President and his National Security Advisor made dutiful pronouncements about the urgent need for a political solution to Arab-Israeli differences, Nixon and Kissinger delegated responsibility for Middle East diplomacy to Secretary of State William P. Rogers, whose star was already on the wane in the Nixon White House, and to his staff of State Department professionals. "For the moment," Kissinger remarked at a National Security Council staff meeting early in 1970, "we're leaving Rogers the Middle East." [4] Without strong White House backing, Rogers's efforts in the Middle East foundered.

Increasingly frustrated by what he saw to be the Soviet Union's attempts to muffle his military preparations in its pursuit of détente with the United States, Sadat tried in vain in 1971–72 to arouse the Nixon Administration's interest. The indecisiveness of Sadat's much ballyhooed "Year of Decision" in 1971 did little to alter the Egyptian leader's ineffectual image in Washington. When Sadat dramatically expelled some ten thousand Soviet military personnel from Egypt in July 1972, both as a signal of his displeasure to the Soviets and of his flexibility to the Americans, he received scant encouragement from the Nixon White House. Amidst the domestic political pressures of a Presidential election campaign, Nixon had no desire to make any new overtures to Egypt; Kissinger, for his part, saw no pressing reason to reward Sadat for his welcome but unilateral action. In a subsequent series of secret conversations with Hafez Ismail, Sadat's National Security Advisor, Kissinger made it clear that he and Nixon considered Sadat's talk about resuming the military struggle against Israel to be nothing more than bombast, and that the U.S. government could not be expected to engage itself in peace efforts until Egypt scaled down its political demands to match its apparent military inferiority.[5]

The October War and the American Response

Against the background of Sadat's ineffectual diplomatic efforts in the early 1970s, the Egyptian assault across the Suez Canal on 6 October 1973, came as a stunning surprise to both the United States and Israel. For Sadat, the October War had a clear Clausewitzian logic: it was designed to help him break out of the political-economic straitjacket of "no war, no peace." Egypt's limited military success, all the more striking when compared to its earlier military disasters, enabled Sadat to shatter the myth of Israeli invincibility that had underpinned much of the Nixon Administration's disinterest in his previous political gestures. Having restored Egyptian pride and achieved his limited military goals, Sadat was in a position to inject new life into the search for a Middle East peace settlement and to bargain with the by-now attentive Nixon Administration for political and economic concessions.

Henry Kissinger perceived from the outset of the October War that Sadat's military adventure created diplomatic opportunities the U.S. government could not afford to ignore. However shortsighted and distracted Kissinger may have been in his approach to Middle East affairs in earlier years, he acted with firmness and vision in the immediate aftermath of the October War to repair America's political stature in the Arab world. During his diplomatic peregrinations in late 1973–early 1974, Kissinger saw clearly that an Egyptian-Israeli disengagement agreement offered not only a means to lift the Arab oil embargo which had caused such consternation in the United States, but also a means of setting in motion a broader peace process. As he sought to invigorate this process, Kissinger—who had become Secretary of State two months before the outbreak of the October War—was handicapped by the deepening preoccupation of President Nixon and his key political advisors with the Watergate scandal. From the vantage point of the embattled Nixon White House, the success of U.S. initiatives in the Middle East was often seen as an antidote to domestic political troubles, and Kissinger was under constant pressure in the months following the October War to engineer diplomatic triumphs to be used to prop up the Nixon Presidency.[6]

From their first meeting in Cairo in November 1973, Sadat and Kissinger developed a close personal rapport. The American Secretary of State was impressed by Sadat's readiness to make tactical sacrifices in the negotiations leading to the Sinai I disengagement agreement in January 1974; the Egyptian President was, in turn, heartened by Kissinger's personal commitment to the peace talks. After three years of dealing with Rogers and his State Department aides, who obviously did not have the full weight of the Nixon Administration behind them, Sadat was at once gratified and reassured to find Kissinger, at this juncture the personification of American foreign policy, so eager to achieve a settlement of Arab-Israeli differences. Like Kissinger, Sadat soon grew impatient with the plodding pace and multilateral wranglings associated with a comprehensive approach to negotiations. After the initial session of the Geneva Middle East Peace Conference in December 1973, Sadat subscribed to Kissinger's notion of a "step-by-step" peace process. In Kissinger's view, pursuit of a comprehensive peace in the immediate aftermath of the October War was bound to run aground on the shoals of Israeli intransigence over the status of Jerusalem and Arab political infighting. As Kissinger later put it, the prospects "of bogging down in niggling detail and of consuming our energies in the pursuit of comprehensive goals more yearned for than attainable . . . induced us to decide instead on a 'step-by-step' approach."[7]

U.S.-Egyptian cooperation, bolstered by the personal rapport between Kissinger and Sadat, was to be the bedrock of this step-by-step process through which the United States hoped to gradually build confidence between Israel and its Arab adversaries. Diplomatic relations between Cairo and Washington were restored shortly after Kissinger's first visit to Egypt, and the newly appointed U.S. ambassador, Hermann Eilts, quickly assembled a small but highly talented Embassy staff. On 18 January 1974, Egyptian and Israeli negotiators initialed a U.S.-sponsored separation of forces agreement, which Sadat hoped would deepen the U.S. commitment to the peace process and to the budding U.S.-Egyptian rapprochement.

When Kissinger and Sadat discussed ways of cementing the U.S.-Egyptian relationship in early 1974, the issue of reviving American economic assistance invariably came to the fore.[8] From the outset, Kissinger's view of a resurrected U.S. aid program was dominated by political concerns, not by any overriding interest in Egypt's chronic economic difficulties. Kissinger and Nixon both realized that their hopes for further political cooperation with Sadat gave them a stake in Sadat's ambitions to modernize the Egyptian economy, and that aid could serve as a powerful inducement to Egyptian moderation in the complicated peace talks which lay ahead. At the same time, they understood that a dramatic rebirth of U.S. aid to Egypt would be greeted with little enthusiasm on Capitol Hill, where attitudes toward economic assistance to Egypt were still colored by memories of Nasser's ingratitude and hostility. Moreover, State Department professionals on the Egyptian desk and elsewhere in the Bureau of Near Eastern and South Asian Affairs, who also had vivid memories of the chequered history of U.S. aid to Egypt, were skeptical about the desirability of any sudden resumption of large-scale aid to the Egyptian government.[9]

Well aware of Congressional constraints and sharing many of the suspicions voiced by his State Department colleagues, Kissinger moved cautiously in 1974 to extend economic assistance in Egypt, always adjusting the pace of his own efforts to Sadat's perceived responsiveness to American political overtures. The first "carrot" Kissinger dangled before Sadat was an offer to help clear the Suez Canal of war debris and assist in reconstruction of the devastated cities bordering the Canal. When the Egyptian government signed the Sinai I accord, Kissinger immediately released $85 million to fund the promised repairs in the Canal area. To reinforce Sadat's interest in the pursuit of a wider Sinai disengagement agreement, the Nixon

Administration decided in March 1974 to request $250 million from Congress to finance Egyptian development projects in fiscal year 1975.[10] President Nixon informed Sadat of this request during his June 1974 trip to Egypt, a journey which strengthened U.S.-Egyptian relations but which failed to save the Nixon Presidency.

The prospect of increased American aid encouraged Sadat not only to contemplate further political concessions in peace negotiations with Israel, but also to accelerate the shift in Egyptian economic policy that he had been experimenting with since 1970–71. As Sadat had come to the conviction in the early 1970s that the United States was a more desirable political partner than the Soviet Union, he had also decided that involvement in the Western economic system was far preferable to Egypt's deepening dependence on Soviet technology and markets. Years of heavy expenditure on defense and on a bloated, ineffectual government bureaucracy, coupled with years of neglect of the economic infrastructure, had severely retarded Egyptian economic development. Sadat determined that the only way out of this economic morass was a policy aimed at re-energizing the Egyptian private sector and attracting foreign investment. Thus was born the policy of *Infitah,* or "opening," which sought to gradually open up the Egyptian economy to the West and economic liberalization. Formally launched by Sadat in a speech in April 1974, *Infitah* provided the economic component of Egypt's historic political-economic shift to the West.

[handwritten margin note: April 74 Infitah. Infitah (opening to the West)]

The summer of 1974 was an exhilarating time for Egyptians. Western trade delegations and businessmen began to explore commercial opportunities in Cairo. Nixon and Sadat spoke with glowing optimism of the possibility of billions of dollars in American public and private investment in Egypt. With the achievement of a Syrian-Israeli disengagement accord in May 1974, Henry Kissinger had returned his attention to a broader Sinai agreement, and many Egyptians confidently expected to reclaim all of Sinai within a matter of months. There were, as John Waterbury puts it, "good reasons to think that peace and an influx of capital were fully within Egypt's reach."[11]

The Ford Administration and the U.S. Aid Program in Egypt

Although hampered at first by domestic political uncertainties in the United States and later by the faltering gait of step-by-step diplomacy, both the American and Egyptian governments made great efforts after the collapse of the Nixon Presidency to preserve the momentum that had been built up in U.S.-Egyptian relations in the months following the October War. As Sadat deepened his reliance on the United States and as his bridges to the Soviet Union and much of the Arab world began to collapse, the Ford Administration demonstrated its faith in the Egyptian President by increasing economic aid to Egypt to about one billion dollars annually in fiscal years 1976 and 1977. Political and economic events in 1975–76 tempered the optimism that had gripped Cairo in the summer of 1974, but the huge and apparently open-ended American commitment to Egyptian economic development helped sustain the hopes that many Egyptians continued to place in partnership with the United States.

As Henry Kissinger surveyed the political landscape in Washington and the Middle East in the fall of 1974, he gradually came to the conclusion that pursuit of a second Egyptian-Israeli disengagement agreement was the best means of revivifying the peace process, dormant since the Syrian-Israeli disengagement agreement the previous May. The absence of strong Presidential leadership, coupled with Israeli hesitations and Kissinger's own reluctance to allow the Soviets a significant role in the peace process, argued against a renewed effort at Geneva to seek a comprehensive settlement. Neither the Rabin government in Israel nor Syrian President Hafiz al-Asad appeared ready to make further concessions on the Golan issue. The prospects for an interim Israeli-Jordanian agreement seemed dim: the Israelis were not eager to concede any part of the West Bank to Jordan, nor was King Hussein ready to expose himself to Arab criticism by acquiescing to Israeli demands for diplomatic recognition and territorial compromise. Furthermore, the Jordanian government was hamstrung by the Rabat Summit's decision in October 1974 to recognize the Palestine Liberation Organization as the sole legitimate representative of the

Palestinian people. Given these apparently unpromising alternatives, Kissinger decided to expand upon the Sinai I agreement between Egypt and Israel.

Much to his dismay, Kissinger discovered in the spring of 1975 that his formidable powers of persuasion could not bridge the gap between the Egyptian and Israeli positions on a second Sinai accord. Sadat insisted that Israel withdraw from the strategic Mitla and Giddi passes and from the Abu Rudeis and Ras Sudr oil fields. In return he was prepared to end the Egyptian economic boycott of Israel and to renounce publicly the use of force as a means of settling Egypt's conflict with Israel. The Rabin government offered only a partial withdrawal from the strategic Sinai passes and the oil fields, and demanded that Sadat formally terminate the state of war between Israel and Egypt. This Sadat refused to do, correctly anticipating that a formal statement of nonbelligerency would estrange him from his erstwhile Arab allies and weaken his bargaining position in future Sinai withdrawal talks. Kissinger and President Ford were sympathetic to Sadat's position, and both men were exasperated by what they perceived to be the obstinacy and lack of vision of the Israeli government. The failure of Kissinger's March 1975 round of shuttle diplomacy between Cairo and Tel Aviv, coming as it did amidst the collapse of South Vietnam, was a powerful blow to the Ford Administration's foreign policy. When Kissinger returned to Washington empty-handed on March 24, Ford announced that the U.S. government would conduct a sweeping "reassessment" of its Middle East policy.[12]

While the Ford Administration pondered its role in the peace process, Sadat's stock in Washington continued to rise. The Egyptian leader met with President Ford in Salzburg in June 1975, and quickly developed an easy rapport with his American counterpart. Shortly after the Salzburg meeting, Sadat formally reopened the Suez Canal, signalling his continuing commitment to a peaceful settlement with Israel.

Kissinger returned to the Middle East in September 1975 and, after much wrangling over details, shepherded Israel and Egypt to a second Sinai agreement. Prime Minister Rabin— anxious to avoid prolonged friction with the United States— made most of the territorial concessions in the Sinai that Sadat had insisted upon, while the Egyptian government moved closer to the political accommodation the Israelis had originally demanded.[13] After signing the Sinai II accord, Sadat paid a formal visit to the United States—the first ever by an Egyptian president. During his visit, Sadat addressed a joint session of Congress, and further endeared himself to the American media, which had already made it a practice to extol his virtues as a statesman and a peacemaker. By all accounts, Sadat's trip was a great success.[14]

The Sinai II agreement was the Ford Administration's highwater mark in the peace process. With the 1976 Presidential election looming on the horizon and the tragic civil war in Lebanon distracting Arab attention, Ford and Kissinger advised Sadat that they planned to postpone further American peace initiatives until 1977. Once reelected, Ford assured Sadat, he would drop the overworked step-by-step approach and seek a comprehensive solution to the Arab-Israeli conflict.[15]

Although a time of relative inactivity on the diplomatic front, 1976 was a year of rapid expansion for the U.S. economic aid program in Cairo. As a reward for Sadat's cooperation in the Sinai II negotiations, Kissinger pledged in the fall of 1975 to provide Egypt with $750 million in grants and concessionary loans and $200 million in PL480 Title I food aid. Like the $250 million in aid that Kissinger had promised in the spring of 1974 and that Congress had finally appropriated in December of that year, the nearly $1 billion in economic assistance that the American Secretary of State proposed in 1975 was a product of political calculations—not of any careful assessment of Egypt's specific needs and absorptive capacity. Kissinger and his colleagues in the Ford Administration aimed to bring Egypt into rough quantitative parity with Israel as a recipient of U.S. economic aid, and in so doing to reinforce Sadat's commitment to partnership with the American govenment.[16]

To be sure, the Egyptian economy needed every bit of outside assistance that Sadat could lay his hands on in the mid-1970s. The most obvious of Egypt's economic difficulties was its deteriorating infrastructure. After decades of mismanagement, overuse, and neglect, Cairo's telephone, transportation, and sewage disposal systems were collapsing. Urban migration aggravated housing problems in Cairo and other large cities. Because water and power systems were inadequate, much of Egypt's industrial plant lay idle or underused.[17] Underlying Egypt's infrastructural dilemmas were the perennial problems of population growth, a debilitating network of commodity subsidies, and an inept, over-sized public sector bureaucracy. Fueled by social and religious traditions, Egypt's 2.5 percent annual rate of population growth showed no signs of diminishing in 1975–76. Subsidies posed another seemingly insoluble problem; largely for political reasons, the Egyptian government clung to a policy of underwriting much of the cost to consumers of necessities like wheat, salt, fuel oil, and electricity. As beneficial as these subsidies were to Cairo's poor, they distorted the rest of the economy and discouraged sound economic planning. The public sector bureaucracy, which by tradition employed all university graduates who would not or could not find work elsewhere, seemed in any event incapable of sound planning, or even of effective management of existing economic projects.

The sheer immensity of the target, coupled with the cumbersome workings of the Egyptian government bureaucracy, posed considerable difficulties for AID planners attempting to channel U.S. assistance in worthwhile directions. After all the high-flown optimism of President Nixon's June 1974 trip, and of Secretary of the Treasury William Simon's follow-up mission in July 1974, had died down, the U.S. Embassy in Cairo found itself hard pressed to make constructive use of the assistance which the Nixon and Ford Administrations secured for the Sadat regime. Ambassador Eilts recalls that "we had a good deal of trouble in early 1975 identifying development projects upon which to expend our aid." [18]

The Ford Administration had no all-encompassing development strategy in mind when it began to shower economic aid upon the Sadat government in 1975 and 1976. U.S. assistance was viewed in Washington primarily as a political tool, designed to impress Egyptians at all levels of society with the value of Sadat's American connection. The Cairo Embassy was directed to do the best that it could to funnel aid quickly into the Egyptian development effort; the result, at least in the early years of the post-1975 aid program, was a scatter-shot approach that embraced a variety of projects. The State Department had no undertaking as dramatic as the construction of the Aswan High Dam upon which to pin American prestige, but it was hoped that the cumulative political effect of a collection of smaller projects would rival the enormous symbolic impact of the High Dam.

To this end, the Ford Administration committed funds to a number of important infrastructure projects in 1975 and 1976. In May 1975, the U.S. government agreed to provide a $30 million grant to underwrite reconstruction of war-damaged power distribution systems in the Suez Canal cities of Suez, Ismailia, and Port Said. This agreement was supplemented a year later by a $141-million commitment to build a new power plant near Ismailia.[19] At the end of June 1975, $44 million was earmarked for two large grain silo complexes, one in Cairo and one in Alexandria. At about the same time, AID signed a $96 million loan agreement to help finance modernization and expansion of a textile plant in the Nile Delta. In July 1976, the United States pledged $90 million for construction of a cement plant south of Suez City.[20]

Assistance for capital projects was one of three types of economic aid which came under the rubric of the Economic Support Fund (ESF) program, through which most U.S. grants and loans to Egypt were channeled in the Sadat years.[21] Since plans for capital projects took a great deal of time and effort to develop, much ESF assistance tended in 1975–76 to flow through the Commodity Import Program (CIP). CIP grants and loans, which underwrote the foreign exchange costs of importing raw materials, capital goods, and spare parts from the United States, accounted for roughly one-third of all ESF aid to Egypt in this period. Technical assistance, the third major component in the ESF program, amounted to about $50 million in fiscal years 1975 and 1976.[22]

In addition to ESF aid, the Ford Administration supplied Egypt with several hundred million dollars worth of PL480 food aid, most of which consisted of Title I concessional sales of wheat and wheat flour. PL480 shipments enabled Sadat to maintain artificially low bread prices, and thus contributed directly to the short-term political stability of his regime. By the end of 1976, one of every three loaves of bread consumed by urban Egyptians was a product of PL480 wheat.[23]

The billion-dollar-a-year program of PL480 and ESF aid which the U.S. government established in Egypt in the mid-1970s was a key element in Sadat's plans for economic liberalization; moreover, it offered tangible proof of the deepening

1976 Egypt abrogates treaty of Friendship w/ USSR

American commitment to the Sadat regime. His confidence bolstered by the rapid growth of the U.S. aid program, Sadat drifted further and further away from the Soviet bloc, unilaterally abrogating the Soviet-Egyptian Treaty of Friendship in March 1976.[24] Sadat clearly believed as 1976 drew to a close that, despite the sputtering of the Ford Administration's Middle East diplomacy and the unknown political inclinations of Gerald Ford's successor, Jimmy Carter, the risks of associating Egypt closely with the United States were made much less onerous by the influx of American economic assistance.

The Road to Jerusalem

1977 was in many ways a frustrating year for Anwar Sadat. The Carter Administration's fitful efforts to reconvene the Geneva Conference and revive a comprehensive approach to the peace process met with some initial success, but by the late fall of 1977 seemed to have bogged down in a mire of procedural difficulties. At home, Sadat faced increasing economic problems, despite massive infusions of American aid. As he had done in 1973, Sadat responded to this combination of political stalemate and economic stagnation with a bold stroke of "electric shock" diplomacy—his historic November 1977 trip to Jerusalem.

Although he entered the White House with very little international experience, Jimmy Carter invested more of his energy and prestige in the business of Middle East peacemaking than had any of his predecessors. In his memoirs, Carter noted: "Looking back on the four years of my Presidency, I realize that I spent more of my time working for possible solutions to the riddle of Middle East peace than on any other international problem."[25] Soon after they took office, Carter and his advisors made it clear that they intended to abandon the step-by-step diplomatic approach employed by Henry Kissinger. As Ford and Kissinger had themselves indicated to Sadat in 1976, step-by-step diplomacy appeared to have outlived its usefulness after Sinai II; in any event, the step-by-step approach was tainted, in President Carter's eyes, by association with the Republican foreign policy that he had inherited and that he was determined to remodel. What Carter, Secretary of State Cyrus Vance, and National Security Adviser Zbigniew Brzezinski hoped to do was to enunciate the principles which they believed should govern final settlement of the Arab-Israeli conflict, nudge the parties to the dispute closer to agreement on these principles, and then reconvene the Geneva Conference to hammer out a detailed peace accord.

To this end, Carter reaffirmed the U.S. commitment to United Nations Security Council Resolution 242, adding that "there has to be a homeland provided for the Palestinian refugees who have suffered for many, many years." [26] Secretary Vance made an exploratory tour of Middle East capitals in February 1977, during which Sadat endorsed the Carter Administration's comprehensive approach. Sadat met Carter for the first time in Washington two months later, and professed great confidence in the new U.S. Administration. But this early optimism in Washington and Cairo gradually diminished over the course of the following six months. In May 1977, Menachem Begin's Likud government came to power in Israel, heralding an era of deeper Israeli inflexibility. The Carter Administration's ill-prepared effort to include the Soviet Union in the peace process, the Soviet-American joint communiqué of October 1977, created a storm of protest in Israel and in the U.S. Congress. Israel's leaders disliked the idea of active Soviet participation in negotiations, and objected to the communiqué's reference to the "legitimate rights" of the Palestinians; Israel's supporters on Capitol Hill had similar reservations about the new Soviet-American statement. [27] The final blow to the Carter Administration's comprehensive initiative came when the Syrian government, on the eve of the scheduled reconvening of the Geneva Conference in November 1977, voiced a number of objections to the negotiating format and announced its refusal to participate. [28] Profoundly discouraged by the developing political stalemate, Sadat was also deeply concerned about domestic economic difficulties. The "Open Door" policy had not produced   the general prosperity that Sadat had promised in 1974. Where economic growth had occurred, it had tended to enrich a small group of upper-middle-class entrepreneurs. These "fat cats"— as they were referred to by their critics—constituted no more than 10 percent of the population, but accounted for perhaps

60 percent of consumer spending.[29] Corruption, always a problem in the governmental bureaucracy and in Egyptian business, was aggravated by the opening up of the private sector.

Meanwhile, Cairo's infrastructure of housing, transportation, sewage, communication, and power systems continued to crumble, and the plight of Cairo's poor continued to worsen. When Deputy Premier for Financial and Economic Affairs Kaissouny attempted to reform the commodity subsidy program in January 1977, food prices rose, and heavy rioting broke out in cities up and down the Nile Valley. For the first time since the revolution of 1952, troops were called out to suppress a civil disturbance. At least 79 Cairenes died in the rioting, and scores more were killed or wounded in Alexandria and Aswan.[30] Sadat hastily repealed Kaissouny's reform measures, sacrificing sound economic planning to the imperatives of domestic politics.

The U.S. aid program did not provide an easy cure for the ills of the Open Door policy in 1977. Two-thirds of the $2.3 billion in grants and loans which the American government had committed to Egypt between 1975 and 1977 had still not been expended by the end of 1977.[31] Bureaucratic inertia in both Cairo and Washington contributed to this "clogged pipeline." AID had its own interminable feasibility studies to conduct; the sluggish workings of Egyptian government ministries made matters worse. American private investors did not materialize in droves, as Sadat had hoped in 1974; many were scared off by the economic disarray they found in Cairo.[32]

In Sadat's eyes, the dismal state of the Egyptian economy and the emerging stalemate in the peace process in November 1977 demanded a response as daring as his decision to launch the October War. Instead of a military crossing, Sadat now envisioned a psychological crossing—a dramatic diplomatic action to disarm the Begin government's suspicions, restore life to Carter's peace plan, and distract attention from Egypt's economic dilemmas.[33] With the boldness and unpredictability that had become his trademarks as a statesman, Sadat flew to Jerusalem on 20 November, and delivered a stirring appeal for peace to the Knesset the next morning. Sadat's gesture elicited streams of abuse from other Arab capitals, but it was enormously popular in Egypt and in the United States. And as he had hoped, his diplomatic "bombshell" gave new impetus to peace negotiations and provided the Egyptian government with a little more domestic breathing space.

Sadat visits Jerusalem - new energy infuses the peace process.

Camp David and Sadat's "Peace Dividend"

Sixteen arduous months after his historic trip to Jerusalem, Sadat penned his signature to documents which formally ended thirty years of Egyptian-Israeli strife and set forth a vague framework for negotiating a settlement of the Palestine problem. Whatever its defects, the Egyptian-Israeli Peace Treaty marked a turning point in Middle East history. Not only was it the first significant break in the long, brutal cycle of Arab-Israeli conflict, it was also the culmination of decades of American efforts to lure Egypt into the Western bloc. From the time of Dwight Eisenhower and John Foster Dulles, American policy-makers had perceived that there could be no lasting accommodation between the United States and Egypt so long as the state of war between Egypt and Israel continued. Jimmy Carter, building on the work of his predecessors, provided Egypt with the incentive which helped make possible the Egyptian-Israeli treaty and the *de facto* U.S.-Egyptian alliance with which it was associated. In the process of winning Egypt's political cooperation, the Carter Administration committed the United States to Egypt's economic rehabilitation. Without an economic "peace dividend" underwritten by billions of dollars of U.S. aid, there could be no guarantee that the Sadat regime would survive, let alone sustain its partnership with the American government.

The path from Sadat's journey to Jerusalem to the Camp David Agreements ten months later was mined with difficulties, many of them emplanted by Menachem Begin. The limited West Bank autonomy plan that Begin proposed to Carter in Washington and to Sadat in Ismailia in December 1977 was not nearly as bold or dramatic a gesture as the Egyptian leader's trip to Israel.[34] Sadat realized that the Begin government sought a separate treaty with Egypt that would leave Israel with a free hand on the West Bank and the Golan Heights. As he later explained to Carter: "They want the West Bank, and are willing to give back the Sinai to me in exchange for the West Bank. They have ignored completely my great gesture."[35]

1979 - Egypt/Israel peace.
E.'s ties to Arab world collapse

Sadat's "Peace Dividend"   191

Nevertheless, Sadat persevered in his talks with the Israelis, at least in part because of the enormous confidence that he had in the U.S. government. At the Camp David summit in September 1978, Jimmy Carter engineered a compromise between Sadat and Begin. As Carter makes clear in his memoirs, it was Sadat's flexibility and willingness to take political risks that made the two Camp David accords possible.[36] However difficult it may have been for Menachem Begin to agree to the evacuation of Israeli settlers from the Sinai, it was Sadat's acceptance of the tenuous link between the bilateral Sinai agreement and the sketchy Camp David formula for West Bank-Gaza autonomy that made the summit a success.

The six months that followed the Camp David meeting were difficult ones for Sadat and his American partners. Sadat's peacemaking efforts were roundly condemned by other Arab leaders—including those from the pro-Western regimes in Saudi Arabia and Jordan—at the Baghdad Summit in November 1978. In the face of threats from his oil-rich Arab benefactors to cut off their subsidies if Egypt signed a formal treaty with Israel, Sadat breathed defiance.[37] "Our ears are closed to the hissing of vipers," Sadat said with the tactlessness that he often demonstrated in responding to his Arab critics, "and we stand aloof from the antics of dwarves." [38]

As Egypt's relations with the rest of the Arab world deteriorated, the Begin government continued to drag out the negotiations for a final peace treaty, which was to have been concluded in December 1978. By the early spring of 1979, Sadat had become deeply discouraged by Begin's intransigence, manifested most vividly in the Israeli resumption of settlement building on the West Bank, which the Egyptians and the Americans both believed to be a clear violation of the Camp David agreements. Again, it was Jimmy Carter's personal intervention which restored Sadat's faith in the peace process. In early March 1979, Carter flew to Egypt and Israel to help resolve the differences over final withdrawal from the Sinai, normalization of relations, and Palestinian autonomy talks that had impeded progress toward a formal treaty. On 26 March 1979, the Egyptian-Israeli Treaty was finally signed in Washington.

With the signing of the treaty, Egypt's already rickety bridges to most of the rest of the Arab world collapsed.[39] Official Arab subsidies ceased to flow into Cairo. At the same time, Sadat's need to produce the long-promised "peace dividend" of economic prosperity grew more and more urgent. In a burst of enthusiasm after the conclusion of the Egyptian-Israeli Treaty, Sadat declared to the Egyptian people that the year 1980 would see "the end of all our troubles."[40] It was clear that Sadat expected Washington to translate his high-flown rhetoric into economic reality.

The promise of U.S. economic aid provided Sadat with an important incentive to negotiate a peace treaty in 1977–79. As Assistant Secretary of State Harold Saunders later explained to the House Foreign Affairs Committee, Sadat "did not attempt to trade his action for our assistance," but he did recognize the economic value of continued partnership with the United States.[41] In the months between the Camp David Summit and the signing of the Egyptian-Israeli Treaty, the Carter Administration fattened the aid carrot, pledging $300 million in post-treaty economic assistance to supplement the ongoing billion-dollar-a-year program. Perhaps more importantly, the U.S. government promised a supplemental package of $1.5 billion in military aid, to be spread over three years.[42] The establishment of a large military assistance program, enabling Sadat to solidify the support of the Egyptian armed forces for his regime and to enhance his stature in regional politics, deepened the Egyptian President's commitment to cooperation with the United States.[43]

The $300 million in supplemental post-treaty economic aid that the Carter Administration provided to Egypt was a modest enlargement of a program which was already by far the largest AID undertaking in the world. Even before Camp David, AID expenditures in Egypt surpassed those in the rest of Africa and Latin America combined.[44] Food aid to Egypt accounted for more than one-third of the total PL480 program.[45] And yet Sadat expected still greater things of the American government. In a series of Al-Ahram interviews in November 1978, Sadat hinted at the scale of the aid program that he envisioned. "I want to tell you something," Sadat was quoted as saying, "I shall ask President Carter for a Carter Plan, on the lines of the Marshall Plan, and I shall ask him openly, before the whole world, the Senate and the Congress." Sadat indicated that this "Carter Plan" would include as much as $15 billion in economic assistance over a five-year period, and "would perform miracles for the country." [46]

As Sadat fanned popular expectations, U.S. officials saw with greater clarity that the economic aid program which had reinforced Egyptian interest in the peace process had become crucial to the survival of the Sadat regime and its foreign policy. As one Congressman put it in the spring of 1979, "To some extent the viability of [the Egyptian-Israeli] peace treaty will be a function of the extent to which President Sadat can demonstrate that there are material benefits of peace to the Egyptian people who really view the peace process, in a way, as a kind of panacea for their problems." [47] If Sadat's American connection did not quickly produce the economic progress that the Egyptian leader had so incautiously promised, both he and his American partners were sure to suffer growing public criticism in Egypt.

Taking Stock: The Aid Program at the End of the Sadat Era

The failure of the American government to deliver an economic "peace dividend" on the grandiose scale envisioned by Anwar Sadat aggravated the internal and external troubles which the Egyptian President faced in his last two years in power. Given Egypt's intractable economic problems and the vastly inflated popular expectations fostered by the Sadat regime, it is doubtful that the U.S. aid program would have been perceived in Cairo as a great success in 1979–1981 even if the Carter and Reagan Administrations had expended the entire $4 billion annual U.S. economic aid budget in Egypt. No "Carter Plan," even if it had approximated the expenditures of the U.S. government in Western Europe after World War II, could have achieved what the Marshall Plan achieved in the late 1940s. The Marshall Plan had been a massive exercise in "priming the pump," in rehabilitating war-torn industrial economies. In Sadat's Egypt, there was no pump to prime; Americans and Egyptians were confronted with the daunting task of building an economic infrastructure while at the same time satisfying the immediate needs of an impoverished, ever-increasing population.

As the State Department and AID grappled with the Egyptian economy, the external and internal difficulties confronting the Sadat regime grew more severe. The peace process stalled almost before the ink had dried on the Egyptian-Israeli Treaty. In what must have sometimes seemed to Sadat to be a carefully orchestrated campaign to discredit him, the Begin government sabotaged the West Bank-Gaza autonomy talks, and went on to provoke the rest of the Arab world with the destruction of the Iraqi nuclear facility near Baghdad, the annexation of the Golan Heights, and the indiscriminate bombardment of Beirut. Egypt's relations with its Arab neighbors continued to deteriorate, amidst new waves of recrimination in Cairo, Damascus, Baghdad, and Riyadh. His Arab critics, said Sadat, were "dwarves and ignoramuses." [48]

Meanwhile, Sadat suffered the loss of his friend Jimmy Carter and struggled to win the attention of Ronald Reagan, who had no special interest in, or knowledge of, the Middle East. Sadat responded enthusiastically when Secretary of State Alexander Haig made a tour of the region in May 1981, twenty-eight years after Foster Dulles's first foray into the Arab world, and issued a call strikingly similar to Dulles's for a cooperative effort to block the spread of Soviet influence. But the Reagan Administration seemed in no particular hurry to push the Israelis in the autonomy talks, nor did it seem to appreciate the pressure Sadat was under to demonstrate that his agreements with the United States and Israel were more than a separate Israeli-Egyptian peace. Sadat privately described his August 1981 meeting in Washington with Reagan as "very disappointing." [49] Worried by the Reagan Administration's apparent indifference to his plight, Sadat could not help but recall a comment that the Shah, paranoid to the end, had made to him at Aswan after his fall from power. The Americans, the Shah told Sadat, "will take everything they can get from you, and then, when you are of no more use to them, they will get rid of you." [50]

Anxious about his American connection, Sadat returned from his visit to Washington to a summer of unrest in Egypt. Despite an 8 percent annual national growth rate, Sadat was losing the "battle for prosperity" which he had launched after the signing of the peace treaty. Egypt's hard currency earnings had grown considerably in the late 1970s as a result of U.S. aid, the recovery of the Sinai oil fields, the expansion of the Suez Canal, increased tourist revenue, and remittances from Egyptians working in the Gulf States. But Sadat, with the memory of the 1977 food price riots fixed in his mind, had shied away from making necessary economic reforms, and as a result, Egypt's underlying economic problems worsened. Inflation and rampant corruption, coupled with the ostentatious lifestyle of the newly enriched upper middle class, strengthened the popular perception that *Infitah* had benefitted the rich at the expense of the poor. To millions of Cairenes living amidst crumbling buildings and open sewers, Sadat's promise that the year 1980 "would see the end of all our troubles" had become a bad joke by the summer of 1981.[51]

Economic stagnation provided a fertile breeding ground for political unrest. Islamic fundamentalists hurled public insults at Sadat, the "fat cats" spawned by *Infitah,* and the Sadat regime's American benefactors. Militant Copts clashed with Moslem extremists, and echoed their criticisms of Sadat. At the same time, Sadat's opponents in the press, the legal profession, and in intellectual circles peppered him with attacks. In a comprehensive effort to silence his critics, Sadat arrested some 1500 dissidents of all political and religious persuasions in September 1981. He was not quite thorough enough. On 6 October 1981, the eighth anniversary of his greatest triumph, the crossing of the Suez Canal, Sadat was assassinated by Islamic extremists.[52]

In the eyes of Sadat's assassins, and in the eyes of many other Egyptians who disapproved of political violence but who had grown dissatisfied with Sadat, the immense American aid program was a part of Sadat's problem, not a part of any solution to Egypt's economic and political troubles. To Sadat's critics, it seemed that American largesse served only to deepen the inequities of *Infitah.* Such criticism tended to overlook the very real contributions that AID had made to Egypt's economic well being, both through the provision of vitally needed foodstuffs and the financing of several important infrastructure projects. But it was based upon a set of political facts: Sadat had promised that U.S. aid would bring prosperity quickly to all Egyptians; Egyptians saw many American officials and consultants bustling about the country; and yet most Egyptians did not perceive any immediate improvement in their standard of living.

To some extent, given the inflated expectations that Sadat had created, it was inevitable that Egyptians would grow impatient with the results of the U.S. aid program. At the same time, however, there were problems connected with the assistance program itself which diminished its political value to the U.S. government. The first and most significant of these problems was the sluggish pace at which AID projects were implemented. Egyptian bureaucratic sloth and inefficiency served as a brake on many of AID's undertakings, but the reams of red tape and the lengthy feasibility studies which the American development agency wrapped around its projects also delayed their completion.[53] As a result, an enormous bottleneck developed in the aid "pipeline" in the 1970s. By the end of 1980, nearly half of the more than $5 billion in economic assistance appropriated by Congress between 1974 and 1980 for use in Egypt remained unspent.[54]

The Suez Cement Project provides a useful illustration of the difficulties that AID experienced in Egypt in the Sadat years. In 1975, AID planners began to consider the feasibility of constructing a cement plant at Suez, which, it was hoped, would underpin the housing programs already underway in the Suez Canal area and in Cairo. An AID project paper completed in June 1976 recommended funding of the plant, which was to be operated by the Suez Cement Company, a new concern partly controlled by private investors. Shortly thereafter, Congress appropriated $90 million to meet the foreign exchange costs estimated in the project paper. According to AID calculations, the plant would become operational in early 1980.

A year and a half after Sadat's death—three years after the completion date originally projected by AID—the Suez plant had still not produced its first bag of cement. In an internal audit of the project conducted in 1982, AID concluded that its initial cost estimates had been "far too low," and that it had failed to supervise the local contractor. Shoddy construction forced several long delays and exasperated U.S. officials. To Egyptians who had been led to expect economic miracles from the United States, the Suez Cement Project was a glaring disappointment.[55]

Disturbed by the slow progress of capital assistance projects like the cement plant, Ambassador Eilts advocated channeling a greater proportion of aid through the PL480 and commodity import programs, which had a more immediate impact upon the Egyptian economy. But by the end of 1978 Egypt was already receiving more than one-third of all PL480 aid distributed by the U.S. government, and Congress was reluctant to approve the increases sought by the American Embassy in Cairo. "We suggest caution by those in Washington who must pass on the Ambassador's request," wrote a staff member of the House Foreign Affairs Committee in early 1979. "Increasing the amount for Egypt would mean that amount not going to some other country, and would risk revival of charges that the food-for-peace program is being used by the U.S. government excessively for political purposes." [56] As a result of such reservations, which were shared by many AID officials, capital programs continued to account for a substantial portion of an overall aid budget in Egypt which was fixed at politically determined levels.

The inability of AID to bring its projects to quick fruition clearly hampered American efforts to produce the "peace dividend" that Sadat needed. A second and perhaps unavoidable flaw in the American effort during the Sadat era centered upon the failure to effectively link economic assistance to economic reform. United States and Egyptian officials agreed that certain basic reforms were prerequisites for modernization of the Egyptian economy. Unless a determined attempt was made to curb the expansion of the government bureaucracy, cut government subsidies, eliminate official corruption, and control the growth of Egypt's population, real economic progress was impossible. But the American government found it difficult to use the lever of economic assistance to pry reform out of the Egyptians; and even if it had been possible to do so, it is certain that large-scale reforms would have created political unrest in Egypt.

The certainty that the Administration would request, and the Congress appropriate, huge amounts of aid so long as Sadat maintained his pro-American political stance made it difficult for U.S. officials in Egypt to condition assistance on needed reforms. At the same time, the certainty that retrenchment in Egypt's subsidy and public sector hiring policies would catalyze popular upheavals like those of January 1977 discouraged both

American and Egyptian policymakers. "The crux of the dilemma for Egypt was," as Congressman Lee Hamilton, chairman of the House Foreign Affairs Subcommittee on Europe and the Middle East, put it in 1981, "that the economic reforms that were necessary to consolidate and expand Egypt's economic revival were the very things that would foster a degree of political discontent." [57] Thus both immediate concerns about political stability in Egypt and institutional constraints created by consistently high levels of aid prevented American diplomats from insisting on the significant modifications in Egyptian economic policies necessary if Sadat were to deliver his peace dividend.

If the clogged AID "pipeline" and the failure to link aid to economic reform hindered the American government in its effort to produce quick economic progress for Sadat, the sheer size and visibility of the AID Mission in Cairo served as a focus for popular disenchantment with Sadat and his American connection. By 1981, the AID Mission in Egypt had become by far the largest AID post in the world, with more than one-hundred professional staff members and numerous attendant consultants and specialists on temporary assignment.[58] As part of the burgeoning 15,000-member American community in Cairo, the large AID Mission was at first an encouraging signal to Egyptians who wanted to believe Sadat's promises of imminent prosperity. But it soon became a convenient target for Egyptians dissatisfied with their peace dividend and sensitive to signs of foreign encroachment. By the end of Sadat's reign, poor Cairenes could see all the trappings of modernity and Americanization—the Coca Cola signs, the blue jeans sported by the children of the *nouveaux riches,* the construction of new hotels for Western tourists and businessmen—but few of the concrete improvements in their standard of living that they had been led to expect. Although considerably smaller than the 40,000-member American community in Tehran in the mid-1970s, the American community in Cairo invited the same sorts of attacks that had accompanied the revolution in Iran. Commenting on the size and visibility of the American presence in Cairo in 1979, Ambassador Eilts said that "all of us remember Iran, and while this is nothing like Iran, it could get out of hand. It is a mistake." [59]

In view of the clear political role which the U.S. economic aid program was designed to play in Sadat's Egypt, it is surprising that American policymakers did not harness it more effectively to their broader political aims. To be sure, Egypt's terrible economic troubles and Sadat's ill-considered claims that U.S. aid would cure them quickly posed enormous difficulties for the American government; still, it is impossible to ignore the fact that the clogged aid-pipeline and the failure to insist upon minimal economic reforms made Sadat's peace dividend even more elusive. At the same time, the growing American presence in Egypt attracted the ire of Egyptians disabused of their faith in an American "quick fix."

The U.S. government provided Egypt with billions of dollars in economic aid after the 1973 War in order to reinforce the Sadat regime's interest in, and ability to pursue, a policy of rapprochement with the United States and conciliation with Israel. In embarking on the risky political course that led to the Camp David agreements, Sadat promised his people that peace would result in massive economic benefits for all Egyptians. The American aid program aimed, in effect, to make good on Sadat's pledge. But Sadat promised more than either he or AID could deliver, and both he and the American government suffered for his extravagant assurances. Within a year after Sadat's death, AID was being described by Egyptian journalists dissatisfied with the pace of development as "an American shadow government in Egypt" and "a tool of American penetration." [60] Gone were the rosy predictions of rapid economic progress that had abounded in Cairo in 1974–75; gone too were many of the hopes that both Egyptians and Americans had had for the economic aid program. U.S. assistance did much, although perhaps not as much as it could have, to reinforce the spectacular improvement in U.S.-Egyptian relations in the Sadat era, but it was never the miracle remedy that Sadat had advertised it to be.

CHAPTER EIGHT

Retrospect and Prospect

By 1982, the Aswan High Dam, the great symbol of Soviet-Egyptian cooperation in the Nasser era, was beginning to show signs of wear. In one of the many ironies of recent Egyptian history, it was the American government, whose refusal to fund the Aswan project a quarter century before had paved the way for Soviet involvement, which now repaired the Dam's cracked turbines. The goals that the Eisenhower Administration had sought to achieve with its Aswan offer—an Egyptian-Israeli peace treaty and a diminution of Soviet influence in Egypt—had been realized. They had been realized not through the barter of economic assistance for political concessions, as some of Eisenhower's advisers had anticipated, but through careful diplomacy and cultivation of shared interests. In the early 1980s, as in preceding years, economic aid served as an important inducement to cooperation with the United States, but it did not give the American government a stranglehold on Egyptian policies.

The American contribution to the repair of the Aswan Dam was a small part of the billion-dollar-a-year economic aid program which Hosni Mubarak inherited from Anwar Sadat.[1] Mubarak came to power in the wake of the assassination committed to the preservation of the special relationship that his predecessor had forged with the United States, as well as to the pursuit of a broader peace with Israel and the continued liberalization of the domestic economy. But he countered Sadat's grandiose promises of domestic prosperity and his "electric-shock" diplomacy with the vocabulary of lowered expectations and quiet efforts to restore Egypt's positions in the Arab and nonaligned worlds. "Don't expect miracles from me," Mubarak said, "I have no magic wands."[2] Widely respected for his personal integrity and incorruptibility, Mubarak cracked down on the excesses of the Sadat era, most notably in the corruption trial of the late President's half-brother Esmet. Disturbed, as were many of his countrymen, by the degree to which Egypt had drifted from the three spheres of influence that Nasser had identified in the mid-1950s, Mubarak began the slow process of rebuilding Egypt's ties to its Arab neighbors, to the nonaligned movement, and to the rest of the Islamic world.

Two corollaries of this trend in Egyptian foreign policy were a slackening of the pace of normalization of Israeli-Egyptian relations and a very gradual shift away from what Mubarak perceived to be overidentification of Egypt with American interests. The first was as much a product of Israeli provocation as of any grand Egyptian design. Recovery of the Sinai in the spring of 1982 made the Egyptian government less hesitant to air its differences with Israel; when the Israelis launched their invasion of Lebanon less than two months after their final withdrawal from the Sinai, the Mubarak regime criticized the Begin government in some of the strongest language used in Egyptian-Israeli relations since the mid-1970s.

Mubarak's moves in 1982–83 to demonstrate that Egypt was something more than an American client were more subtle. He refused to allow the United States to establish a permanent air force base at Ras Banas on the Red Sea, although he made it clear that the U.S. Rapid Deployment Force could make use of the military facilities at Ras Banas for training or during an actual emergency. He voiced staunch support for the Reagan Peace Initiative but continued to advocate a direct U.S. dialogue with the Palestine Liberation Organization. He insisted upon greater Egyptian control over the disbursement of American aid funds, and obtained it.

And yet Mubarak realizes that Egypt is more dependent on American assistance now than at any other time in the postrevolutionary era. With income from oil production, tourist revenues, and foreign remittances all decreasing, with one million more mouths to feed every ten months and with an entrenched public sector bureaucracy and politically sensitive subsidies policies to contend with, the outlook for the Egyptian economy has rarely seemed bleaker.[3] The Mubarak regime cannot afford to jeopardize its American aid connection; at the same time, it cannot appear to kowtow to American desires.

Mubarak's position is made even more delicate by the fact that Egypt's disproportionate share of the U.S. government's dwindling aid expenditures—Egypt now receives more than 25 percent of all U.S. food aid and some 30 percent of the total Economic Support Fund budget—will insure careful Congressional scrutiny of Egyptian policies.[4] Should any significant U.S.-Egyptian differences emerge, the huge American aid program will tempt American legislators with visions of potential political leverage. That possibility lends urgency to the need to review the lessons learned in the past thirty years about the objectives, application, and effects of American aid policy toward Egypt.

Objectives

Since 1955, American aid policy toward Egypt has had three broad sets of objectives: those relating specifically to Egyptian behavior; those relating to American domestic concerns; and those relating to broader international interests, like Soviet-American competition in the Third World or the need to appease allies. In America's generally adversarial relationship with Nasser's Egypt, American policymakers sought, among other things, to contain the growth of Soviet influence in Egypt, to engineer an Arab-Israeli peace settlement, and to curb Egyptian attacks on Western interests in the Arab world and in Africa. In the more congenial times that followed the October War, the U.S. government used economic assistance on a massive scale to reinforce Sadat's inclination to cooperate with the United States in the Camp David peace process. Underpinning all of these aims was a persistent American tendency to overestimate the political utility of economic aid.

This interminable optimism, surely one of the most remarkable aspects of the U.S.-Egyptian aid relationship in the Nasser era and a lingering feature of American thinking in the Sadat era, seems to have been at least partly the result of a mistaken application of the American domestic experience to U.S.-Egyptian relations. Lyndon Johnson was certainly not the only American politician or government official in the 1950s and 1960s to presume that Third World leaders would respond to the same sorts of inducements and threats to which American Senators responded: he was simply the most prominent. The promise, or threatened withdrawal, of economic favors was an effective way of securing political concessions on Capitol Hill. It was widely assumed in the American government, particularly but not exclusively in Congress, that the manipulation of economic carrots and sticks would be an effective means of dealing with the Nasser regime. American national ambitions have historically been bound up with visions of economic progress, and it was quite natural for American officials unfamiliar with the chemistry of Third World nationalism to suppose that economic modernization would be the overriding ambition of the leaders of developing countries. The assumption that Third World governments would be willing to enter into detailed political bargains in order to attract American economic assistance was thus a logical, if seriously flawed, outcome of American experience and American expectations.

Throughout the Nasser and Sadat eras, U.S. efforts to use aid to regulate Egyptian behavior were influenced by American domestic political concerns. When John Foster Dulles decided to cancel the Aswan offer in the summer of 1956, he was motivated as much by a desire to avoid attacks on aid to Yugoslavia and on the Executive Branch's control of aid policy as by an interest in altering Egyptian conduct. Similarly, the Johnson Administration's restrictive aid policy in 1965 was aimed at Congressional and public opinion in the United States as well as at Egyptian behavior.

The Nasser regime was never oblivious to the connection between the American government's bilateral and domestic goals. As Ali Sabri's comments to John Badeau about the link between Egypt's restrained behavior at the 1962 Nonaligned Economic Summit in Cairo and progress of the foreign aid bill indicated, Nasser and his advisers understood that domestic considerations played a role in the making of U.S. aid policy.[5] But Nasser never demonstrated the sophisticated appreciation of the Washington policy-making process that Sadat did. After the October War, Sadat met with hundreds of members of Congress, in Cairo and in Washington.[6] His personal attention to Congressional views, as well as his spirited courtship of the American media, contributed greatly to the success that Sadat enjoyed in obtaining assistance from the United States.

In addition to its interest in influencing Egyptian behavior and its domestic goals, the American government had a broader set of objectives linked to competition with the Soviet Union and relations with United States allies. Part of the rationale behind the original American offer to help finance the Aswan High Dam had to do with offsetting the influence that the Soviet Union was developing in Egypt through arms shipments. When the Eisenhower Administration dropped the Aswan offer less than a year later, it did so in part because of pressure from American allies to reprimand Nasser.

A further distinction to be noted when considering the objectives of aid policy, that between publicized and unpublicized goals, can also be illustrated with reference to the Aswan affair. The key initial aim of U.S. aid policy in 1955–56, to obtain Nasser's signature on a peace agreement with Israel in return for construction of the High Dam, was shrouded in the secrecy of the Anderson mission. A broader publicized goal of the Aswan offer was to impress Third World leaders with the advantages of cooperation with the United States in its struggle against the Soviet Union. In the first instance, it was feared that publicity would undermine American aims; in the second, publicity was deemed essential to the realization of U.S. goals.

Application

The American government employed a wide variety of tactics in its aid policy toward the Nasser and Sadat regimes. When American policymakers wished to reinforce desirable patterns of Egyptian behavior, aid was offered as an inducement. In the early 1960s, this took the form of a gradual escalation of the quantity, quality, and duration of aid proffered by the United States—a tactic that culminated in the three-year PL480 agreement of 1962. A similar policy was pursued in the mid-1970s, as Henry Kissinger sought to coax concessions from the Sadat government.

Contrary Egyptian behavior was met with an array of sanctions, ranging from the withdrawal of the Aswan offer to the suspension of food aid shipments in early 1965 to the provision of a tightly restricted six-month PL480 arrangement in 1966 instead of the longer term, more generous, accord that Nasser had wanted. As has been noted earlier, the distinctions between inducements and sanctions were rarely as clear cut in practice as they might seem in theory. Economic carrots and sticks were usually mixed to maximize political leverage in Egypt. At the same time that the Eisenhower Administration scrapped its Aswan aid proposal in the summer of 1956, for example, it hinted that assistance might be forthcoming in the future if Nasser modified his policies.

Since its objectives generally extended beyond Egyptian behavior, the American government had to accommodate its tactics to domestic and broader foreign policy aims as well as to those relating more narrowly to the U.S.-Egyptian relationship. This was no easy task, as the Johnson Administration's experience in 1965 illustrated. After the suspension of food aid shipments to Egypt at the beginning of 1965, some of Johnson's advisers detected a moderation of Egyptian attitudes toward American interests in the Arab world and in Africa. Ambassador Lucius Battle argued for a resumption of aid, contending that modest PL480 shipments would help induce Nasser to continue to moderate his policies. But the Johnson Administration stalled for several more months, less because of the presumed effect procrastination would have on Nasser than because of its concern about running the rest of its foreign aid appropriations through the Congressional gauntlet. When the foreign aid bill had been passed, the Administration unblocked PL480 shipments to Egypt and began to consider actively a new food aid agreement.

Effects

It is difficult to establish a clear cause and effect relationship between American aid policy and Egyptian behavior, or, for that matter, between aid policy and domestic events or developments in the Soviet-American rivalry or changing attitudes in the Third World. But there can be no doubt that Kennedy's food aid program in the early 1960s helped improve U.S.-Egyptian relations, that Johnson's sanctions in 1965 had some moderating influence on Nasser's conduct in the Congo, and that the massive post-1974 assistance program reinforced a trend toward U.S.-Egyptian cooperation. Domestic economic modernization was an important goal of the Nasser and Sadat regimes, and both appreciated the fact that foreign aid was crucial to their hopes for development. Even Nasser, as sensitive as he was to foreign encroachment, was willing to make some minor political concessions to ensure the continued flow of American aid. There was always, however, a threshold beyond which Egyptian positions and policies were non-negotiable, no matter how much aid the United States offered. It was not possible to buy an Arab-Israeli peace with aid for the Aswan project, as Herbert Hoover, Jr., had hoped in 1955–56, just as it was not possible to force Nasser out of Yemen by threatening to cut off PL480 aid, as some Congressmen and Senators had hoped in 1964–65. Nor, in more recent memory, could the United States trade increased aid for permanent military bases in Egypt. As important as economic modernization was to the Nasser and Sadat governments and as important as U.S. economic aid was to the modernization program, neither Nasser nor Sadat was prepared to abandon or substantially modify foreign policy aims that he considered essential to his personal or national ambitions in order to promote domestic economic development.

From the point of view of the Nasser regime, economic aid became an irritant rather than a lubricant in U.S.-Egyptian relations because of the American government's persistence in thinking that it could expect significant political returns on its economic investments in Egypt. Nothing was more deeply embedded in the Nasser regime's approach to foreign affairs than a powerful aversion to any form of foreign control of Egyptian policies. Nasser was once quoted as saying that "all of Egypt's ills, whether economic, social, or political, derive from the fact of foreign domination." [7] Despite the obvious inadequacies of this explanation of the problems that Nasser and his successors faced, it is clear that the regime's strident anti-imperialism struck a responsive chord in Egypt and in the rest of the Arab world.

By the 1970s, this revolutionary ardor had cooled somewhat, but sensitivity to foreign domination was still an important feature of Egyptian foreign policy. Sadat's expulsion of Soviet advisers in 1972 was, after all, at least partly a reaction against

Egypt's growing dependence on the Soviet Union. The growth of American influence in Egypt after the October War was more a source of concern for his critics than for Sadat himself, but on more than one occasion Sadat made it clear that he did not intend to become a vassal of the United States. In a speech in June 1980, for example, the Egyptian president asserted that "if America commits a wrong against Egypt and wants to impose its will on Egypt, we will have a new position toward America." [8]

The Egyptian government's sensitivity to foreign encroachment was most acute in those instances in which the United States made a clumsily disguised attempt to barter aid for political concessions, as it did during Robert Anderson's pioneering venture in shuttle diplomacy in 1955–56. But Egyptian anxieties about foreign domination, real or imagined, also manifested themselves during times in which more open-ended aid agreements were in effect. Indeed, the sheer size and liberality of the three-year PL480 accord signed in 1962 created both domestic and regional pressures on Nasser to demonstrate that, even when blessed with unprecedented American largesse, he was not a pawn of the United States. By the end of 1963, the American government had discovered to its chagrin that it had locked itself into an expensive, long-term aid commitment which, ironically, activated some of Nasser's most pronounced anti-imperialist instincts.

Although U.S.-Egyptian ties are far stronger today than at any time in the Nasser era, the fact that the size and generosity of the current American economic assistance program creates risks for both the Egyptian and American governments is worth underlining. Because he receives a billion dollars worth of U.S. economic aid every year, as well as a similar amount of military aid, Hosni Mubarak will continue to feel pressure in Egypt and in the rest of the Arab world to demonstrate periodically that he is not in thrall to the United States. The American government, for its part, will find that it cannot trim aid disbursements—whether because of budgetary troubles in Washington, a clogged aid-pipeline in Egypt, or anything else—without encountering political difficulties in Cairo. Decreasing U.S. economic aid will aggravate the Egyptian government; increasing it, however, is unlikely to give the American government any greater political leverage in Egypt.

If there is a general lesson to be learned about the effect of aid policy on Egyptian behavior, it is that economic assistance, however it is dispensed, does not in itself furnish a foundation for U.S.-Egyptian cooperation—it reinforces an interest in mutual accommodation derived from more basic shared political objectives. Henry Byroade's admonitions to John Foster Dulles in July 1956 seem as sound today, and as relevant to the U.S.-Egyptian aid relationship, as they did during the Aswan affair:

> Economic assistance provides a very useful lubricator for foreign policy operations. . . . assistance does not (repeat not) in itself establish basic common bonds between us and recipients and it does not (repeat not) buy repudiation of national objectives which may not (repeat not) coincide with our programs and policies.[9]

Determining whether or not aid policy was a "success" in terms of domestic aims is, like consideration of effects on Egyptian conduct, a difficult endeavor. It is also a rather pointless one, unless all of the side effects, both long run and short run, of particular policies are taken into account. Cancellation of aid for the Aswan High Dam may have rescued the assistance program in Yugoslavia and preserved Executive Branch supremacy in the making of foreign aid policy, but it also did considerable damage to American relations with Egypt. Similarly, President Johnson's punitive aid policy in 1965–66 may have staved off a Congressional revolt and helped modify, temporarily, Egyptian policies, but in the long run it probably reinforced Nasser's suspicions about the United States and aggravated his hostility toward the Johnson Administration. There was nothing inherently antagonistic about the relationship between domestic concerns and objectives related to Egyptian behavior; in the early 1960s, for instance, a domestic interest in disposing of surplus agricultural commodities fit neatly into the Kennedy Administration's plans to expand the Food for Peace program in Egypt. Foreign aid will always be a subject of contention on Capitol Hill, however, and situations will continue to arise in which satisfaction of domestic aims (i.e., passage of an aid bill, or of some other bit of legislation desired by the Administration) will lead to aid policies which have damaging effects on relations between donor and recipient.

The effects that American aid policy toward Egypt had on the course of the Soviet-American rivalry or on U.S. relationships with allies cannot be defined precisely. The Eisenhower Administration's withdrawal of the Aswan offer, intended partly as a lesson to aspiring neutralists on the perils of flirtation with the Soviet Union, damaged America's reputation in the Third World. On the other hand, Kennedy's efforts to court Nasser with food aid made a generally favorable impression on other developing countries, and helped offset earlier Soviet gains in the Third World. Cancellation of Aswan aid pleased Britain and France, but they were soon to feel the adverse side-effects of that decision. One of the subsidiary aims of the Aswan cancellation had been to satisfy British and French demands to punish Nasser; an indirect effect of the withdrawal of aid was the tension that surfaced in U.S. relations with Britain and France during the Suez affair.

The American fear that the Soviets would gain complete control over Egyptian policies through manipulation of their aid relationship with Nasser and Sadat proved as groundless as American expectations that U.S. aid could produce similar leverage. The Soviet experience in Egypt, like the American experience, demonstrated that the use of economic aid as a political lever had no more than a marginal effect on the policies Nasser deemed to be vital to his nation's interests. When Soviet and Egyptian interests coincided—as they did in the mid-1950s when both governments sought to sabotage Western regional defense plans—economic and military aid served to reinforce bilateral bonds. But when major Soviet-Egyptian differences arose—as they did in the late 1950s over the issue of Soviet support for the Kassem regime in Iraq—it was clear that Soviet aid did not in itself produce enough leverage to force an adjustment of Egyptian policies.[10]

It is worth noting that the Soviet government did nevertheless enjoy a number of advantages over the American government in its efforts in the Nasser era to exploit the marginal political leverage produced by economic aid to Egypt. In the first place, the Soviets did not need to rely as heavily on economic aid as a diplomatic instrument as the Americans did, since they had in their military aid program a more potent means than economic aid of influencing Egyptian behavior. By manipulating, or threatening to manipulate, the flow of weaponry, ammunition, and spare parts, the Soviet government could compel the Egyptian government—which consistently gave a higher priority to military development than to economic development in the Nasser era—to give serious consideration to modifying Egyptian policies to conform to Soviet desires. Secondly, Soviet economic aid was channeled into highly visible development projects, like the Aswan High Dam and the Helwan Iron and Steel Works, in contrast to the more obscure American food shipments, which were equated in the Egyptian popular mind with a desire to keep the beneficiary country in a state of agricultural backwardness.[11] American efforts to balance expensive industrial projects with support for agricultural development were sometimes regarded as part of a neocolonialist scheme to retard Egyptian modernization and keep Egypt dependent on Western industry.[12] The fact that PL480 aid was, if anything, a boon to the Egyptian industrial program, since it freed foreign exchange for use in industrial projects, was often lost in the maze of Egyptian suspicions.

Moreover, the use of food aid as a political lever had a stigma attached to it that similar use of capital or technical assistance did not have. Shipping wheat to Egypt was not the same as shipping tractors or industrial equipment: as John Badeau later noted, "food was so vital, so personal, so connected with basic human needs, that conditions, restrictions, and fluctuations in supplying it aroused violent reactions."[13] Finally, the centralized, secretive style of Soviet decision-making made it possible for the Soviets to provide economic aid to Egypt without the public discussion of political demands, the encumbering legislative restrictions, and the interminable delays that proved so debilitating to the U.S.-Egyptian aid relationship.

The issue of publicity—with which the Soviets did not really have to contend—deserves special mention. Publicization of the aims of American aid policy antagonized Nasser throughout the 1950s and 1960s. Congressional attempts in the mid-1960s to tie aid to Egyptian withdrawal from Yemen and the dismantling of Egypt's guided missile program only served to increase the Nasser regime's intransigence. But on some occasions publicity served other American aims. John Foster Dulles's public cancellation of the Aswan offer, for example, was designed to calm a restive Congress and impress an audience of newly independent Third World states with the hard realities of Cold War politics. Whatever gains such publicity may have yielded in domestic or broader international terms, however, it nearly always undermined attempts to moderate Nasser's behavior.

Economic Aid and the Limits of Influence

What lessons does the American experience in the Nasser and Sadat eras hold for current aid policy? Such lessons are, in contrast to the more specific points made at the end of Chapter Seven about unclogging the aid-pipeline, linking aid to reform, and reducing the size and visibility of the American presence, applicable not only to the American aid relationship with Mubarak's Egypt, but also to U.S. aid policy toward other developing countries. The first of these lessons may seem hackneyed, but the failure of successive Administrations to learn it during the Nasser years underscores the need to repeat it. Before American policymakers can begin to set intelligent objectives, develop tactics, or consider effects, they must first understand the constraints imposed upon them by the domestic concerns, interests, and fears of the government that they hope to influence. Whether it was Foster Dulles and Herbert Hoover, Jr., discussing the economic price of an Arab-Israeli peace settlement, Chester Bowles extolling the political virtues of aid to Egypt to President Kennedy, Senator Gruening explaining to his colleagues the ease with which the cut off of aid could be used to force Egyptian troops out of Yemen, or Lyndon Johnson tightening the leash on Gamal Abdel Nasser, the dominant image of American policymaking in the period 1955–1967 was that of officials confusing their own vision of what Egyptian priorities should be with the real priorities of the Nasser regime. Inflated American expectations, coupled with deep Egyptian anxieties about foreign encroachment, produced a highly combustible aid relationship.

In the Sadat era, inflated Egyptian expectations, publicly fanned by Sadat himself, posed real dangers for American policymakers. Again, it is clear that no sensible aid policy could be developed without taking Egypt's domestic mood into account. The political influence that one country derives from *must remember domestic concerns of recipient* [handwritten marginal note]

the provision of economic assistance to another is not the neat mathematical product of a simple calculus of economic costs and benefits: it results from the complicated interaction of the needs, perceptions, and ambitions of the donor with those of the recipient.

Several other lessons emerge from past American experience in Egypt. Given the variety of objectives that the American government invariably pursues, it is important to sort out aims, assigning priorities and adhering to them with some consistency. In this connection, publicization of goals must be carefully managed, always in full awareness of the negative impact that publicizing political quid pro quos is likely to have on Egyptian behavior. Aid policy should then be applied to fit the rough hierarchical arrangement of objectives devised by American policy-makers. If modification or reinforcement of a particular aspect of Egyptian foreign policy is the highest American priority, the quantity, quality, and duration of aid programs should not be constantly juggled in pursuit of other domestic or foreign policy goals. Any consideration of the effects or "success" of aid policy must include a comprehensive look at side effects. Whenever a number of interconnected objectives are pursued, each will be affected to some degree by shifts in aid policy, in the long run if not in the short run. Finally, it is important to underline the fact that economic assistance, however it is dispensed, does not in itself furnish a basis for U.S.-Egyptian cooperation.

The provision of economic aid can reinforce an interest in mutual accommodation derived from more fundamental shared political objectives. The promise, threatened withdrawal, or actual withdrawal of aid can also, if discreetly applied, earn modest political concessions from the recipient. But the political value of economic assistance must not be overestimated. A large aid program, even one as extensive as the current program for Mubarak's Egypt, cannot effectively be used as a political bludgeon; moreover, the sheer size of such a program creates considerable risks for both donor and recipient. For those who may be tempted to think that the Mubarak regime's dependence on American assistance gives the U.S. government a vice grip on Egyptian policies, the lessons of the Nasser and Sadat eras are worth remembering.

Appendix 1

Initial Draft of Aswan Cancellation Statement, 18 July 1956

The Aswan Dam project is one of great magnitude. It would require an estimated twelve to fifteen years to complete at a total cost currently estimated at some $1,500,000,000, of which about $1,100,000,000 represents local currency costs. The project involves not merely the rights and interests of Egypt but of other states whose waters are contributory, such as the Sudan, Ethiopia, and Uganda. Such a gigantic undertaking could succeed only in an atmosphere of international tranquility and with close and understanding co-operation between the Government and peoples of Egypt who provide the internal effort and those abroad who provide the foreign exchange portion of the effort. In the absence of such an atmosphere the project could generate ill will and success would be improbable.

Last year the Government of the United States hoped that such an atmosphere could be created and that indeed the launching of the first phase of the Aswan Dam project would assist in that respect. Since then, developments seem to put into question the basic premises referred to.

Under the circumstances, the United States government has informed the Egyptian government through its Ambassador at Washington that the United States government is not now disposed to proceed with its part of the projected plan.

This decision in no way involves any alteration in the friendly relations of the Government and people of the United States toward the Government and people of Egypt. Neither does it involve any decision not to assist the Egyptian economy and to help the Government of Egypt to remedy the conditions of economic distress which afflict so many of the Egyptian people. Rather, it is designed to avoid embarking upon a vast project when the conditions are not auspicious.

Source: Eisenhower Library, Foster Dulles Papers.

Appendix 2

Aswan Cancellation Statement, 19 July 1956

At the request of the Government of Egypt, the United States joined in December 1955 with the United Kingdom and with the World Bank in an offer to assist Egypt in the construction of a high dam on the Nile at Aswan. This project is one of great magnitude. It would require an estimated twelve to sixteen years to complete at a total cost estimated at some $1,300,000,000, of which over $900,000,000 represents local currency requirements. It involves not merely the rights and interests of Egypt but of other states whose waters are contributory, including Sudan, Ethiopia, and Uganda.

The December offer contemplated an extension by the United States and United Kingdom of grant aid to help finance certain early phases of the work, the effects of which would be confined solely to Egypt, with the understanding that accomplishment of the project as a whole would require a satisfactory resolution of the question of Nile water rights. Another important consideration bearing upon the feasibility of the undertaking and thus the practicability of American aid was Egyptian readiness and ability to concentrate its economic resources upon this vast construction program.

Developments within the succeeding seven months have not been favorable to the success of the project, and the United States Government has concluded that it is not feasible in present circumstances to participate in the project. Agreement by the riparian states has not been achieved, and the ability of Egypt to devote adequate resources to assure the project's success has become more uncertain than at the time the offer was made.

This decision in no way reflects or involves any alteration in the friendly relations of the Government and people of the United States toward the Government and people of Egypt.

The United States remains deeply interested in the welfare of the Egyptian people and in the development of the Nile. It is prepared to consider at an appropriate time and at the request of the riparian states what steps might be taken toward a more effective utilization of the water resources of the Nile for the benefit of the peoples of the region. Furthermore, the United States remains ready to assist Egypt in its efforts to improve the economic condition of its people and is prepared, through its appropriate agencies, to discuss these matters within the context of funds appropriated by the Congress.

Source: CR, vol. 97, part 2, 21 August 1957: p. 14073.

Appendix 3

U.S. Economic Commitments to Egypt 1952–67* (millions of U.S. dollars)

	1952–56	1957	1958	1959	1960	1961	1962	1963	1964	1965	1966	1967	Total
Food Aid (PL480)	63	—	48	82	88	114	126	120	176	176	67	—	1060
Title I	20	—	48	73	80	92	81	100	168	164	41	—	866
Title II	—	—	—	—	—	—	24	—	—	—	—	—	24
Title III	43	—	—	9	8	22	21	20	8	12	12	—	156
Title IV	—	—	—	—	—	—	—	—	—	—	14	—	14
Capital Aid	47	—	—	13	12	27	40	51	6	—	—	11	207
Technical Aid	19	1	—	1	2	2	2	2	1	2	1	1	35

* Fiscal years (1 July–30 June) in which commitments made rather than actual dispersal of benefits.

Source: Faulkner, "Economic Effects of PL480 in UAR," p. 73 (table 3.2)

Appendix 4

U.S. Economic Commitments to Egypt: FY 1975–1981 (Millions of Dollars as of November 15, 1981)

I. GENERAL ECONOMIC SUPPORT	L/G	FY 1975 250.0	FY 1976* 518.1	FY 1977 647.1	FY 1978 500.85	FY 1979 564.6	FY 1980 702.8	FY 1981 601.0
A. Balance of Payments (Sub-Total)		248.1	501.1	620.7	476.5	547.1	660.0	588.0
Commodity Import Program	L	(150.0)	(315.0)	(440.0)	(300.0)	(250.0)	(280.0)	(70.0)
Commodity Import Program	G	(—)	(—)	(—)	(—)	(85.0)	(55.0)	(230.0)
PL-480 Title I	L	(98.1)	(186.1)	(180.7)	(176.5)	(212.1)	(325.0)	(275.0)
B. Development Planning		1.9	17.0	26.4	24.35	17.5	42.8	13.0
Technical and Feasibility Studies	G	(0.9)	(15.0)	(18.0)	(12.0)	(5.0)	(6.0)	(8.0)
Technology Transfer and Workforce Development	G	(1.0)	(2.0)	(4.5)	(4.0)	(10.0)	(6.0)	(5.0)
Applied Science and Technology Research	G	(—)	(—)	(3.9)	(4.2)	(—)	(16.3)	(—)
Development Planning Studies	G	(—)	(—)	(—)	(3.8)	(—)	(12.0)	(—)
Sinai Planning Studies	G	(—)	(—)	(—)	(—)	(2.5)	(2.5)	(—)
Review of U.S. Assistance to Egypt	G	(—)	(—)	(—)	(0.35)	(—)	(—)	(—)
Summary: Loan Component		248.1	501.1	620.7	476.5	462.1	605.0	345.0
Grant Component		1.9	17.0	26.4	24.35	102.5	97.8	243.0

II. INFRASTRUCTURE

	L/G	FY 1975 30.0	FY 1976* 173.0	FY 1977 123.01	FY 1978 221.0	FY 1979 305.8	FY 1980 193.1	FY 1981 276.0
Electric Power Distribution Equipment	G	(30.0)	(—)	(—)	(—)	(—)	(—)	(—)
Ismailia Electric Power Plant	G	(—)	(99.0)	(42.0)	(—)	(—)	(—)	(—)
National Energy Control Center	L/G	(—)	(24.0)	(19.0)	(17.0)	(—)	(2.5)	(—)
Gas Turbines Generators (Helwan/Talkha)	L	(—)	(50.0)	(17.01)	(—)	(—)	(—)	(—)
Urban Electric Power Distribution	L/G	(—)	(—)	(30.0)	(20.9)	(—)	(10.0)	(31.0)
Cairo Water System	L	(—)	(—)	(15.0)	(—)	(—)	(—)	(—)
Alexandria Sewerage I	L	(—)	(—)	(—)	(—)	(87.3)	(—)	(—)
Alexandria Sewerage System Expansion	G	(—)	(—)	(—)	(—)	(—)	(—)	(74.1)
Cairo Sewerage	G	(—)	(—)	(—)	(25.0)	(36.0)	(—)	(—)
Canal Cities Water and Sewage Systems	L/G	(—)	(—)	(—)	(60.0)	(80.0)	(—)	(—)
Telecommunications I, II, III	L/G	(—)	(—)	(—)	(40.0)	(80.0)	(80.0)	(—)
Low-Cost Housing and Community Upgrading	G	(—)	(—)	(—)	(50.0)	(—)	(28.1)	(1.9)
Shoubra Power Thermal Electric Plant	G	(—)	(—)	(—)	(—)	(100.0)	(—)	(90.0)
Summary: Loan Component		—	74.0	81.01	146.0	—	—	—
Grant Component		30.0	99.0	42.0	75.0	305.0	193.1	276.0

III. DECENTRALIZATION

	L/G	FY 1975	FY 1976*	FY 1977	FY 1978 1.4	FY 1979 2.5	FY 1980 127.3	FY 1981 94.0
Decentralization Support Fund	G				(—)	(—)	(50.0)	(—)
Development Decentralization	G				(1.4)	(2.5)	(7.3)	(15.0)
Basic Village Services	G				(—)	(—)	(70.0)	(—)
Neighborhood Urban Services	G							(20.0)
Provincial Cities	G							(20.0)

IV. TRANSPORTATION, INDUSTRY, COMMERCE AND FINANCE

	L/G	FY 1975	FY 1976*	FY 1977	FY 1978	FY 1979	FY 1980	FY 1981
		35.0	255.6	21.0	180.9	54.0	70.8	80.5
Suez Canal Rehabilitation	G	(22.0)	(2.6)	(—)	(—)	(—)	(—)	(—)
Road Building Equipment	G	(10.0)	(4.0)	(—)	(—)	(—)	(—)	(—)
Cargo Handling Equip. (Alexandria Port)	L	(—)	(31.0)	(—)	(—)	(—)	(—)	(—)
Suez Cement Plant	G	(—)	(90.0)	(—)	(—)	(—)	(10.0)	(—)
Mahalla Textile Plant Rehabilitation	L	(—)	(96.0)	(—)	(—)	(—)	(—)	(—)
Development Industrial Bank I	L/G	(—)	(32.0)	(—)	(2.0)	(—)	(—)	(—)
Hydrographic Survey for Suez Canal	G	(—)	(—)	(8.0)	(—)	(—)	(—)	(—)
Port Said Salines Production Plant	G	(—)	(—)	(13.0)	(—)	(—)	(—)	(—)
Suez Port Development	L	(—)	(—)	(—)	(30.0)	(—)	(—)	(—)
Industrial Production	L/G	(—)	(—)	(—)	(53.9)	(16.0)	(25.0)	(50.0)
Quattamiya Cement Plant	L	(—)	(—)	(—)	(95.0)	(—)	(—)	(—)
Private Investment Encouragement Fund	G	(—)	(—)	(—)	(—)	(33.0)	(—)	(—)
Private Sector Feasibility Studies	G	(—)	(—)	(—)	(—)	(5.0)	(—)	(—)
Vehicle Maintenance Training	G	(—)	(—)	(—)	(—)	(—)	(4.5)	(—)
Industrial Productivity Improvement	G	(—)	(—)	(—)	(—)	(—)	(8.5)	(30.5)
Mineral, Petroleum and Groundwater Assessment	G	(—)	(—)	(—)	(—)	(—)	(20.7)	(—)
Tax Administration	G	(—)	(—)	(—)	(—)	(—)	(2.1)	(—)
Helicopter Transfer	G	(3.0)	(—)	(—)	(—)	(—)	(2.1)	(—)
Summary: Loan Component		35.0	159.0	21.0	171.4	54.0	70.8	80.5
Grant Component			96.6		9.5			

V. FOOD AND AGRICULTURE

	L/G	FY 1975 44.3	FY 1976* 32.5	FY 1977 83.84	FY 1978 13.8	FY 1979 105.5	FY 1980 78.0	FY 1981 64.0
Grain Storage Facilities	L	(44.3)	(—)	(—)	(—)	(—)	(—)	(—)
PVC Pipe Drainage	L	(—)	(31.0)	(—)	(—)	(—)	(—)	(—)
Water Use and Management	G	(—)	(1.5)	(0.8)	(1.5)	(3.2)	(—)	(6.0)
Canal Dredging Equipment	L/G	(—)	(—)	(26.0)	(—)	(—)	(—)	(—)
Food Grain/Veg. Oil Storage and Dist. Factory	L	(—)	(—)	(42.0)	(—)	(—)	(—)	(—)
Irrigation Equipment	L/G	(—)	(—)	(11.0)	(—)	(—)	(8.0)	(—)
Agricultural Development Systems	G	(—)	(—)	(1.2)	(3.8)	(7.9)	(—)	(—)
Poultry Improvement	G	(—)	(—)	(0.47)	(3.5)	(0.6)	(—)	(8.0)
Rice Research and Training	G	(—)	(—)	(2.37)	(1.5)	(5.9)	(—)	(12.0)
Aquaculture Development	G	(—)	(—)	(—)	(3.5)	(—)	(—)	(—)
Major Cereals	G	(—)	(—)	(—)	(—)	(30.0)	(24.0)	(—)
Small Farmer Production	G	(—)	(—)	(—)	(—)	(25.0)	(17.0)	(—)
Agriculture Cooperative Development	G	(—)	(—)	(—)	(—)	(5.0)	(—)	(—)
Small Scale Agriculture Activities	G	(—)	(—)	(—)	(—)	(1.7)	(—)	(—)
Agricultural Mechanization	G	(—)	(—)	(—)	(—)	(21.0)	(19.0)	(—)
Agricultural Management Development	G	(—)	(—)	(—)	(—)	(—)	(5.0)	(—)
Agricultural Data Collection and Analysis	G	(—)	(—)	(—)	(—)	(—)	(5.0)	(—)
Irrigation Management Systems	G	(—)	(—)	(—)	(—)	(—)	(—)	(38.0)
Summary: Loan Component		44.3	31.0	79.0	—	—	—	—
Grant Component			1.5	4.84	13.8	105.5	78.0	64.0

	L/G	FY 1975 12.6	FY 1976* 7.4	FY 1977 17.0	FY 1978 17.2	FY 1979 33.7	FY 1980 112.8	FY 1981 165.5
Strengthen Rural Health Delivery System	G	(—)	(1.8)	(—)	(1.8)	(4.2)	(—)	(—)
Family Planning	G	(—)	(—)	(4.0)	(6.0)	(6.5)	(10.0)	(18.5)
Integrated Social Work Training Centers	G	(—)	(—)	(1.0)	(1.5)	(1.5)	(—)	(—)
Urban Health Delivery	G	(—)	(—)	(—)	(—)	(5.0)	(20.3)	(12.0)
Peace Fellowships Program	G	(—)	(—)	(—)	(—)	(—)	(30.0)	(24.0)
Suez Canal Univ.—Fac. of Medicine	G	(—)	(—)	(—)	(—)	(—)	(2.7)	(—)
University Linkages	G	(—)	(—)	(—)	(—)	(—)	(27.5)	(—)
Control of Diarrheal Diseases	G	(—)	(—)	(—)	(—)	(—)	(—)	(26.0)
Basic Education	G	(—)	(—)	(—)	(—)	(—)	(—)	(39.0)
PL-480 Title II a	G	(12.6)	(5.6)	(12.0)	(6.5)	(14.0)	(15.0)	(31.0)
TOTAL A.I.D. ASSISTANCE (Excluding PL-480 Program)		261.2	794.9	699.25	750.75	835.0 c	865.0 d	829.0
PL-480 PROGRAM		110.7	191.7	192.7	183.0	226.1	340.0	306.0
GRAND TOTAL U.S. ECONOMIC ASSISTANCE b		371.9	986.6	891.95	933.75	1,061.1	1,205.0	1,135.0

* Includes Interim Quarter
L = Loan; G = Grant
a Includes Estimated Ocean Freight Costs
b Does Not Include Egyptian Pound Grants
c Includes $85 Million Supplemental Peace Allotment
d Includes $55 Million Supplemental Peace Allotment

Notes

Introduction

[1] For the purposes of this study, "economic aid" can be defined as the concessional transfer of capital, goods, or services from one government to another. The United States program in Egypt consisted at various times of capital aid—loans and grants designed to expand the concrete physical means of production, through financing of factories, roads, ports, irrigation works, and grain storage facilities; technical aid—the transfer of skills and knowledge to the Egyptians; and food aid—concessional shipments of surplus US agricultural commodities.

[2] See "The Nature of the US-UAR Relationship," Benjamin Read to McGeorge Bundy, 10 August 1964, Johnson Library, National Security File (NSF), Countries, UAR, vol. 2.

[3] James E. Dougherty, "The Aswan Decision in Perspective," *Political Science Quarterly*, March 1959, p. 21.

[4] Constance Parry Faulkner, "The Economic Effects of US PL480 in the UAR" (University of Utah, Ph.D. thesis, 1969), p. 1.

[5] "Interim Evaluation and Termination Report," Athens Embassy Telegram (Embtel) 25, 22 July 1967.

[6] The best known defense of the syllogism noted above is probably Max F. Millikan and Walt W. Rostow, *A Proposal: Key to an Effective Foreign Policy* (New York: Harper, 1957).

[7] See Sidney Weintraub (editor), *Economic Coercion and US Foreign Policy* (Boulder, Colorado: Westview Press, 1982), pp. 19–20. Weintraub's section on "theory and analysis" (pp. 3–72) provides valuable insights into the potential and limits of economic instruments of foreign policy. The introductory and concluding chapters of this book owe much to Weintraub's careful assessment.

[8] Hugh Thomas, *Suez* (New York: Harper and Row, 1966), p. 31.

[9] Henry A. Byroade to author.

Chapter One

[1] *New York Times,* 22 October 1955.

[2] See State Department Office of Intelligence and Research (OIR) report #7577.1, "Egypt: Motivations, Capabilities, and Trends," 4 September 1957. National Archives, Diplomatic Branch.

[3] For a thoughtful analysis of Egyptian foreign policy in the 1950s, see Malcolm Kerr's unpublished paper entitled "Egyptian Foreign Policy and the Revolution" (n.d.), found in the Egyptian press clippings file of the Middle East Centre Library, St. Antony's College, Oxford.

[4] Nasser suggested in a series of articles in the Egyptian weekly *Akher Sa'a* in the latter part of 1953 that Egypt was destined to play a leading role in three geopolitical "circles": the Arab circle, the African circle, and the Islamic circle. See Nasser's *Philosophy of the Revolution,* translated by Richard H. Nolte (Cairo: American Universities Field Staff, March 1954), pp. 31–43.

[5] *Al Ahram,* 31 December 1965.

[6] See Adeed Dawisha's *Egypt in the Arab World: The Elements of Foreign Policy* (London: Macmillan, 1976).

[7] See Karen Dawisha, *Soviet Foreign Policy Towards Egypt* (London: Macmillan, 1979), pp. 178–79.

[8] See Cairo Embtel 1352, 12 January 1955. Washington National Records Center (WNRC), Record Group (RG) 84, Box 264.

[9] *New York Times,* 8 August 1952.

[10] Barry Rubin provides an invaluable account of US-Egyptian relations in the early 1950s in chapter 14 ("Egypt's Revolution, Israel, and America: 1950–56") of his *The Arab States and the Palestine Conflict* (Syracuse: Syracuse University Press, 1981). I am indebted to Dr. Rubin for his kind advice in the early stages of my research.

[11] In 1950, two-thirds of the world's proven oil deposits were located in the Middle East (for the purposes of this study, the "Middle East" refers to Morocco, Algeria, Tunisia, Libya, Egypt, Sudan, Israel, Lebanon, Jordan, Syria, Turkey, Iraq, Saudi Arabia and the countries of the Arabian Peninsula, and Iran). Although the United States was not dependent on Middle East oil in this period, America's NATO allies relied on the Middle East for about 60 percent of the oil that they consumed annually. See Finer, pp. 12–13.

[12] Raymond Hare, oral history, Columbia University Oral History Collection (COH), p. 56.

[13] The Free Officers enlisted Naguib to lend credibility to their efforts and to reinforce the moderate image that they sought to project. Naguib describes his role in the revolution candidly in his memoirs. The Free Officers, said Naguib, "realized that a successful revolution could not be carried out by a group of junior officers unless they were led by a senior officer with special qualifications. I was that senior officer." See Mohamed Naguib, *Egypt's Destiny* (Garden City, N.Y.: Doubleday, 1955), p. 29.

[14] Cairo Embtel 271, 5 August 1952. WNRC, RG 84, Box 220.

[15] In a 1955 study of Arab public opinion, 90 percent of those questioned held the United States—either alone or with the other Western powers—

responsible for the creation of Israel and the partition of Palestine. The author of the study concluded that "American policy toward Palestine is the principal Arab grievance against the United States." See H.P. Castleberry, "The Arabs' View of Postwar American Foreign Policy: Retrospect and Prospect." *Western Political Quarterly*, March 1959, p. 19.

[16] Parker Hart to Joseph Kraft in Kraft's "Those Arabists in the State Department," *New York Times Magazine*, 7 November 1971, p. 82.

[17] Henry Byroade to author.

[18] Miles Copeland's *The Game of Nations* (London: Weidenfeld and Nicolson, 1969) has often been misinterpreted, particularly in Egypt, to suggest that the CIA organized or supported the Free Officers' coup. The available evidence indicates that the Cairo CIA station was caught by surprise on the night of 22–23 July 1952, and that the Cairo Embassy first made contact with the Free Officers after the revolt had begun through Lt. Col. David Evans, the assistant Air Force attaché. Kermit Roosevelt to author. See also Mohamed Hassanein Heikal, *The Cairo Documents* (Garden City, N.Y.: Doubleday, 1973), p. 34; Jean and Simone Lacouture, *Egypt in Transition* (London: Methuen, 1962), p. 212; and Cairo Embtel 140, 23 July 1952. WNRC, RG 84, Box 228.

[19] Wilbur Crane Eveland, *Ropes of Sand: America's Failure in the Middle East* (New York: Norton, 1980), p. 103.

[20] Rubin, p. 223, and Kermit Roosevelt to author. See also Eveland, p. 104; and Copeland, pp. 64–108.

[21] The best study of US-Egyptian arms negotiations in the early 1950s can be found in Chapter 6 ("Arms for Egypt: The Litmus Test") of Paul Jabber's *Not by War Alone* (Berkeley: University of California Press, 1981).

[22] See Egyptian request of 15 October 1952 in WNRC, RG 84, Box 218.

[23] Greco Memorandum for Caffery, 21 October 1952, WNRC, RG 84, Box 218.

[24] See Caffery to Acheson, 26 September 1952 and Acheson to Caffery, 2 October 1952, in WNRC, RG 84, Box 218.

[25] Kermit Roosevelt to author.

[26] *New York Times*, 4 September 1952.

[27] Byroade to author. See also Jabber, pp. 133–134; Love, p. 280; Anthony Nutting, *Nasser* (London: Constable, 1972), p. 46; and Heikal, *Cairo Documents*, p. 37.

[28] The 1936 Anglo-Egyptian Treaty of Alliance, unilaterally abrogated by the Farouk government in October 1951, provided for a British military presence at Suez. Expanded during the Second World War, the Suez Canal Base had become by 1953 the largest Western military installation outside Britain and the United States, housing some 75,000 British troops. See *The Guardian*, February 19, 1953.

[29] Nutting, *Nasser*, p. 49; and Jabber, pp. 136–139. See also Air Chief Marshal Sir William Elliot's letter to the Chairman of the Joint Chiefs of Staff, General Omar Bradley, and Bradley's reply of 23 January 1953 in National Archives, Modern Military Branch, Bradley Files, Box 5.

[30] See Foster Dulles memoranda for Eisenhower, 15 June 1953 and 17 June 1953. Eisenhower Library, Foster Dulles Papers, Box 1.

[31] Lakeland memcon, 15 November 1952. WNRC, RG 84, Box 216.

[32] For more detailed consideration of the Sabri mission, see Jabber, pp. 133–134; Heikal, *Cairo Documents*, pp. 37–39; and Copeland, pp. 145–46.

[33] Copeland, p.146.

[34] Cairo Embtel 1268, 21 November 1952. WNRC, RG 84, Box 216.

[35] See, for example, Caffery to Acheson, 3 January 1953; and Caffery to Dulles, 2 March 1953. WNRC, RG 84, Box 216.

[36] See Dulles's confidential testimony to the Senate Foreign Relations Committee (SFRC), 3 June 1953, in *Executive Sessions of the Senate Foreign Relations Committee*, vol. 5 (1953), (Washington: Government Printing Office, 1978), pp. 439–40.

[37] President Eisenhower repeated Dulles's promise of aid in a letter to Naguib dated 15 July 1953. See Eisenhower Library, Eisenhower Papers, International Series, Box 8. The United States had already begun to furnish Point Four technical aid to Egypt. Between 1951 and 1955, Point Four aid to Egypt totalled about $20 million, and involved more than one hundred American advisers. See "Point Four and the UAR," *Egyptian Economic and Political Review*, January 1961.

[38] See "Conclusions on Trip," February 1953, and "Important Points of Trip," probably late May or early June 1953, Foster Dulles Papers, Princeton University, Box 73.

[39] Caffery to Dulles, 31 March 1954. WNRC, RG 84, Box 2672.

[40] Rubin, p. 223.

[41] Dulles to Stassen, 27 July 1954. Eisenhower Library, Foster Dulles Papers, Telephone Conversations Series, Box 3.

[42] Cairo Embtel 144, 2 August 1954. WNRC, RG 84, Box 221.

[43] See Jabber, p. 150.

[44] The Tripartite Declaration, issued by the United States, Britain, and France on 25 May 1950, expressed the three Powers' concern over the possible development of an arms race between the Arab states and Israel. The Declaration conditioned future arms shipments to the protagonists in the Arab-Israeli conflict on assurances that such weaponry would not be used for any aggressive purpose. See text in J.C. Hurewitz, *Diplomacy in the Near and Middle East: A Documentary Record* (Princeton: Van Nostrand, 1956), ii, p. 308.

[45] *U.S. News and World Report*, 13 August 1954.

[46] Cairo Embtel 268, 29 August 1954. WNRC, RG 84, Box 2671.

[47] See Burdett's memcon, 31 August 1954. WNRC, RG 84, Box 2671. The Moslem Brotherhood, founded in 1928 by Hasan el-Banna, was dedicated to the expulsion of the British from Egypt by violent means and to the application of Islamic law to Egyptian society. The Moslem Brothers and the Free Officers had cooperated in the 1952 coup, but friction between the RCC and the Brotherhood developed and increased rapidly in 1953–54. The Wafd, the largest political party in prerevolutionary Egypt, retained considerable support in the countryside after July 1952, and sniped constantly at RCC policies in hopes that it might one day displace the Free Officers and regain power. The tiny Egyptian Communist party struggled against the RCC much as it had struggled against the Farouk government.

[48] See Cairo Embtel 271, 30 August 1954. WNRC, RG 84, Box 2671. The United States eventually provided the Egyptian government with $40 million in economic aid in fiscal year 1955 (1 July 1954 to 30 June 1955).

[49] For detailed accounts of the Gerhardt-Eveland mission, see Eveland, pp. 90–112; Copeland, pp. 123–30; and Jabber, p. 150.

[50] Nutting, *Nasser*, pp. 72–73.

[51] Rubin, p. 224.

[52] Sherman Adams, *Firsthand Report* (New York: Harper, 1961), pp. 247–48.

[53] For an incisive study of the Israel lobby, see Kennan Lee Teslik, *Congress, the Executive Branch, and Special Interests* (Westport, Conn.: Greenwood, 1982), pp. 31–46.

[54] See Earl Dean Huff, "Zionist Influences Upon United States Foreign Policy: A Study of American Policy Toward the Middle East from the Time of the Struggle for Israel to the Sinai Conflict" (University of Idaho Ph.D. thesis, 1971), p. 22.

[55] Steven Fred Windmueller, "American Jewish Interest Groups: Their Roles in Shaping U.S. Foreign Policy in the Middle East: A Study of Two Time Periods: 1945–48, 1955–58" (University of Pennsylvania Ph.D. thesis, 1973), p. 151.

[56] Russell Warren Howe and Sarah Hays Trott, *The Power Peddlers* (Garden City, N.Y.: Doubleday, 1977), p. 288.

[57] See Teslik, p. 31.

[58] Love, p. 272. One common criticism of the American media's treatment of the Arab-Israeli conflict in this period is that it made little effort to improve the American public's understanding of the Arab world, and in fact helped to perpetuate widely-held myths about Arab malevolence. See, for example, Michael Suleiman, "National Stereotypes as Weapons in the Arab-Israeli Conflict," *Journal of Palestine Studies*, Spring 1974; Robert H. Trice, "The American Elite Press and the Arab-Israeli Conflict," *Middle East Journal*, Summer 1979; and Shelley Slade, "The Image of the Arab in America: Analysis of a Poll on American Attitudes," *Middle East Journal*, Spring 1981.

[59] See William B. Quandt, "Domestic Influences on U.S. Foreign Policy in the Middle East: The View From Washington," in Willard A. Beling, *The Middle East: Quest for an American Policy* (Albany, N.Y.: State University of New York, 1973), p. 282.

[60] Huff, p. 41. In the 1950s, 87 percent of American Jews lived in metropolitan areas; the American Jewish community was the most highly urbanized ethnic group in the United States. See Windmueller, p. 151.

[61] Isaiah Kenen to author.

[62] Stephen D. Isaacs, *Jews and American Politics* (Garden City, N.Y.: Doubleday, 1974), p. 152.

[63] See Robert J. Donovan, *Eisenhower: The Inside Story* (London: Hamish Hamilton, 1956), p. 67; and Huff, p. 166.

[64] Finer, pp. 13–14. This comment exposed Eisenhower to groundless charges of anti-Semitism. As Judah Nadich writes in *Eisenhower and the Jews* (New York: Twayne, 1953), p. 20: "Eisenhower's treatment of the Jewish displaced persons whom his armies liberated from the Nazi concentration

camps was marked by understanding and sympathy. His friendship for the Jews left no room for doubt."

[65] Finer, p. 14.

[66] Between 1948 and 1952, for example, Israel received $173 million in United States economic aid; similar aid to the Arab states *totalled* less than $36 million. See Huff, p. 159.

[67] See Kraft, p. 88.

[68] See Teslik, pp. 31–46.

[69] Nick Thimmesch, "These Men Have a Pipeline to the Heartland," *Washington Post Magazine*, 20 June 1976, p. 14.

[70] See Leonard Mosley, *Dulles: A Biography of Eleanor, Allen, and John Foster Dulles and Their Family Network* (New York: Dial, 1978), p. 384.

[71] Byroade to author. See also Eveland, pp. 90–92.

[72] See, for example, Dulles's account of a conversation with Naguib in "Important Points of Trip," Dulles Papers, Princeton, pp. 1–2.

[73] See William C. Burdett's memorandum of conversation with Ambassador Abba Eban, Minister Reuven Shiloah, and Assistant Secretary of State Byroade, 30 July 1954. WNRC, RG 84, Box 2672; and General Walter Bedell Smith's memorandum of conversation with Ambassador Eban and Minister Shiloah, 5 August 1954. WNRC, RG 84, Box 2671.

[74] Dulles to Caffery, 3 August 1954. WNRC, RG 84, Box 2671.

[75] Francis Russell to author; Francis Russell, oral history, John Foster Dulles Oral History Collection (DOH), Princeton University; and Eveland, p. 125. For the Alpha Group's estimate of the financial contribution that the United States government would have to make to underwrite the costs of Palestinian resettlement and regional development, see Russell to Foster Dulles, 14 February 1955. Eisenhower Library, Foster Dulles Papers, Box 3.

[76] Byroade to author; Parker Hart to author. Nasser later told Assistant Secretary of State George Allen that Foster had "promised" Egypt $60 million worth of military equipment. See Cairo Embtel 632, 10 October 1955.

[77] With the loss of the Suez Base, Britain had begun to build up its political-military position in Iraq, where it had base rights that were due to expire in October 1957. According to the Foreign Service officer then serving as the Middle East specialist in the United States Embassy in London, the British government "seized upon the idea of Iraqi membership in a regional alliance as a means of promoting its own objectives in the Middle East." Evan Wilson to author. See also Lord Selwyn Lloyd, *Suez 1956* (New York: Mayflower, 1978), pp. 26–27.

[78] Jabber, pp.153–154.

[79] *New York Times*, 4 April 1955.

[80] On 1 March 1955, the American Embassy in Cairo reported that "Nasser sincerely feels he was cast aside by the United States in favor of Nuri of Iraq," and that the Egyptian leader believed that the Eisenhower Administration had deliberately rejected Nasser's scheme of an Egyptian-dominated Arab alliance loosely associated with the West in favor of a formal defense arrangement between the West and some Arab states. See Cairo Embtel 1261, 1 March 1955.

[81] For detailed consideration of the Gaza Raid, see Love, Chapter 1.

[82] Rubin, p. 226.

[83] Eban, oral history, DOH, p. 16.

[84] See Moshe Dayan, *Story of My Life* (New York: William Morrow, 1976), pp. 176–77.

[85] See Gideon Rafael, *Destination Peace* (London: Weidenfeld and Nicolson, 1981), pp. 36–41.

[86] Love, Chapter 1. See also Cairo Embtel 1270, 2 March 1955; Cairo Embtel 1282, 4 March 1955; Cairo Embtel 1306, 8 March 1955; Cairo Embtel 1396, 24 March 1955; and George Allen to Foster Dulles, "United States Reaction to Israeli Attack on Gaza," 9 March 1955.

[87] Anwar Sadat, *In Search of Identity* (New York: Harper and Row, 1977), p. 135.

[88] One member of the RCC later described the state of the Egyptian military at the time of the Gaza Raid as follows: "We were desperately weak. Our armed forces were short of everything. At the time of the Gaza Raid, Egypt had six serviceable planes, about thirty others were grounded for lack of spare parts: Britain had stopped deliveries. We estimated that our tank ammunition would last for a one hour battle. Nearly 60 percent of our tanks were in need of major repairs. Our artillery was in the same deplorable state. We were even short of small arms." Saleh Salem to Patrick Seale in Seale's *The Struggle for Syria* (London: Oxford, 1965), p. 234. See also OIR report #7042, "The Mainsprings of Egyptian Foreign Policy", 12 September 1955. National Archives, Diplomatic Branch.

[89] See OIR report #6830.4, "Developments Relating to the Bandung Conference," 1 April 1955. National Archives, Diplomatic Branch.

[90] See Gail Meyer, pp. 118–120. *The United States and Egypt: The Formative Years*, (Rutherford, N.J.: Fairleigh Dickinson University Press, 1980).

[91] Meyer, p. 119.

[92] *Egyptian Gazette*, 26 April 1955. Also quoted in Meyer, p. 119.

[93] Meyer, p. 120.

[94] "The Soviet Union and Egypt," CIA Office of Current Intelligence, 8 May 1964. Johnson Library, President's Office Files (POF), Countries, UAR Series.

[95] In October 1954, for example, the Soviet government made a $2-million loan to Afghanistan to finance the cost of paving the streets of Kabul, a commitment that reflected the Soviet penchant for dramatic "impact" projects that focused maximum popular attention upon Soviet aid. On a highly publicized Asian tour early in 1955, Khrushchev also announced that the Soviet government would build the Bhilai steel mill for India, at an estimated cost to the USSR of $136 million. See Marshall Goldman, *Soviet Foreign Aid* (New York: Praeger, 1967), p. 115. For more detailed consideration of Kremlin infighting over policy in the Third World, see Uri Ra'anan, *The USSR Arms the Third World* (Cambridge, Mass.: MIT, 1969), pp. 86–102.

[96] "The Soviet Arms Offer to Egypt," CIA Office of Current Intelligence, p. 1.

[97] Ra'anan, pp. 145–46.

[98] See Cairo Embtel 1881, 9 June 1955; Byroade's testimony to the Senate Foreign Relations Committee (SFRC) in SFRC *Hearings on the Eisenhower*

Doctrine (1957), p. 714; *New York Times*, 14 November 1955. Byroade, formerly Assistant Secretary of State for Near Eastern Affairs, had served to the rank of Brigadier General in the United States Army during the 1930s and 1940s. Foster Dulles thought that Byroade's military background and relative youth (he was thirty-seven, the same age as Nasser, when he took up the Cairo post) would enable him to get on well with Nasser and the other members of the RCC. Byroade to author.

⁹⁹ Byroade, Parker Hart, and Fraser Wilkins to author. See also *New York Times*, 14 November 1955; and Dwight D. Eisenhower, *Waging Peace* (London: Heinemann, 1965), p. 24, for Eisenhower's comment that the State Department had been "confident that Nasser was short of money" when it made its offer of cash sales.

¹⁰⁰ See "The Soviet Arms Offer To Egypt," CIA Office of Current Intelligence, pp. 1–5.

¹⁰¹ Kermit Roosevelt to author. See also Eveland, p. 132.

¹⁰² Eveland, p. 147n.

¹⁰³ Peter Lyon, *Eisenhower: Portrait of a Hero* (Boston: Little Brown, 1974), p. 683.

¹⁰⁴ Ra'anan, pp.152–54.

¹⁰⁵ See Heikal, *Cairo Documents*, p. 46; and Meyer, p. 121.

¹⁰⁶ For more detailed consideration of the Shepilov visit, see Heikal, *Sphinx and Commissar*, pp. 59–60; Jabber, p. 166; Love, p. 244; Nutting, *Nasser*, pp. 103–104; and Ra'anan, pp. 152–54.

¹⁰⁷ "The Soviet Arms Offer to Egypt," CIA Office of Current Intelligence, pp. 2–3; and Cairo Embtel 234, 15 August 1955.

¹⁰⁸ Byroade to author. See also Byroade's retrospective comments on Nasser's need to respond to pressures from the military in September 1955 in Cairo Embtel 2515, 16 June 1956.

¹⁰⁹ Kermit Roosevelt to author. See also Cabell to Foster Dulles, 29 August 1955. Eisenhower Library, Dulles Papers, Telephone Conversations Series, Box 4; and Jabber, p. 167.

¹¹⁰ Dulles to Hoover, 20 September 1955. Eisenhower Library, Dulles Papers, Telephone Conversations Series, Box 4.

¹¹¹ Kermit Roosevelt and Miles Copeland to author. See also Copeland, pp. 134–36.

¹¹² Love, p. 248. Moshe Dayan, pp. 179–80, claims that as a result of the September 1955 arms agreement Egypt received "three hundred medium and heavy tanks of the latest Soviet type, two hundred armored personnel carriers, one hundred armored self-propelled guns, 200 MIG–15 jet fighters, fifty Ilyushin bombers, transport planes, radar systems, two destroyers, four minesweepers, twelve torpedo boats, ammunition, spare parts, ground equipment for aircraft, hundreds of battle vehicles of various types, and thousands of semiautomatic rifles." Although the scope of the initial Egyptian arms arrangement with the Soviet bloc is still unclear, contemporary estimates were somewhat less extravagant than Dayan's. See, for example, *New York Times*, 24 September 1955; OIR report #6675/s, "Recent Developments in Trade Relations Between Egypt and the Soviet Bloc," 18 January 1956. National Archives, Diplomatic Branch; and the testimony of Admiral Arthur

Radford, Chairman of the Joint Chiefs of Staff, to SFRC, *Executive Sessions (1957)*, p. 147. For text of Nasser's 27 September speech and summary of Cairo press comments, see Cairo Embtel 585, 28 September 1955; Cairo Despatch 359, 29 September 1955; and Cairo Embtel 602, 29 September 1955.

[113] See Lyon, p. 684.

[114] Dulles to Hoover and Dulles to Allen, 28 September 1955. Eisenhower Library, Dulles Papers, Telephone Conversations Series, Box 4. Dulles and Hoover had by this point begun to lose confidence in Byroade, who had had a public row with Nasser on the evening of 26 September over alleged mistreatment of the American Embassy's labor attaché. See Copeland, pp. 137–139; and Mosley, pp. 389–391.

[115] Parker Hart to author. Nasser did assure Allen that he was "even more concerned to prevent Communist activity . . . than Secretary Dulles could possibly be, because Egypt is the country directly involved." See Allen's report of his first meeting with Nasser in Cairo Embtel 632, 1 October 1955. See also Love, pp. 285–89.

[116] J.C. Hurewitz, "Our Mistakes in the Middle East," *Atlantic Monthly* (December 1956), p. 46. Also quoted in Rubin, p. 235.

[117] Finer, p. 28.

[118] See Meyer, pp. 124–25.

[119] Rubin, p. 234.

[120] Rubin, p. 234.

[121] Board of National Estimates to Allen Dulles, 29 November 1955. Allen Dulles Papers, Princeton University; and Barry Rubin's unpublished paper, "America and the Egyptian Revolution, 1950–57," p. 23. See also Rubin, *Arab States and Palestine Conflict*, p. 230.

[122] Fraser Wilkins to author.

[123] Rubin, *Arab States and Palestine Conflict*, p. 234.

Chapter Two

[1] Raymond Hare to author.

[2] OIR report #7074, "The Outlook for U.S. Interests in the Middle East," 14 November 1955. National Archives, Diplomatic Branch, p. 3. In an Anglo-American discussion of the arms deal on 3 October in Washington, Raymond Hare noted that "it now seems clear, following the talks of the British ambassador and Assistant Secretary Allen with Nasser, that blocking the deal completely is out of the question and that even the possibility of substantial modification is doubtful." Memcon, "Call of the British Foreign Secretary Regarding the Soviet-Egyptian Arms Agreement," 3 October 1955, p. 1. For a similar argument, see Allen Dulles to Foster Dulles, n.d. (probably October or November 1955). Eisenhower Library, Foster Dulles Papers, White House Memoranda Series, Box 8.

[3] Byroade to author. See also Cairo Embtel 661, 5 October 1955; and Cairo Embtel 668, 6 October 1955.

[4] Dulles to Hoover, 27 September 1955. Eisenhower Library, Foster Dulles Papers, Telephone Conversations Series, Box 4.

[5] Byroade, Parker Hart, and Kermit Roosevelt to author. See also Sherman Adams, p. 197.

[6] Memcon, "Call of British Foreign Secretary," 3 October 1955, p. 2.

[7] Memcon, "Call of British Foreign Secretary," p. 2.

[8] See Foster Dulles's Memorandum of Conversation with President Eisenhower and Robert Anderson, 11 January 1956. Eisenhower Library, Foster Dulles Papers, White House Memoranda Series, Box 4.

[9] See Francis Russell's comments in "Call of British Foreign Secretary," p. 3.

[10] See Robert W. Rycroft and Joseph S. Szyliowicz, "The Technological Dimensions of Decision Making: The Case of the Aswan High Dam," *World Politics* (October 1980), p. 42.

[11] See Keith Wheelock, *Nasser's New Egypt* (New York: Praeger, 1960), pp. 181–82; Sadat, p. 129; John Waterbury, *Hydropolitics of the Nile Valley* (Syracuse, N.Y.: Syracuse University, 1979), pp. 100–102; "The High Dam", *Egyptian Economic and Political Review* (September 1954); Yusuf A. Shibl, "The Aswan High Dam" (Beirut: The Arab Institute for Research and Publishing, 1971), pp. 29–31; and UAR Ministry of Power, "The Aswan High Dam" (Aswan: High Dam Authority Public Relations Department, May 1964).

[12] See Rycroft and Szyliowicz, p. 42.

[13] This board consisted of five Americans, one Frenchman, and one German. UAR State Information Service, "Egypt's High Dam" (Cairo: n.d.), p. 8. See also Meyer, pp. 130–31; Tom Little, *High Dam at Aswan: The Subjugation of the Nile* (New York: John Day, 1965), pp. 69–92; Eugene Black, oral history, DOH, pp. 1–2; and Wheelock, p. 180.

[14] See Rycroft and Szyliowicz, pp. 43–44.

[15] *The Times*, (London) 31 January 1956.

[16] The immediate source of Sudanese-Egyptian discord in 1955 was Egyptian meddling in the Sudanese elections in the spring of 1955. For further background on Sudanese-Egyptian tensions and on the Nile Waters controversy, see *The Times*, (London) 12 April 1956; Wheelock, pp. 183–189; James E. Dougherty, "The Aswan Decision in Perspective," *Political Science Quarterly* (March 1959), p. 23n; and Sudan Ministry of Irrigation and Hydroelectric Power, "The Nile Waters Question" (Khartoum, December 1955).

[17] See Meyer, pp. 132–33; Rycroft and Szyliowicz, p. 48; and Dougherty, p. 23n.

[18] See Eugene Black, oral history, DOH, pp. 1–3; Edward S. Mason and Robert E. Asher, *The World Bank Since Bretton Woods* (Washington, D.C.: Brookings, 1973), pp. 629–632; Love, pp. 301–302; and Waterbury, *Hydropolitics of the Nile Valley*, p. 103.

[19] See Black to Eisenhower, 22 April 1953. Eisenhower Library, Ann Whitman Papers, International Series, Box 8; and Black, oral history, DOH, pp. 2–3. The indefatigable Adrien Daninos had tried unsuccessfully to interest the Truman Administration in the High Dam project in the late 1940s and early 1950s. See Daninos to Acheson, 18 September 1952. WNRC, RG 84, Box 219.

[20] *Al Ahram*, 7 October 1953. Also quoted in Meyer, p. 132.

[21] See Eugene Black, oral history, DOH, p. 4.

[22] In a cable to Dulles on 26 May 1956, Byroade recalled that "word that the Russians might do the [Aswan] project prompted a desire on our part for quick action." See Cairo Embtel 2347, 26 May 1956.

[23] *New York Times*, 11 October 1955.

[24] *Al Akhbar*, 12 October 1955 and *New York Times*, 13 October 1955. See also *Le Journal d'Egypte*, 18 and 21 October, 1955.

[25] See Heikal, *Cairo Documents*, pp. 58–59; Saleh Salem to Patrick Seale in *Struggle for Syria*, p. 336; and Burdett to Wilkins, 12 October 1955.

[26] Byroade to author. In a cable to Dulles on 25 November, Byroade emphasized that Nasser "unquestionably prefers Western assistance to Soviet aid regarding which performance unknown and untested." Cairo Embtel 1016, 25 November 1955.

[27] See Heikal, *Cairo Documents*, p. 59; Byroade to author; Miles Copeland to author; and OIR report #6675/s, "Recent Developments in Trade Relations Between Egypt and the Soviet Bloc."

[28] Nutting, *Nasser*, p. 130. See also David Carlton, *Anthony Eden* (London: Allen Lane, 1981), pp. 390–91.

[29] In a *Sunday Times* interview in 1962, Nasser complained about what he had perceived to be Eden's condescending attitude during their 1955 meeting, asserting that Eden had treated him "like a junior official who could not be expected to understand politics." *Sunday Times*, 24 June 1962. See also Heikal, *Cairo Documents*, pp. 77–81; Nutting, *Nasser*, p. 89; Nutting, *No End of a Lesson* (London: Constable, 1967), p. 21; Selwyn Lloyd, p. 27.

[30] Sir Harold Beeley to author; Nutting, *No End of a Lesson*, pp. 22–23. Eden had played a prominent personal role in the compromise arrangements which ended the Korean and Indochina wars, the Yugoslav-Italian conflict over Trieste, the East-West conflict over Austrian independence, and the Suez Base dispute.

[31] Sir Anthony Eden, *Full Circle* (London: Cassell, 1960), p. 420; Selwyn Lloyd, pp. 28–29; and Harold Macmillan, *Tides of Fortune* (London: Macmillan, 1969), pp. 639–642. Eden has sometimes been erroneously portrayed as having been unenthusiastic about Western aid for the High Dam in this period. See, for example, Dougherty, p. 25; and Richard Neustadt, *Alliance Politics* (New York: Columbia University, 1970), p. 11n.

[32] Winthrop Aldrich, oral history, DOH, pp. 6–7; *Washington Post*, 8 January 1957; and Evan Wilson to author.

[33] Roger Makins (now Lord Sherfield) to author; Sir Willie Morris to author.

[34] Macmillan, *Tides of Fortune*, p. 642. See also Selwyn Lloyd, p. 29.

[35] Roger Makins, oral history, DOH, p. 5.

[36] See John Hollister, oral history, DOH, pp. 44–45; State Department Telegram (Deptel) 580 to Cairo, 3 March 1955. WNRC, RG 84, Box 264; Finer, pp. 37–38; and Morton Berkowitz, P.G. Bock, and Vincent J. Fuccillo, *The Politics of American Foreign Policy* (Englewood Cliffs, N.J.: Prentice Hall, 1977), p. 78.

[37] Kermit Roosevelt and Miles Copeland to author.

[38] See George Allen, oral history, DOH, pp. 30–31; George Allen, oral history, COH, pp. 69–70; and Finer, p. 51.

[39] Byroade to author; Cairo Embtel 1034, 28 November 1955. See also Love, p. 305.

[40] During the Eisenhower years, Humphrey was the ringleader of the "4H Club," a group of tightfisted government officials which included Herbert Hoover, Jr., Budget Director Rowland R. Hughes, and ICA Director John B. Hollister. The "4H Club" waged an intermittent bureaucratic struggle against a small circle of aid supporters led by Vice President Nixon and Secretary of State Dulles. See Robert P. Donovan, p. 388.

[41] George Humphrey, oral history, DOH, p. 23. See also Eugene Black, oral history, DOH, p. 25; George Humphrey, *The Basic Papers of George Humphrey, 1953–57*, edited by Nathaniel R. Howard (Cleveland: Western Reserve Historical Society, 1965), pp. xxv–xxvi; and Hoopes, p. 338.

[42] See Emmet John Hughes, *The Ordeal of Power* (London: Macmillan, 1963), pp. 71–74.

[43] Andrew Rice, "Building a Constituency for the Foreign Aid Program: The Record of the Eisenhower Years" (Syracuse University Ph.D. thesis, 1963), p. 19.

[44] See Samuel Huntington, "Foreign Aid: For What and For Whom," *Foreign Policy* (Winter 1970–71 and Spring 1971), p. 118.

[45] For a lucid exposition of this theme, see Robert Packenham, *Liberal America and the Third World* (Princeton: Princeton University, 1976 paperback edition).

[46] Joan Nelson, *Aid, Influence, and Foreign Policy* (New York: Macmillan, 1968), p. 5.

[47] During the Marshall Plan years, polls showed that better than 80 percent of the American public approved of the foreign assistance program. By the mid-1950s, that figure had been cut in half. See H. Field Haviland, "Foreign Aid and the Policy Process: 1957," *American Political Science Review* (September 1958), p. 700; and Michael Kent O'Leary, *The Politics of American Foreign Aid* (New York: Atherton Press, 1967), pp. 22–26.

[48] See David A. Baldwin, *Foreign Aid and American Foreign Policy* (New York: Praeger, 1966), p. 5.

[49] Baldwin, p. 6.

[50] Dan Morgan, *Merchants of Grain* (New York: Viking, 1979), p. 301. See also Douglas Cater, *Power in Washington* (London: Collins, 1965), p. 149.

[51] John Montgomery, *The Politics of Foreign Aid* (New York: Praeger, 1962), p. 199.

[52] See Frank Coffin, *Witness for AID* (Boston: Houghton Mifflin, 1964), Chapter 4; and William D. Anderson, "The Intersection of Foreign and Domestic Policy: The Examples in Public Law 480" (University of Illinois Ph.D. thesis, 1970), pp. 221–222.

[53] Isaiah Kenen to author.

[54] Kenen to author; *New York Times*, 16, 29 November 1955 and 7 February 1956; Don W. Harrell, "The Attitudes of the Congress Toward the Middle East" (American University M.A. thesis, 1963), pp. 32–33; Huff, pp. 190–192; and Eisenhower, *Waging Peace*, p. 25.

[55] Abba Eban, oral history, DOH, pp. 30–31. See also Jacob Javits, oral history, DOH; and Windmueller, p. 264.

[56] State Department memorandum, "U.S. Policy on Financing the High Aswan Dam in Egypt," 2 December 1955.

[57] Minutes of Bipartisan Legislative Leaders Meeting, 13 December 1955. Eisenhower Library, Ann Whitman Papers, Ann Whitman Diary Series, Box 7; Sherman Adams, p. 197; and Love, p. 324. Interestingly enough, the Soviet government apparently feared that Western aid for the Dam would bind Egypt to the West for a decade or more. At about the same time that Dulles was reassuring Lyndon Johnson, the Soviet ambassador in Cairo reportedly confided to his Indian counterpart that he believed that Egypt "would remain on the Western side for twenty years if the West built the High Dam." See Humphrey Trevelyan, *The Middle East in Revolution* (Boston: Gambit, 1970), p. 49.

[58] Eisenhower to Foster Dulles, 5 December 1955. Eisenhower Library, Foster Dulles Papers, White House Memoranda Series, Box 3.

[59] Eisenhower to Foster Dulles, 5 December 1955.

[60] Foster Dulles to Eisenhower, 29 November 1955. Eisenhower Library, Foster Dulles Papers, Telephone Conversations Series, Box 11.

[61] See text of Dulles's address (State Department press release #5.7, 26 August 1955) and an earlier draft of the speech in Eisenhower Library, Foster Dulles Papers, Subject Series, Box 1. See also Foster Dulles to Eisenhower, 19 August 1955. Eisenhower Library, Foster Dulles Papers, White House Memoranda Series, Box 3; Francis Russell to Foster Dulles, 14 February 1955. Eisenhower Library, Foster Dulles Papers, White House Memoranda Series, Box 3; and Francis Russell to author.

[62] Hagerty to Foster Dulles, 29 August 1955, Eisenhower Library, Foster Dulles Papers, Telephone Conversations Series, Box 10.

[63] Foster Dulles to Eisenhower, 1 September 1955. Eisenhower Library, Foster Dulles Papers, White House Memoranda Series, Box 3.

[64] Byroade to author. Parker Hart confirmed that Nasser had expressed some interest in Dulles's Alpha proposals, but Hart was less sanguine than Byroade about Nasser's sincerity. Hart to author.

[65] See Eden, p. 330; Macmillan, *Tides of Fortune*, p. 631; Wilton Wynn, *Nasser of Egypt: The Search for Dignity* (Cambridge, Mass.: Arlington Books, 1959), pp. 128–146; and *New York Times*, 27 November 1955.

[66] See Dulles's comments on "pushing Egypt along on a settlement with Israel" in "Call of British Foreign Secretary," 3 October 1955, p. 4.

[67] Foster Dulles's memcon with Eisenhower and Robert B. Anderson, 11 January 1956. Eisenhower Library, Foster Dulles Papers, White House Memoranda Series, Box 4.

[68] Byroade to author. See also Love, pp. 304–305; Eveland, p. 156; and Chester Cooper, *The Lion's Last Roar* (New York: Harper and Row, 1978), p. 95.

[69] Love, p. 307.

[70] Eisenhower diary, 11 January 1956. Eisenhower Library, Ann Whitman Papers, DDE Diary Series, Box 12.

[71] *New York Times*, 12 December 1955.

[72] Roger Makins, oral history, DOH, p. 8; Eugene Black oral history, DOH, p. 8; Sir Willie Morris and Fraser Wilkins to author. See also Deptel 1067 to Cairo, 23 November 1955; and Cairo Embtel 1053, 30 November 1955.

[73] See State Department memorandum, "U.S. Policy on Financing the High Aswan Dam in Egypt," 2 December 1955; Rycroft and Szyliowicz, pp. 53–54; *New York Times*, 18 December 1955; *The Observer*, 18 December 1955; *Guardian*, 19 December 1955; *The Times*, 19 December 1955; and Eisenhower, *Waging Peace*, p. 31. On 14 December 1955, the United States government had also agreed to provide the Egyptians with $17 million worth of surplus wheat. See Faulkner, p. 106; and *New York Times*, 23 January 1956.

[74] See U.S. *aide mémoire*, 16 December 1956, Eisenhower Library, Foster Dulles Papers.

[75] See Waterbury, *Hydropolitics of the Nile Valley*, p. 105; and Love, p. 310.

[76] Kaissouny did express some concern to Byroade about the vagueness of the Western commitment to the final stages of the project. See Cairo Embtel 1203, 28 December 1955.

[77] Cairo Embtel 1214, 29 December 1955. See also Cairo Embtel 1203, 28 December 1955; Meyer, pp. 134–135; M.L. Cooke, *Nasser's Aswan Dam: Panacea or Politics?* (Washington: Public Affairs Institute, 1956), p. 13; Trevelyan, pp. 50–51; and Heikal, *Cairo Documents*, p. 60.

[78] See Heikal, *Cairo Documents*, pp. 60–61; Love, pp. 310–312; and Waterbury, *Hydropolitics of the Nile Valley*, pp. 105–106.

[79] Dulles to Black, 23 January 1956. Eisenhower Library, Foster Dulles Papers, Telephone Conversations Series, Box 5; and Black oral history, DOH, pp. 7–8.

[80] Black, oral history, DOH, p. 8; and *The Financial Times*, 26 January 1956.

[81] See Black, oral history, DOH, pp. 8–9; Love, pp. 311–312; and Heikal, *Cairo Documents*, p. 61.

[82] Kermit Roosevelt and Parker Hart to author; Nutting, *Nasser*, p. 134; and Love, p. 312. See also Rountree's comment to Hoover on 7 February 1956 that "the discussions between Mr. Black of the IBRD and the Egyptians have recently taken a turn for the better" in Rountree to Hoover, 7 February 1956.

[83] See Trevelyan, pp. 52–53; and Rycroft and Szyliowicz, p. 54.

[84] Quoted in Love, p. 313.

[85] Unpublished World Bank Board report quoted in Meyer, p. 34. See also *New York Times*, 10, 13 February 1956; *The Times*, 11 February 1956; and Cairo Embtel 1548, 10 February 1956.

[86] Black, oral history, DOH, p. 11; Love, p. 312. As part of an apparent attempt to drag negotiations out until the United States and Britain modified the terms set out in their *aides-mémoires*, Nasser decided two weeks later to postpone preliminary work on the Dam until agreement on the Nile waters issue had been reached with the Sudanese government. See Cairo Embtel 1665, 23 February 1956.

[87] Black did tell Nasser privately, on Foster Dulles's authorization, that the Eisenhower Administration had secured informal assurances from Congres-

sional leaders that no legislative barriers would be placed in the path of United States aid for the second stage of the High Dam project. Dulles to Black, 23 January 1956; Black oral history, DOH, p. 9.

[88] Black, oral history, DOH, pp. 9–10.

[89] Black, oral history, DOH, p. 22; Byroade to author; and Love, p. 312.

[90] Eisenhower diary, 11 January 1956. Eisenhower Library, Ann Whitman File, DDE Diary Series, Box 12.

[91] See Francis Russell to Foster Dulles and Allen Dulles to Foster Dulles, 23 December 1955. Eisenhower Library, Foster Dulles Papers, Telephone Conversations Series, Box 4; Allen Dulles to Foster Dulles, 6 January 1956. Eisenhower Library, Foster Dulles Papers, Telephone Conversations Series, Box 5; Francis Russell to author; Foster Dulles to Eisenhower, 19 August 1955. Eisenhower Library, Foster Dulles Papers, White House Memoranda Series, Box 3; Eveland, pp. 155–158; and William Bragg Ewald, Jr., *Eisenhower the President: Crucial Days 1951–60* (Englewood Cliffs, N.J.: Prentice Hall, 1981), pp. 191–194.

[92] Byroade to author. See also Byroade's recollection of his reaction to news of the Anderson mission in Cairo Embtel 2347, 20 May 1956. Byroade's relationship with his superiors in the State Department was by this point quite strained. Before he returned to his post in February, Byroade was informed by Foster Dulles that he would probably be reassigned in the spring or summer of 1956. Byroade to author.

[93] Memcon, 11 January 1956. Eisenhower Library, Foster Dulles Papers, White House Memoranda Series, Box 4.

[94] Memcon, 11 January 1956.

[95] Memcon, 11 January 1956.

[96] Memcon, 11 January 1956. See also Ewald, p. 196; and Macmillan, *Tides of Fortune*, pp. 631–633.

[97] Memcon, 11 January 1956.

[98] Memcon, 11 January 1956.

[99] Love, p. 307.

[100] Ewald, p. 194; and Memcon, 11 January 1956.

[101] See Eisenhower to Nasser and Eisenhower to Ben Gurion, 9 January 1956. Eisenhower Library, Ann Whitman File, DDE Diary Series, Box 12. Anderson's mission had been preceded in the summer of 1955 by an unsuccessful private effort by Elmore Jackson, a prominent American Quaker, to arrange direct high-level Egyptian-Israeli peace talks. See Gideon Rafael, pp. 42–44.

[102] Kermit Roosevelt to author; Ewald, pp. 194–195.

[103] Kermit Roosevelt to author.

[104] Kermit Roosevelt and Miles Copeland to author; Heikal, *Cairo Documents*, pp. 55–56; and Ewald, p. 196.

[105] Francis Russell to author; Francis Russell, oral history, DOH, pp. 15–16. See also Rafael, pp. 48–52.

[106] Byroade to author.

[107] Byroade to author. See also Love, p. 309.

[108] Byroade to author; Eugene Black, oral history, DOH, p. 22; Parker Hart to author.

[109] See Eveland, p. 158; and Foster Dulles to Anderson, 3 January 1956. Eisenhower Library, Foster Dulles Papers, Telephone Conversations Series, Box 5.

[110] See Macmillan, *Tides of Fortune*, pp. 653–656; Eden, pp. 341–343; and Selwyn Lloyd, pp. 29–31.

[111] Hermann Eilts (then serving as political officer, U.S. Embassy, Baghdad) to author. See also Macmillan, *Tides of Fortune*, pp. 654–656; and Trevelyan, p. 56.

[112] Macmillan, *Tides of Fortune*, p. 656.

[113] See Trevelyan, p. 57; Meyer, p. 137; and Eden, p. 343.

[114] See King Hussein I of Jordan, *Uneasy Lies the Head* (New York: Bernard Geis Associates, 1963), pp. 91–94; OIR report #7134, "Jordan, the Baghdad Pact and the Arab Legion," 10 January 1956. National Archives, Diplomatic Branch; and Meyer, p. 137.

[115] Sir Harold Beeley to author. See also Eden, p. 343; and Trevelyan, p. 57.

[116] See Eden, pp. 332–333; and *Guardian*, 30 January 1956.

[117] Memcon, 30 January 1956. Eisenhower Library, Ann Whitman File, International Series, Box 20.

[118] Eden, p. 335.

[119] See King Hussein, pp. 107–114; Lieutenant General Sir John Bagot Glubb, *A Soldier With the Arabs* (London: Hodder and Stoughton, 1957), pp. 423–427; Trevelyan, p. 63; and Love, pp. 207–210.

[120] Anthony Nutting, *No End of a Lesson* (London: Constable, 1967), p. 18.

[121] Sir Willie Morris to author. See also Nutting, *No End of a Lesson*, pp. 17–33; Eden, pp. 347–352; and Carlton, pp. 397–398.

[122] Selwyn Lloyd, pp. 41–58.

[123] Nutting, *No End of a Lesson*, pp. 34–35.

[124] Selwyn Lloyd, pp. 59–61.

[125] Lloyd, p. 68; Roger Makins to author.

[126] See Eden to Eisenhower, 15 March 1956, and Eisenhower to Eden, 20 March 1956. Eisenhower Library, Ann Whitman File, International Series, Box 19. See also Sir Willie Morris to author.

[127] Fraser Wilkins to author.

[128] Tehran Embtel 37, 23 December 1955. WNRC, RG 84, Box 264.

[129] Eden, p. 421.

[130] See George Allen's confidential testimony to SFRC, 8 May 1956, in *Executive Sessions (1956)*, p. 199; and Robert Murphy, *Diplomat Among Warriors* (Garden City, N.Y.: Doubleday, 1964), p. 376.

[131] See Chester Cooper, pp. 88–90; Love, pp. 144–145; and Maurice Couve de Murville, oral history, DOH, pp. 11–16.

[132] See Hollister to Hoover, 9 December 1955.

[133] United States Department of State *Bulletin*, 16 January 1956, p. 82.

[134] United States Senate, Committee on Appropriations, Hearings: "Financing of the Aswan High Dam in Egypt" (84th Congress, 2nd session, January 26, 1956), p. 2.

[135] Abba Eban, oral history, DOH, pp. 30–31; Isaiah Kenen to author; and Alan Richard Balboni, "A Study of the Efforts of the American Zionists to

Influence the Formulation and Conduct of United States Policy During the Roosevelt, Truman, and Eisenhower Administrations" (Brown University Ph.D. thesis, 1973), p. 210. See also American Zionist Committee for Public Affairs, "Report From Washington," 16 April 1956, analyzing Foster Dulles's 24 February 1956 testimony on High Dam aid before the SFRC.

[136] SFRC *Executive Sessions (1956)*, p. 46.

[137] "Financing of the Aswan High Dam in Egypt," pp. 5, 16.

[138] "Financing of the Aswan High Dam in Egypt," pp. 10–14, 21–22.

[139] "Financing of the Aswan High Dam in Egypt," pp. 11, 22, 24. See also Hoover's report of conversation with Kaissouny in Deptel 1067 to Cairo, 23 November 1955.

[140] Adams, p. 198.

[141] J. William Fulbright to author. See also Finer, p. 49.

[142] Nasser to Eisenhower, 6 February 1956. Eisenhower Library, Ann Whitman File, International Series, Box 8.

[143] Eisenhower to Nasser, 27 February 1956. Eisenhower Library, Ann Whitman File, International Series, Box 8. See also Eisenhower to Ben Gurion, 27 February 1956. Eisenhower Library, Ann Whitman File, International Series, Box 8; and Francis Russell to author.

[144] Henry Byroade, Kermit Roosevelt, and Miles Copeland to author; Ewald, p. 161n; and Ben Gurion, pp. 294–325. See also Rafael, pp. 51–52.

[145] Eisenhower diary, 13 March 1956. Eisenhower Library, Ann Whitman File, DDE Diary Series, Box 9.

[146] Eisenhower diary, 13 March 1956.

[147] Eisenhower diary, 13 March 1956. See also Eisenhower to Anderson, 20 March 1956. Eisenhower Library, Ann Whitman File, DDE Diary Series, Box 14; and Foster Dulles to Anderson, 22 March 1956. Eisenhower Library, Foster Dulles Papers, Box 100.

[148] See Colonel Andrew Goodpaster's memcon with President Eisenhower and Undersecretary Hoover, 6 March 1956. Eisenhower Library, Ann Whitman File, DDE Diary Series, Box 13; Waterbury, *Hydropolitics of the Nile Valley*, p. 106; and Dayan, pp. 179–182.

[149] Ben Gurion to Eisenhower, 16 March 1956. Eisenhower Library, Ann Whitman File, International Series, Box 13. See also Foster Dulles's memorandum for Eisenhower, 23 April 1956. Eisenhower Library, Ann Whitman File, White House Memoranda Series, Box 10; and Ben Gurion, pp. 294–325.

[150] Dwight Eisenhower, oral history, DOH, pp. 29–30.

[151] Eisenhower diary, 8 March 1956. Eisenhower Library, Ann Whitman File, DDE Diary Series, Box 13.

[152] See Goldman, pp. 63–64.

[153] Heikal, *Cairo Documents*, pp. 59–60.

[154] Eisenhower diary, 8 March 1956. Eisenhower Library, Ann Whitman File, DDE Diary Series, Box 13.

Chapter Three

[1] See Colonel Andrew Goodpaster's memorandum of conversation with Joint Chiefs of Staff, 16 March 1956. Eisenhower Library, Ann Whitman File, DDE Diary Series, Box 13.

[2] Selwyn Lloyd, pp. 53–54.

[3] Eisenhower to Foster Dulles, 10 March 1956. Eisenhower Library, Ann Whitman File, DDE Diary Series, Box 14.

[4] The other participants in the 24 March meeting were Kim Roosevelt and James Jesus Angleton of the CIA, and Herbert Hoover, Jr., George Allen, Francis Russell, William Rountree, and Herman Phleger of the State Department. See Foster Dulles to Allen Dulles, 23 March 1956 and Foster Dulles to Herbert Hoover, Jr., 27 March 1956 in Eisenhower Library, Foster Dulles Papers, Telephone Conversations Series, Box 4.

[5] Foster Dulles to Eisenhower, 28 March 1956. Eisenhower Library, Ann Whitman File, DDE Diary Series, Box 13.

[6] Foster Dulles to Eisenhower, 28 March 1956.

[7] Eisenhower diary, 28 March 1956. Eisenhower Library, Ann Whitman File, DDE Diary Series, Box 9.

[8] See Goodpaster's memorandum of 28 March conference. Eisenhower Library, Ann Whitman File, Dulles-Herter Series, Box 5.

[9] See Selwyn Lloyd, pp. 59–61. (Cross reference to pp. 66–67).

[10] Kermit Roosevelt, Miles Copeland, and Raymond Hare to author. See also Eveland, pp. 168–172, 180–181, 192; Raymond Hare, oral history, DOH, p. 22; Goodpaster memorandum of conference with Joint Chiefs of Staff, 2 April 1956. Eisenhower Library, Ann Whitman File, DDE Diary Series, Box 15; Eisenhower diary, 10 April 1956. Eisenhower Library, Ann Whitman File, DDE Diary Series, Box 15; Eisenhower to Foster Dulles, 10 April 1956. Eisenhower Library, Foster Dulles Papers, Telephone Conversations Series, Box 11; and Hoover to Eisenhower, n.d. (probably early May 1956). Eisenhower Library, Ann Whitman File, International Series, Box 8.

[11] Roger Makins to author; Rountree to Hoover, "Meeting with Ambassador Makins Concerning the Aswan Dam," 3 April 1956.

[12] Selwyn Lloyd, p. 66.

[13] Lloyd, pp. 68–69.

[14] See Cooper, p. 92; and Heikal, *Cairo Documents*, pp. 61–62.

[15] See Nutting, *Nasser*, pp. 137–139; Yitzhak Shichor, *The Middle East in China's Foreign Policy, 1949–77* (New York: Cambridge University, 1979), pp. 45–46; Mon'im Nasser Eddine, *Arab-Chinese Relations, 1950–71* (Beirut: The Arab Institute for Research and Publishing, 1972), pp. 102–105; and *New York Times*, 28 May 1956.

[16] See *New York Times*, 28 April 1956; and Love, p. 259. On Eden's talks with Khrushchev concerning Middle East issues, see Eisenhower to Eden, 5 April 1956. Eisenhower Library, Ann Whitman File, DDE Diary Series, Box 14.

[17] With the approval of the Eisenhower Administration, the French government had sold twelve Mystère fighters to the Israelis in April 1956. John

Robinson Beal and W. Tyler Kefauver both allege that Nasser recognized the PRC chiefly as a means of striking back at the United States government for its approval of the Mystère sale. See Beal, *John Foster Dulles* (New York: Harper, 1959), p. 257 and Kefauver, "The Influence of Foreign Policy in the Election of 1956" (American University M.A. thesis, 1968), pp. 5–6.

[18] Shichor, p. 46.

[19] Shichor, p. 46.

[20] See Henry Byroade's confidential testimony to SFRC, in *Executive Sessions (1957)*, p. 225.

[21] By the summer of 1965, Egypt was exporting 17 percent of its cotton crop to the People's Republic of China. See Eddine, p. 99; and Goldman, p. 64.

[22] From the vantage point of the Peking government, Egyptian recognition was seen as a first step toward the enlargement of Chinese influence in the Arab world and in Africa. As Yeh Chih-Chuang, the Chinese Minister of Foreign Trade, put it at the time: "We greet the establishment of diplomatic relations between China and Egypt, furthermore, because the significance and effects of this great landmark in Sino-Egyptian relations are not confined to our two countries alone. We have here a sign of closer ties between China and the Arab countries which are being strengthened every day. It is a contribution to the promotion of friendship and cooperation among all Asian and African countries, and to the consolidation of world peace." Quoted in Eddine, p. 111.

[23] Foster Dulles to C.D. Jackson, 23 May 1956. Eisenhower Library, Foster Dulles Papers, Telephone Conversations Series, Box 5.

[24] United States Department of State *Bulletin*, 4 June 1956, p. 920. See also *New York Times*, 23 May 1956; and Foster Dulles to William Rountree, 22 May 1956. Eisenhower Library, Foster Dulles Papers, Telephone Conversations Series, Box 5.

[25] *New York Times*, 24 September 1956. See also Foster Dulles to John Snyder (Hagerty's deputy), 23 May 1956. Eisenhower Library, Foster Dulles Papers, Telephone Conversations Series, Box 11.

[26] *Washington Post*, 18 May 1956.

[27] *New York Herald Tribune*, 20 May 1956.

[28] George Allen, oral history, DOH, p. 33. See also Lyon, p. 623.

[29] See Foster Dulles to Allen Dulles, 18 May 1956. Eisenhower Library, Foster Dulles Papers, Telephone Conversations Series, Box 5.

[30] See Heikal, *Cairo Documents*, pp. 62–63; and *New York Times*, 18 May 1956.

[31] President Eisenhower claims in his memoirs that Nasser "gave Black a series of counterproposals" at the 20 June meeting, "some of which would be totally unacceptable to all three of the financing authorities." Black later denied emphatically that Nasser added any new points to his *contre mémoire* of January 1956. See Eisenhower, *Waging Peace*, p. 32; Black oral history, DOH, p. 13; and *New York Times*, 22 June 1956.

[32] Black, oral history, DOH, pp.13–14. Black reaffirmed the World Bank's confidence in the Egyptian economy's ability to bear the burden of High Dam construction in a letter to Egyptian Finance Minister Kaissouny on 9

July 1956, ten days before Dulles cancelled the Western offer. See Love, p. 316.

33 *New York Times,* 2 April 1956.

34 See Dougherty, p. 23; Robert St. John, *The Boss* (New York: McGraw Hill, 1960), p. 219; and Allen to Hoover, "The Aswan High Dam," 3 July 1956.

35 *New York Times,* 18 June 1956. See also Sadat, p. 142.

36 *The Times's* story differed with the *New York Times* report only in that it suggested that the repayment period for the Soviet loan was sixty years, not twenty years.

37 *Al Ahram,* 30 June 1956.

38 Dougherty, p. 24.

39 See Foster Dulles to George Allen, 27 June 1956. Eisenhower Library, Foster Dulles Papers, Telephone Conversations Series, Box 5; *New York Times,* 23 July 1956.

40 Southern Senators sensitive to threats to regional cotton interests continued to lead the fight against High Dam aid on Capitol Hill. Senator James Eastland (D-Miss.) later boasted to his constituents that he was "personally responsible for killing the Aswan aid program." See Andrew Eliot Rice, "Building a Constituency for the Foreign Aid Program: The Record of the Eisenhower Years" (Syracuse University Ph.D. thesis, 1963), p. 34.

41 Loy Henderson, oral history, DOH, pp. 23–24.

42 See United States Senate, Committee on Appropriations, Hearings: "Mutual Security Act of 1957," pp. 23–25, 55–65. See also Senator William Knowland to Foster Dulles, 28 June 1956. Eisenhower Library, Foster Dulles Papers, Telephone Conversations Series, Box 5.

43 Fraser Wilkins to author. See also Cooper, p. 96.

44 Drummond and Coblentz, p. 151.

45 See John Hollister, oral history, DOH, pp. 47–51; Hollister to Hoover, 22 March 1956; and Rountree to Hoover, 14 May 1956. Byroade informed Nasser of the American decision to allow the 1956 appropriation to lapse in late May. See Deptel 2815 to Cairo, 24 May 1956; and Wilkins to Rountree, 7 June 1956.

46 United States Senate, Committee on Appropriations, Hearings: "Mutual Security Act of 1957," pp. 23–25.

47 See Foster Dulles to Eisenhower, 16 July 1956. Eisenhower Library, Ann Whitman File, Dulles-Herter Series, Box 5; and Robert G. Barnes to George Allen, 19 June 1956.

48 Foster Dulles to Eisenhower, 16 July 1956; Barnes to Allen, 19 June 1956.

49 *New York Times,* 17 July 1956.

50 Foster Dulles to Barnes, 16 July 1956. Eisenhower Library, Foster Dulles Papers, Telephone Conversations Series, Box 5.

51 Dulles to Eisenhower, 16 July 1956.

52 For a description of Eisenhower's meeting with the Senate leadership, see Foster Dulles to Sherman Adams, 17 July 1956. Eisenhower Library, Foster Dulles Papers, Telephone Conversations Series, Box 11.

[53] Knowland to Dulles, 17 July 1956. Eisenhower Library, Foster Dulles Papers, Telephone Conversations Series, Box 5. Dulles was scheduled to depart for Panama, the first stop on a brief tour of Latin America, on Saturday, 21 July.

[54] Beal, p. 260.

[55] Henry Byroade to author.

[56] For more detailed accounts of the 13 July Gettysburg meeting, see Eisenhower, *Waging Peace*, p. 32; Hoopes, p. 339; Cooper, p. 98; and Love, p. 322.

[57] Beal, p. 259.

[58] Cairo Embtel 2347, 26 May 1956.

[59] Cairo Embtel 2515, 16 June 1956.

[60] Deptel 52 to Cairo, 9 July 1956.

[61] Cairo Embtel 70, 13 July 1956.

[62] Fraser Wilkins and Raymond Hare to author.

[63] See *Egyptian Gazette*, 17 July 1956; *New York Times*, 21 July 1956; and Love, p. 313.

[64] See Heikal, *Cairo Documents*, pp. 64–65; and Nutting, *Nasser*, p. 139.

[65] BBC Third Program, "Suez: Ten Years After." Edited and introduced by Anthony Moncrieff (London: BBC, 1967). See also, Heikal, *Cairo Documents*, p. 65.

[66] See *The Financial Times*, 16 July 1956; and *The Guardian*, 16 July 1956.

[67] Love, p. 321. Some writers have argued, inaccurately, that Nasser was completely surprised by Dulles's cancellation of the Aswan offer. See, for example, Deane and David Heller, *John Foster Dulles: Soldier for Peace* (New York: Holt, Rinehart and Winston, 1960), p. 248.

[68] *Washington Post*, 18 July 1956. Byroade had reported about a week earlier that Hussein would accept the Western offer. See memcon, Ronald Bailey (Counselor, British Embassy, Washington), Willie Morris, and William C. Burdett (Deputy Director, Office of Near East Affairs, State Department), 11 July 1956.

[69] Cabinet meeting minutes, 18 July 1956.

[70] See Robert Bowie, oral history, DOH, pp. 28–31; Francis Russell, oral history, DOH, pp. 11–13; Bowie to Calvocoressi in BBC, "Suez: Ten Years After," pp. 39–40; and Mosley, p. 401.

[71] For full text of draft statement, see appendix 1.

[72] See Bowie, oral history, DOH, p. 32; and Hoopes, p. 340. For full text of final cancellation statement, see appendix 2.

[73] Love, p. 325.

[74] Foster Dulles to Allen Dulles, 19 July 1956 (3:40 P.M.). Eisenhower Library, Foster Dulles Papers, Telephone Conversations Series, Box 5.

[75] Rountree's memcon, 19 July 1956. See also George Allen, oral history, DOH, p. 36; Deptel 127 to Cairo, 19 July 1956; and Deptel 139 to Cairo, 21 July 1956.

[76] Knowland to Dulles, 19 July 1956. Eisenhower Library, Foster Dulles Papers, Telephone Conversations Series, Box 5.

[77] Foster Dulles to Allen Dulles, 19 July 1956 (5:30 P.M.). Eisenhower Library, Foster Dulles Papers, Telephone Conversations Series, Box 5. Am-

bassador Hussein did not evidently bear any personal hard feelings toward the Secretary of State. He later told Georgiana Stevens that he "did not regard Secretary Dulles as being at fault in the Aswan Dam matter." Hussein felt that "Secretary Dulles acted completely honorably with respect to the dam and in his dealings with [the Egyptian Embassy]." The Stevens-Hussein conversation was recorded by Francis Russell in his oral history, DOH, p. 19.

[78] William Macomber, oral history, DOH, pp. 54–55.

[79] *New York Times*, 21 July 1956.

[80] Eden, p. 422.

[81] Lloyd, p. 71.

[82] Macmillan, *Tides of Fortune*, p. 98.

[83] Aldrich, oral history, DOH, p. 12.

[84] Murphy, p. 377.

[85] Richard Goold-Adams, *The Time of Power* (London: Weidenfeld and Nicolson, 1962), p. 211. See also Hugh Thomas, p. 30.

[86] Makins to author. Makins very kindly allowed the author to read his recent correspondence with the Foreign Office on the issue of Anglo-American consultation on the withdrawal of the High Dam offer.

[87] In a meeting on 13 July, Dulles had discussed the Aswan issue with Makins, and had told the British ambassador that his "present inclination" was to formally withdraw the American offer of aid for the High Dam. Memcon, 13 July 1956.

[88] Makins to author. See also Makins oral history, DOH, pp. 6–7.

[89] Nutting, *Nasser*, p. 140; and Nutting, *No End of a Lesson*, pp. 44–45.

[90] Makins to author.

[91] Foster Dulles to Allen Dulles, 19 July 1956 (3:40 P.M.).

[92] *New York Times*, 21 July 1956.

[93] *Parliamentary Debates (Hansard)*, Commons, Fifth Series, 25 July 1956, vol. 557, c. 412.

[94] See *New York Times*, 21 July 1956.

[95] Sir Willie Morris and Evan Wilson supported Makins's account in interviews with the author. See also George Allen, oral history, DOH, p. 36; and William Rountree, oral history, DOH, p. 13.

[96] On the neutralist summit, see *Egyptian Gazette*, 12, 14, and 21 July 1956; and Mosley, pp. 403–404.

[97] *Egyptian Gazette*, 12, 14, and 21 July 1956; and Mosley, pp. 403–404.

[98] Nasser to Erskine Childers in BBC, "Suez: Ten Years After", p. 42. See also Cairo Embtel 108, 20 July 1956, which includes the report of a "journalist confidant of Nasser" (probably Mohamed Heikal) on Nasser's reaction to the United States withdrawal of Aswan aid.

[99] Without Anglo-American backing, the World Bank was forced to withdraw its loan offer on 23 July. Eugene Black, who had learned of the impending American cancellation from Herbert Hoover, Jr., during a golf game at Burning Tree Country Club near Washington on 18 July, later described the withdrawal of the Western offer as "the greatest disappointment of my professional life. It was a classic case where long-term policy was sacrificed because of short term problems and irritations." See Black, oral

history, DOH, p. 21; Henry Byroade to author; and Black to Kennet Love, in Love, p. 296.

[100] *New York Times*, 22 July 1956.

[101] See *Le Journal d'Egypte*, 25 July 1956; and *New York Times*, 25 July 1956.

[102] *Le Journal d'Egypte*, 25 July 1956; and *New York Times*, 25 July 1956.

[103] *Le Journal d'Egypte*, 25 July 1956. See also Cairo Embtel 126, 24 July 1956; and Allen to Hoover, "Nasser's Comments on the Withdrawal of the Aswan Dam Offer," 24 July 1956.

[104] Dulles to Hoover, 23 July 1956. Eisenhower Library, Foster Dulles Papers, Telephone Conversations Series, Box 5.

[105] See *New York Times*, 23 July 1956; and OIR report #7317, "Reactions to the Egyptian Crisis," 13 August 1956. National Archives, Diplomatic Branch. Secretary Dulles also received a number of personal letters congratulating him on the Aswan renege. Former New York Governor Thomas E. Dewey, who had been Dulles's political mentor in the late 1940s, wrote a few days after the Dulles-Hussein meeting that "the week-end blowup over the dam seems to have been all to the good. It took guts and might even clear the air for sound progress." Dewey to Dulles, 20 July 1956 (with postscript several days later). Foster Dulles Papers, Princeton, Box 102. See also Ferdinand Mayer to Dulles, 24 July 1956. Foster Dulles Papers, Princeton, Box 100; and Vincent Sheean to Dulles, 21 July 1956. Foster Dulles Papers, Princeton, Box 106.

[106] The State Department anticipated that Nasser would react to the Aswan renege by terminating America's modest technical aid program in Egypt, which he described in his 24 July speech as a "danger to our independence and a dagger in our backs." On 25 July, the Office of Near East Affairs prepared a press release on the cancellation of the technical aid program "as a contingency planning measure." See Cairo Embtel 126, 24 July 1956; and Rountree to Hoover, "Press Release for Issuance If Nasser Terminates the Point Four Program," 25 July 1956.

[107] For text, see FBIS, *Daily Report*, Foreign Radio Broadcasts, 27 July 1956. Nasser and his advisers had begun to consider the possibility of nationalizing the Canal Company before its concession expired in 1968 as early as November 1954. Although Eisenhower, Foster Dulles, and Selwyn Lloyd, among others, later alleged that Nasser had provoked the West in the Aswan affair so that he would have a pretext for nationalizing the Canal Company, there is no evidence to suggest that Nasser decided to nationalize the Company until after 19 July 1956. In any case, Nasser exaggerated Egypt's ability to finance the High Dam with Canal revenues, which amounted to only about $30 million per year exclusive of unusual expenditures for Canal improvements. See Love, p. 321; Dougherty, pp. 41–43; BBC, "Suez: Ten Years After," p. 43; Heikal, *Cairo Documents*, pp. 65–66; Eisenhower, oral history, DOH, p. 30; Dulles to Andrew Berding in Berding, *Dulles on Diplomacy* (Princeton: Van Nostrand, 1965), p. 107; and Lloyd, p. 69. The State Department had considered nationalization of the Canal Company to be one of the more improbable of several possible Egyptian responses to the Aswan

cancellation. See George Allen, oral history, DOH, p. 39; and Fraser Wilkins to author.

[108] Hugh Thomas, p. 31.

[109] Eden to Eisenhower quoted in Eden, p. 428. Robert Murphy, who had been sent to London immediately after Nasser's nationalization of the Canal Company to restrain Eden from impulsive action, later wrote that he "was left in no doubt that the British government believed that Suez was a test which would be met only by the use of force." Murphy, pp. 462–464.

[110] Meyer, p. 153.

[111] For good recent accounts of the Suez Crisis, see Donald Neff, *Warriors at Suez* (New York: Simon and Schuster, 1981); Meyer, Chapter 7; and Carlton, Chapter 11.

[112] Minutes of Bipartisan Legislative Leaders Meeting, 12 August 1956. Eisenhower Library, White House Office Papers, Office of Staff Secretary Series, Box 11. See also Sherman Adams, pp. 199–200. It is worth noting that the Joint Chiefs of Staff had begun contingency planning for military action in support of Britain and France in late July 1956. In a report to the President on 31 July, the Joint Chiefs stressed the urgency of the situation, concluding that "if action short of the use of military force cannot reasonably be expected to . . . establish a friendly and responsible authority over the Suez Canal . . . the United States should consider the desirability of taking military action in support of the United Kingdom, France, and others as appropriate." See JCS report, 31 July 1956. National Archives, Modern Military Branch, JCS Files.

[113] See Eisenhower, *Waging Peace*, pp. 669–671. The Suez Canal was far less important to the U.S. economy than it was to the British economy. In 1956, for example, only 4 percent of total U.S. oil requirements were transported through the Canal. See J.H. Lichtblau, "Is the Tank Running Low?" *The Reporter* (21 March 1957), p. 17.

[114] Meyer, p. 155.

[115] Meyer, p. 155.

[116] See Moshe Dayan, *Diary of the Sinai Campaign 1956* (London: Sphere Books, 1967), pp. 12–21; and Rafael, pp. 53–54.

[117] For a well-informed recent account of Anglo-French-Israeli collusion in the Suez Crisis, see Geoffrey Warner, " 'Collusion' and the Suez Crisis of 1956," *International Affairs* (April 1979).

[118] For text of the Anglo-French ultimatum, see RIIA, *Documents on International Affairs 1956* (London: Oxford University Press, 1957), p. 261.

[119] See Adams, p. 256; Allen Dulles, *The Craft of Intelligence* (London: Weidenfeld and Nicolson, 1963), p. 166; Andrew Tully, *CIA: The Inside Story* (New York: William Morrow, 1962), p. 110; and Lyon, p. 705. Foster Dulles fell ill on 2 November with the cancer that was later to kill him, and spent most of November recuperating from exploratory surgery.

[120] See United States Department of State *Bulletin*, 12 November 1956; and Meyer, p. 168.

[121] United States economic pressure on Britain took two forms. First, the Eisenhower Administration refused categorically to alleviate the oil shortage in Britain caused by Nasser's blockage of the Suez Canal and Syrian sabotage

of several major pipelines unless Britain and France agreed to a ceasefire and to unconditional withdrawal of their troops from Suez. Second, the American government made its approval of an IMF loan to Britain to stave off a run on sterling contingent on a ceasefire and troop withdrawal. See Macmillan, *Riding the Storm*, pp. 164–165; and Adams, p. 262.

[122] In a series of steps which embittered Israel's supporters in America, the Eisenhower Administration suspended economic aid to Israel, threatened to lift the tax exemption of the United Jewish Appeal, and threatened to support United Nations sanctions against Israel if the Israelis did not withdraw from Sinai. See *New York Times*, 6 February 1957; Rafael, p. 62; Lyon, pp. 731–732; and Isaacs, pp. 250–251.

[123] *New York Times*, 10 November 1956.

[124] Macmillan, *Riding the Storm*, p. 198. In one of the many ironies of the Suez Crisis, it was Macmillan, by all accounts one of the most hawkish members of the Cabinet during the crisis, who succeeded Eden as Prime Minister.

[125] Mohieddin to Humphrey Trevelyan in Trevelyan, p. 55.

[126] Nasser to Kennedy, 22 August 1961. Kennedy Library, President's Office Files (POF), Countries, UAR Correspondence, p. 20.

[127] Black, oral history, DOH, p. 15.

Chapter Four

[1] Raymond Hare to author.

[2] The United States Treasury also froze about $40 million worth of Egyptian assets in the United States, pending settlement of compensation claims made by Suez Canal Company stockholders. See *New York Times*, 13 August, 1 October 1956; 1 January, 17 March, 3 May, 30 November 1957; 1 May 1958; and Glenn Earl Perry, "U.S. Relations with Egypt, 1951–63: Egyptian Neutralism and American Alignment Policy" (University of Virginia Ph.D. thesis, 1964), pp. 340–356.

[3] *New York Times*, 1 May 1958.

[4] Eisenhower, *Waging Peace*, p. 178.

[5] Eisenhower to Dulles, 12 December 1956. Eisenhower Library, Ann Whitman File, DDE Diary Series, Box 12.

[6] Eisenhower, *Waging Peace*, p. 178.

[7] Fraser Wilkins to author. See also United States Department of State *Bulletin*, 21 January 1957, pp. 83–86; and text of Doctrine in Public Law 85-7, 85th Congress, first session, House Joint Resolution 117, 9 March 1957.

[8] Hoopes, p. 406.

[9] In closed Senate Foreign Relations Committee hearings on the Eisenhower Doctrine, Senator John F. Kennedy (D-Mass.) observed presciently that, in failing to distinguish between ideological Communism and tactical alliances with Moscow, the Administration ran the risk of pushing Egypt, Syria, and

some of the more moderate Arab states into deeper opposition to Western interests in the Middle East. See SFRC *Executive Sessions (1957)*, pp. 174–175.

[10] The two key features of the Administration's campaign to promote the Eisenhower Doctrine were King Saud's official visit to the United States in February 1957, and former Congressman James P. Richards's fifteen nation swing through the Middle East in March–April 1957. See Eisenhower, *Waging Peace*, pp. 193–194; Adams, p. 223; and National Security Council staff note #62, "Reactions to the Eisenhower Doctrine," 9 January 1957. Eisenhower Library, Ann Whitman File, DDE Diary Series, Box 12.

[11] See Meyer, pp. 185–187.

[12] See Patrick Seale, *The Struggle for Syria* (London: Oxford University Press, 1965), pp. 283–306; and Eisenhower, *Waging Peace*, pp. 197–203.

[13] See Seale, pp. 307–326; and Malcolm Kerr, *The Arab Cold War*, pp. 1–5. From this point onward in the text, "UAR" and "Egypt" are used interchangeably.

[14] See Allen Dulles Briefing Notes, 14 July 1958. Eisenhower Library, White House Office Files, Office of Staff Secretary, International Series, Box 11.

[15] Adams, p. 232.

[16] See Kerr, pp. 16–18; and Uriel Dann, *Iraq Under Kassem* (New York: Praeger, 1969), pp. 19–27.

[17] In January 1958, the Soviet government had pledged $175 million in economic aid to modernize Egyptian heavy industry. See Goldman, p. 65.

[18] OIR report #7848, "Soviet-UAR Differences and Related Developments in Syria and Iraq," 22 October 1958. National Archives, Diplomatic Branch. On the Soviet-Egyptian rift, see also Heikal, *Sphinx and Commissar*, pp. 76–102; and Karen Dawisha, pp. 21–30.

[19] Goldman, p. 65, See also OIR report #7997, "Economic Implications of the Soviet-UAR Aswan High Dam Agreement", 8 April 1959. National Archives, Diplomatic Branch.

[20] See OIR report #7961, "Nasir and the Pan-Arab Conflict With Communism," 2 March 1959 and OIR report #7979, "Soviet-UAR Relations Since the Iraqi Coup Attempt," 24 March 1959, both in National Archives, Diplomatic Branch.

[21] Kamel to author. Kamel had arrived in Washington in mid-July 1958, just as the Iraqi, Lebanese, and Jordanian crises were erupting.

[22] Kamel to author. As Egypt's per capita agricultural production declined, Egyptian wheat imports increased from 0.1 percent of total imports in 1955 to 18.6 percent of total imports in 1964. In 1958, domestic production provided for little more than one-half of Egypt's consumption of wheat and wheat flour. Meanwhile, the gold and foreign exchange reserves of the National Bank of Egypt dropped from $957 million in 1951 to $214 million in December 1959. See Mohamed Hassan Fouad, "The Economics of Foreign Aid: The UAR Experience With the United States and USSR Programs, 1952–1965" (University of Southern California Ph.D. thesis, 1968), p. 172.

[23] Raymond Hare to author. See also Heikal, *Sphinx and Commissar*, p. 101.

[24] See National Security Council Policy Memorandum 5820/1, "U.S. Policy Toward the Near East," 4 November 1958. National Archives, Modern Military Branch, NSC File.

[25] *Congressional Record* (CR), volume 105, part 5, 16 April 1959: p. 6124. See also Jacob Kaplan, *The Challenge of Foreign Aid* (New York: Praeger, 1967), pp. 50–52; and Earl Butz, oral history, COH, p. 20.

[26] See Frances M. Lappé and Joseph Collins, *Food First* (Boston: Houghton-Mifflin, 1977), p. 329.

[27] See Dan Morgan, *Merchants of Grain* (New York: Viking, 1979), p. 98.

[28] Morgan, p. 98.

[29] Lappé and Collins, p. 329. See also William and Paul Paddock, *Famine 1975* (Boston: Little Brown, 1967), p. 175.

[30] Morgan, p. 98.

[31] See Peter Toma, *The Politics of Food for Peace* (Tucson: Arizona State University Press, 1967), p. 2.

[32] United States Senate, Committee on Agriculture, "Food for Peace 1954–78" (Washington: GPO, 26 April 1979), p. 3.

[33] Between 1954 and 1962, the U.S. government retained 30 percent of accumulated soft currency for its own uses; between 1962 and 1965, 15 percent; and after 1965, 20 percent. "Food for Peace 1954–78," pp. 10–12.

[34] "Food for Peace 1954–78," pp. 5–6.

[35] Initially, PL480 financed about one-fourth of United States wheat exports; but in 1959—an especially bleak year for the grain trade—PL480 accounted for four-fifths of U.S. wheat exports. See Morgan, p. 101.

[36] United States Department of Agriculture, Economic Research Service, Foreign Agricultural Report #142, "PL480 Concessional Sales" (Washington: GPO, December 1977), p. 9.

[37] United States food shipments fueled the Allied war effort in both World Wars I and II. Herbert Hoover, Sr., director of the United States Food Administration during the First World War, had used the threat of a food aid cut-off to forestall Bolshevik uprisings in Austria and Hungary in 1919. Food shipments comprised 29 percent of Marshall Plan aid in the late 1940s. See Congressional Research Service, "Use of U.S. Food for Diplomatic Purposes" (Washington: GPO, January 1977), p. 23; Dan Caldwell, "Food Crises and World Politics", Sage Professional Papers in International Studies, 5, (London: Sage Publications, 1977), p. 41; and Morgan, pp. 257–258.

[38] See William Anderson, pp. 109–110. At least one USDA official did conceive of PL480 as a political lever. He later told William and Paul Paddock (p. 171): "I could see the possibility of the American government controlling a couple of dozen countries through these free-food shipments. In its simplest form this is how I foresaw these food shipments would work. A country with riots coming on could be controlled by letting our wheat ships sit outside the port like a carrot on a stick. A leader whom we considered dangerous would lose the support of the masses because everyone would know we were not going to unload the wheat if he became top man or even if the government in power went overboard to the Communist Left or to the Junta Right."

[39] See Anderson, p. 11; and OIR report #6809/R, "The Use of Agricultural Surpluses to Promote Economic Development in Underdeveloped Countries," 7 September 1955. National Archives, Diplomatic Branch.

[40] See Mitchel B. Wallerstein, *Food for War—Food for Peace* (Cambridge, Mass.: MIT Press, 1980), p. 38.

[41] See Anderson, p. 101.

[42] See Wallerstein, pp. 38–40; and Don Paarlberg, oral history, Columbia Oral History Collection (COH), pp. 20–22.

[43] See Balboni, pp. 224–226; and Isaiah Kenen to author. Kenen recalls that "we argued that PL480 aid enabled Egypt to grow more cotton, which in turn enabled Nasser to barter for more Soviet arms. Unfortunately, this line of thinking did not become popular on Capitol Hill until 1962 or 1963."

[44] Anderson, pp. 421–422.

[45] Anderson, pp. 421–422. See also Faulkner, pp. 85–86.

[46] Raymond Hare to author.

[47] It is worth noting that the American government's more conciliatory approach toward Nasser began while Foster Dulles was still serving as Secretary of State. Dulles was forced to resign because of ill health on 15 April 1959, and died of cancer the next month. He was succeeded as Secretary by his deputy, Christian A. Herter.

[48] OIR report #8235, "Outlook for the United Arab Republic," 11 March 1960. National Archives, Diplomatic Branch, p. 33.

[49] In August 1960, the Soviet government agreed to provide $225 million for the second and third stages of the High Dam project. Despite their gratitude for Soviet financial support, the Egyptians complained about the heavyhandedness of Soviet technical advisers and the inadequacy of Soviet construction equipment. See Ivan Komzin, *The High Aswan Dam* (Moscow: Foreign Languages Publishing House, n.d.); and Goldman, pp. 65–69.

[50] See Heikal, *Sphinx and Commissar*, pp. 76–78.

[51] A marked increase in revenue from the tourist trade and Suez Canal tolls in 1959–1960 also helped alleviate the foreign-exchange problem. See Harry Ellis, p. 4; and Haven D. Umstott, "PL480 and other Economic Aid to Egypt" (Washington: USDA, June 1964), pp. 4–5.

[52] Ellis, p. 4; and Umstott, pp. 4–5.

[53] OIR report #8235, p. 35.

[54] Gamal Abdel Nasser, *Speeches and Press Interviews 1959* (Cairo: Ministry of Information, 1960), p. 589.

[55] See G. Bernard Noble, *Christian A. Herter* (New York: Cooper Square, 1970), pp. 135–140.

Chapter Five

[1] Arthur Schlesinger, Jr., *A Thousand Days* (London: Andre Deutsch, 1965), p. 527.

[2] Faulkner, p. 1.

[3] Battle to author. See also Battle, oral history, JOH, pp. 20–22.

[4] See United States Ambassador to the Soviet Union Llewelyn Thompson's cable describing Khrushchev's 6 January 1961 address, 19 January 1961. Kennedy Library, POF, Box 127.

[5] Schlesinger, p. 605. See also Rusk's confidential testimony to an Executive Session of the SFRC, 28 February 1961. National Archives, Legislative Branch.

[6] Kennedy, State of the Union message, 11 January 1962, in United States Department of State *Bulletin*, 29 January 1962, p. 161.

[7] Dean Rusk to author.

[8] Dean Rusk to author. See also John Badeau, oral history, Kennedy Oral History Collection (KOH), p. 2; and Badeau to author.

[9] Kennedy, 1959, quoted in J. Katz, "Kennedy and the Middle East," *New Outlook* (January 1964), p. 4.

[10] See William Polk, *The United States and the Arab World* (Cambridge, Mass.: Harvard University Press, third edition, 1975), pp. 330–344.

[11] Polk to Walt Rostow, 7 April 1964. Johnson Library, NSF, Countries, UAR, vol. 1.

[12] Bowles to Rusk (Addis Ababa Airgram A–74), 21 February 1962. Kennedy Library, POF, Countries, UAR Security, p. 4. Bowles had been sacked as Undersecretary of State in November 1961 because of his alleged administrative incompetence. See Schlesinger, pp. 389–394; and Warren I. Cohen, *Dean Rusk* (Totawa, N.J.: Cooper Square, 1980), p. 103.

[13] See Joan Nelson, pp. 19–20.

[14] Packenham, p. 52.

[15] See Millikan and Rostow, *Key to an Effective Foreign Policy*. Rostow served as McGeorge Bundy's deputy on Kennedy's National Security Council staff, as director of the State Department's Policy Planning Staff, and finally as Johnson's National Security Adviser.

[16] See Millikan and Rostow.

[17] George McGovern, oral history, KOH, p. 18. See also the report of the Kennedy transition team's task force on the Food for Peace program, 19 January 1961. Kennedy Library, POF, Food for Peace. McGovern had just lost a very close Senate race in South Dakota to the incumbent Republican, Karl Mundt. The "coat-tail" of the young, Catholic, Democratic Presidential nominee had not done much for McGovern in staid, Protestant South Dakota; indeed, Kennedy had lost the State by 52,000 votes, while McGovern had lost by only 14,500 votes. Kennedy reportedly telephoned McGovern the night after the election and told him: "I think I cost you an election." McGovern believed that he was appointed Director of Food for Peace in order to put him in a favorable position for another campaign in South Dakota in 1962 or 1964. See McGovern, oral history, KOH, p. 16; and McGovern, *Grassroots* (New York: Harper, 1977), pp. 83–84.

[18] McGovern in CR, vol. 111, part 10, 17 June 1965; p. 13999.

[19] Total PL480 exports increased by roughly 40 percent during the Kennedy years. See USDA *1978 Annual Report*, p. 52; and Wallerstein, pp. 7–8, 40–42, 180–181. The expansion of the PL480 program was part of the Kennedy Administration's general restructuring of the economic aid program. In the spring of 1961, Kennedy created the Agency for International Development (AID) as an umbrella economic aid organization. During the Kennedy era,

U.S. economic aid commitments to developing countries averaged about $4 billion annually, compared to an average of $2.5 billion annually in the period 1956–1960. See Packenham, p. 60.

[20] See Anderson, p. 423.

[21] In a letter to the author, Mr. William Langdon, Assistant Director, Program Department, CARE, noted that the Title II program in Egypt in the Kennedy era constituted CARE's "largest feeding operation." According to Langdon's figures, CARE used PL480 donations to operate a school lunch program for three million Egyptian children in the period 1961–63. Title II contributions to the Egyptian operations of CARE and Catholic Relief Services were suspended briefly in 1963 because of alleged mismanagement of funds. See "End of Tour Report," C.A. Cabooris, Food for Peace Officer, Cairo, 25 September 1965. U.S. AID Library, Washington.

[22] Faulkner, p. 132 (table 4.2).

[23] Faulkner, viii–ix. PL480 aid was supplemented in this period by a modest program of technical aid and dollar loans. See appendix 3.

[24] Badeau to author.

[25] Benjamin Read (Executive Secretary to Dean Rusk) to President Kennedy, 5 May 1961. Kennedy Library, POF, Countries, UAR Security.

[26] Rusk to author.

[27] Badeau, oral history, KOH, pp. 10–11; and Badeau, oral history, COH, pp. 322–323.

[28] Isaiah Kenen to author. Myer ("Mike") Feldman, who had been one of Kennedy's legislative aides during his Senate career, served as the Kennedy White House's liaison with the American Jewish community.

[29] Mustapha Kamel first met Kennedy in 1958, and reported to Cairo that the young Massachusetts Senator seemed committed to a genuinely "even-handed" approach to the Palestine problem. Kamel to author. See also Don Peretz, "The United States, the Arabs, and Israel: Peace Efforts of Kennedy, Johnson, and Nixon," *The Annals of the American Academy of Political and Social Science* (May 1972), p. 118.

[30] Nasser to Kennedy, 22 August 1961. Kennedy Library, POF, Countries, UAR.

[31] For detailed accounts of the efforts of Dr. Joseph E. Johnson to devise a formula for repatriation or resettlement of the displaced Palestinians, see Peretz, pp. 119–120; and Joseph E. Johnson, "Arab v. Israel: A Persistent Challenge," *Middle East Journal* (Winter 1964).

[32] See Badeau's comments on Egyptian attitudes toward the Arab-Israeli conflict in 1961–62 in Cairo Airgram A-737, 11 April 1964. Johnson Library, NSF, Countries, UAR.

[33] See "The Soviet Union and Egypt", CIA Special Report, 8 May 1964, p. 3.

[34] Geoffrey Arthur (Political Counselor, British Embassy Cairo, 1961–63) and Ahmed al-Zant (staff assistant to Foreign Minister Fawzi, 1960–64) to author. Soviet aid personnel and their dependents in Egypt were openly ridiculed by many Egyptians for their alleged stinginess, aloofness, and cliquishness. See OIR report #7998, "A Comparison of U.S. and Soviet Aid

Personnel in Less Developed Countries," 16 April 1959. National Archives, Diplomatic Branch.

[35] Badeau, oral history, COH, p. 303. See also Malcolm Kerr, pp. 21–25.

[36] See Kerr, p. 25; and A. Kapehink, "Nasser Turns to Home Front," *New Outlook* (December 1961), pp. 10–14. See also Nasser's speech of 29 September 1961 in *Nasser's Speeches 1961*, p. 17; and his speech of 22 February 1962 in *Nasser's Speeches 1962*, pp. 5–6. For symbolic reasons, Nasser continued to refer to Egypt as the "United Arab Republic" after the breakup.

[37] Badeau, oral history, COH, p. 297.

[38] See Badeau, "Crisis in Confidence," *Foreign Affairs* (January 1965), p. 287.

[39] See Robert Stookey, *America and the Arab World* (New York: John Wiley, 1975), p. 169; and CIA Office of National Estimates, "Nasser's Policy and Prospects in Black Africa," 9 January 1964. Johnson Library, NSF, Countries, Africa, General, vol. 1.

[40] BBC, *Summary of World Broadcasts*, iv, 21 February 1961: p. 571.

[41] Nasser to Kennedy, 20 February 1961. Kennedy Library, POF, Countries, UAR Security.

[42] See Bowles to Kennedy, 27 February 1961; and text of Kennedy letter in Deptel 1666 to Cairo, 1 March 1961. Both documents in Kennedy Library, POF, Countries, UAR Security.

[43] Unnumbered Deptel to Cairo, "Objectives of Bowles Mission," 25 January 1962. Kennedy Library, POF, Countries, UAR Security. See also Rusk to President Kennedy, 20 January 1962. Kennedy Library, POF, Countries, UAR Security.

[44] Bowles's Addis Ababa Airgram A-74, 21 February 1962. See Cairo Embtel 1217, "First Bowles-Nasser Meeting," 16 February 1962; Cairo Embtel 1234, "Second Bowles-Nasser Meeting," 18 February 1962; Khartoum Embtel 477, "Bowles's Summary of Meetings," 19 February 1962; and Cairo Airgram A-284, "Bowles's Mission", 20 February 1962. All four documents in Kennedy Library, POF, Staff Memoranda, Chester Bowles, Box 62. See also Chester Bowles, *Promises to Keep* (New York: Harper and Row, 1971), pp. 371–372.

[45] Edward S. Mason, "Report on Mission to UAR," 25 March 1962. Kennedy Library, POF, Countries, UAR Security; and Mason to author.

[46] Kamel to author. The four year, $1.3 billion Title I pledge made by the American government to India in May 1960 provided a precedent for Kamel's proposal. See Wallerstein, p. 185.

[47] Bergus and Harold Beeley (then serving as British ambassador in Cairo) to author.

[48] Talbot to Bundy, 27 February 1962. Kennedy Library, POF, Countries, UAR Security.

[49] See *Washington Post*, 28 April 1962.

[50] Despite the marked improvement in U.S.-Egyptian relations in the period, and despite the relative popularity of PL480 aid, Nasser's antagonists in Congress had not been completely quiescent in 1961–62. Representative Seymour Halpern (D-NY.) had introduced four amendments to the foreign aid bill in 1961, aimed at restricting aid to Nasser unless he opened the Suez Canal to Israeli shipping, and abandoned the Arab boycott of firms

dealing with Israel. Halpern had also cosponsored, with Senator Kenneth Keating (D-NY.), a 1962 amendment aimed at cutting off aid to Egypt unless Nasser ceased his "military and propaganda" attacks on other recipients of U.S. aid. The Halpern and Keating amendments expressed the "sense of the Congress" regarding aid to Nasser, but were not binding upon President Kennedy. See Bhanwar Lal Maheshwari, "Foreign Aid and the Policy Process: A Study of the Struggle over Foreign Aid in Congress, 1961–65" (University of Pennsylvania Ph.D. thesis, 1966), pp. 219–220.

[51] Kamel to author; *New York Times*, 9 October 1962.

[52] Badeau, oral history, COH, p. 352.

[53] For a good recent account of the Yemen Civil War, see Robert W. Stookey, *Yemen* (Boulder Colorado: Westview, 1978), Chapter 8.

[54] See Patrick Seale, "The War in Yemen," *New Republic* (26 January 1963), p. 11.

[55] *New York Times*, 9 November 1962.

[56] CIA, President's Daily Intelligence Checklist, "Egypt and Yemen," 15 October 1962.

[57] See John Badeau, *The American Approach to the Arab World* (New York: Harper, 1968), Chapter 7. See also Badeau, COH, p. 339: "It seemed to us that the time had come for the United States to cut loose from the policy of simply supporting these conservatives and this was a kind of test case, to see whether or not we could do this."

[58] Deptel 323 to Cairo, 27 September 1962. Kennedy Library, POF, Countries, UAR Security.

[59] Badeau, oral history, COH, pp. 332–336.

[60] Manfred Wenner, *Modern Yemen* (Baltimore: Johns Hopkins, 1967), pp. 198–199.

[61] Donald Bergus to author. See also Robert Stookey, pp. 179–189.

[62] See Seale, "The War in Yemen," p. 11; and Wenner, p. 203.

[63] British Ambassador to Egypt Harold Beeley recommended recognition of the Yemen Arab Republic, citing the backwardness of the Imamate and the expanding popular base of the Sallal regime, but was overruled by his superiors in London, who feared that a republican success in Yemen would destabilize the Arabian Peninsula and threaten the British position in Aden. The British government's refusal to recognize the Sallal regime heartened Nasser's most determined antagonist in Britain, Anthony Eden. On 22 October 1962, Eden wrote to Lord Beaverbrook that "Nasser wants, from a base in Yemen, to threaten Aden and infiltrate Saudi Arabia where lies the American oil he wants to control through a rebel Saudi government. As we cannot defend the Persian Gulf without Aden, the stakes are high." Beeley to author; and Carlton, p. 475. See also Macmillan, *At the End of the Day: Memoirs 1961–63* (London: Macmillan, 1973), Chapter 9.

[64] See James Cortada, "The Yemen Crisis," unpublished paper presented to UCLA Institute of International and Foreign Studies, 1965. Cortada was United States Chargé d'Affaires in Yemen from February 1963 until August 1964.

[65] United States Department of State *Bulletin*, 7 January 1963, pp. 11–12.

[66] Wenner, pp. 203–204.

[67] See Nasser's speech at Aswan, 9 January 1963, in *Nasser's Speeches 1963*, p. 30.

[68] Bergus to author.

[69] See *Washington Post*, 7 January 1963; and United States Department of State *Bulletin*, 21 January 1963, pp. 90–91. The despatch of the jet fighter squadron was part of "Operation Hard Surface," a scheme developed by White House aide Robert Komer to reassure the nervous Saudi regime of American support. None of the top-level policy-makers involved in the planning of "Hard Surface" seemed particularly certain about what the United States Air Force squadron was to do if it was engaged by Egyptian MIGs. Rusk to author.

[70] See text of Kennedy letter in Heikal, *Cairo Documents*, pp. 219–220.

[71] See Stookey, pp. 185–186.

[72] Badeau, oral history, COH, p. 353. See also text of Kennedy message to Nasser in Deptel 1958 to Cairo, 18 March 1963. Kennedy Library, POF, Countries, UAR Security.

[73] Wenner, p. 207.

[74] Badeau, oral history, COH, p. 356.

[75] Rusk news conference, 29 May 1963 in United States Department of State *Bulletin*, 17 June 1963, p. 937.

[76] See Dana Adams Schmidt, *Yemen: The Unknown War* (London: The Bodley Head, 1968), pp. 257–273.

[77] See text of Kennedy letter in Heikal, *Cairo Documents*, pp. 222–223.

[78] Kim Roosevelt and Donald Bergus to author.

[79] Roosevelt and Bergus to author.

[80] Hare to author.

[81] See Nadav Safran, *From War to War* (New York: Pegasus, 1969), pp. 148–158.

[82] *New York Times*, 25 December 1962.

[83] Badeau, oral history, COH, p. 410.

[84] Reported in CR, vol. 111, part 1, 26 January 1965: p. 1194.

[85] See Safran, pp. 148–149; and Lewis A. Frank, "Nasser's Missile Program," *Orbis* (Fall 1967), pp. 746–749.

[86] See United States House of Representatives, Committee on Foreign Affairs, Hearings: Foreign Assistance Act of 1963: p. 1735.

[87] Myer Feldman, Kennedy's liaison with the American Jewish community, was apparently the guiding force behind the HAWK sale. Feldman to author; Joseph Kraft, p. 88. See also Badeau, oral history, KOH, p. 12; Badeau, oral history, COH, p. 290–291; and Kenen to author.

[88] Cairo Embtel 331, 24 August 1962. Kennedy Library, POF, Countries, UAR Security. See also Deptel 190 to Cairo, 22 August 1962.

[89] For announcement of the HAWK sale, see *New York Times*, 27 September 1962.

[90] Badeau recalled that "we had practically no immediate reaction in Egypt to the arms sales: no newspaper attacks, no artificially created crowds, people continued to come to my parties." Badeau, oral history, KOH, p. 12.

[91] Glassman estimated the value of the June 1963 agreement at "anywhere from $220 million to $500 million." Glassman, *Arms for the Arabs* (Baltimore: Johns Hopkins, 1975), pp. 24–25.

[92] SFRC Executive Session, 5 June 1963. National Archives, Legislative Branch.

[93] McCloy used a sightseeing trip with his daughter as "cover" for his mission in Egypt. See Deptel 3480 to Cairo, 15 June 1963; and Deptel 945 to Cairo, 18 June 1963. Both documents in Kennedy Library, POF, Countries, UAR Security.

[94] Eilts to author.

[95] Cairo Embtel 2470, 28 June 1963. Kennedy Library, NSF, UAR, UAR/Israel Arms Limitation.

[96] Cairo Embtel 2491, 30 June 1963. Kennedy Library, NSF, UAR, UAR/Israel Arms Limitation. Having failed to persuade Nasser to consider dismantling his missile program, McCloy returned to Washington without visiting Tel Aviv.

[97] Mason to author. After this visit, Mason revised his earlier prediction that the growth in Egyptian national income would substantially exceed the rate of population growth and estimated that—given the concentration of resources on military and other nondevelopment-related spending—growth of Egyptian national income would barely keep pace with population growth. For a similar assessment, see Robert Mabro, *The Egyptian Economy 1952–72* (London: Oxford University Press, 1974), pp. 183–185.

[98] Dean Rusk to author.

[99] Rusk to author.

[100] Parker Hart to author. Hart added that he doubted that Prince Feisal and his advisers really believe that the cessation of American aid would force Nasser out of Yemen, but were eager to drive a wedge between the United States and Egypt.

[101] See Cortada, pp. 20–21.

[102] See "Gruening Report," Chapter 4, excerpted in CR, vol. 109, part 15, 30 October 1963: p. 20570.

[103] SFRC Hearings: Foreign Assistance Act of 1963, p. 497.

[104] See full text of Dutton letter in CR, vol. 109, part 15, 30 October 1963: pp. 205–210.

[105] Fulbright to author.

[106] See comments of Congressman Thomas Morgan (D-Pa.), Chairman of the House Foreign Affairs Committee, in CR, vol. 109, part 12, 11 October 1963: p. 15605. See also Gruening comments, CR, vol. 109, part 15, 30 October 1963: p. 20567.

[107] Rusk news conference, 8 November 1963. United States Department of State *Bulletin*, 13 November 1963, p. 811.

[108] See account of Brandt meeting in Cairo Embtel 1092, 9 November 1963. Kennedy Library, POF, Countries, UAR Security.

[109] Bundy to Fulbright, 11 November 1963. Kennedy Library, POF, Countries, UAR Security.

[110] Bergus to author.

[111] Kamel to author.

Chapter Six

[1] Philip Geyelin, *Lyndon B. Johnson and the World* (New York: Praeger, 1960), p. 156.

[2] Packenham, p. 89.

[3] Quoted in Geyelin, p. 268. See also William Gaud, oral history, JOH, p. 15.

[4] Faulkner, p. 132 (table 4.2).

[5] Robert Kleeman's chapter ("Suspension of PL480 aid to the United Arab Republic in 1965") in Sidney Weintraub's *Economic Coercion and U.S. Foreign Policy* provides detailed consideration of Johnson's aid policy in 1964–65.

[6] Text of Johnson letter of 17 February 1964 in Heikal, *Cairo Documents*, p. 231.

[7] Kamel to author.

[8] Heikal, *Cairo Documents*, pp. 226–227. Kennedy's successor is still referred to disparagingly in Cairo government and journalistic circles as "that cowboy Johnson." Eilts to author.

[9] See *New York Times*, 7 February 1964; and CIA Intelligence Information Cable, "Nasser Reaction to Weizmann Institute Speech," 13 February 1964.

[10] Cairo Radio Domestic Broadcast, 10 February 1964. Senator Gruening drew a similar conclusion, praising the Weizmann Institute speech as "a reversal of the U.S. policy of tying American fortunes in the Middle East to Nasser's Egypt." CR, vol. 110, part 3, 28 February 1964: p. 3955.

[11] Quoted in Huff, p. 244.

[12] Isaiah Kenen to author.

[13] McGeorge Bundy to Oxford seminar, 25 May 1981.

[14] The Saudis temporarily set aside their differences with Nasser over Yemen after the conference. It is also worth noting that the Palestine Liberation Organization was created at the Cairo Summit. See CIA Office of Current Intelligence, "Nasser's Arab Policy," 28 August 1964; and CIA Intelligence Information Cable, "Nasser's Comments on Arab Summit," 9 January 1964.

[15] Cairo Embtel 1643, 21 January 1964. Johnson Library, NSF, Countries, UAR, vol. 1.

[16] Rusk to author.

[17] London Embtel 4713, 25 March 1964. Johnson Library, NSF, Countries, UAR, vol. 1. See also CIA Intelligence Information Cable, "Nasser's Comments on Talbot Meeting," 5 March 1964.

[18] The High Dam proved to be a mixed blessing for Egypt. Although completion of the Dam did regularize the flow of the Nile, it also created or exacerbated problems connected with coastal erosion, water salinity, silt deprivation, evaporation, and the spread of bilharziasis. For more detailed discussions of the economic and ecological impact of the Dam, see Waterbury, *Hydropolitics of the Nile Valley*, pp. 116–153; Claire Sterling, "Superdams: The Perils of Progress," *Atlantic* (June 1972); and Mabro, pp. 83–106.

[19] To smooth Khrushchev's path, Nasser had suspended his campaign against Egyptian Communists in March 1964. See Kerr, "Coming to Terms

With Nasser," p. 76. See also Cairo Embtel 2856, 26 May 1964. Johnson Library, NSF, Countries, UAR, vol. 1; and Heikal, *Sphinx and Commissar,* Chapter 7.

[20] Khrushchev's promise of economic aid would provide about 10 percent of the funds needed to finance Egypt's second five-year plan (1965–1970). See Goldman, pp. 73–74; and Thomas C. Sorenson (Special Counsel to President Johnson) to Robert Komer, 25 May 1964. Johnson Library, NSF, Countries, UAR, vol. 1.

[21] Cairo Embtel 2856, 26 May 1964.

[22] Cairo Airgram A-737, 11 April 1964; and *New York Times,* 22 February 1964.

[23] Baida Embtel 84, 19 March 1964; and *New York Times,* 26 February 1964.

[24] Badeau to author; and Cairo Embtel 2316, 5 April 1964. Johnson Library, NSF, Countries, UAR, vol. 1.

[25] See Winston Burdett, *Encounter With the Middle East* (London: André Deutsch, 1970), pp. 188–189.

[26] CR, vol. 110, part 8, 12 May 1964: p. 10650.

[27] CR, vol. 110, part 8, 18 May 1964: p. 11180.

[28] CR, vol. 110, part 6, 20 April 1964: p. 8439.

[29] CR, vol. 110, part 10, 10 June 1964: p. 13255.

[30] See text of Stratton Amendment in CR, vol. 110, part. 10, 10 June 1964: p. 13254.

[31] For an account of the debate on the Stratton Amendment, see Maheshwari, p. 222.

[32] See text in CR, vol. 110, part 16, 2 September 1964: p. 21436.

[33] CR, vol. 110, part 16, 2 September 1964: p. 21448.

[34] See Maheshwari, p. 224.

[35] See *New York Times,* 6 October 1964.

[36] Badeau to President Johnson, 3 January 1964. Johnson Library, NSF, Countries, UAR, vol. 1.

[37] Battle, oral history, JOH, p. 13.

[38] Hedrick Smith to author.

[39] Heikal, *Cairo Documents,* pp. 227–228.

[40] Battle to author; and Cairo Embtel 1945, 3 December 1964. Johnson Library, NSF, Countries, UAR, vol. 2.

[41] Heikal, *Cairo Documents,* p. 228.

[42] *New York Times,* 19 December 1964; and Dean Rusk's confidential testimony to SFRC, 27 January 1965. National Archives, Legislative Branch.

[43] Stino was anxious to work out an aid arrangement quickly because a new U.S. regulation requiring dollar payment for the transportation of surplus commodities was to take effect in January 1965. See Battle, oral history, JOH, p. 16.

[44] Battle to author; Battle, oral history, JOH, p. 16. See also Cairo Embtel 2251, 30 December 1964, Johnson Library, NSF, Countries, UAR.

[45] See Heikal, *Cairo Documents,* p. 229; and Battle to author.

[46] Heikal, *Cairo Documents*, p. 158. See also Heikal, *Sphinx and Commissar*, pp. 138–139; Nutting, *Nasser*, p. 358; and Battle, oral history, JOH, pp. 14–16.

[47] CIA Office of Current Intelligence, "Nasser's Port Said Speech," 24 December 1964.

[48] Heikal, *Cairo Documents*, pp. 229–230.

[49] CIA Intelligence Information Cable, 13 January 1965.

[50] Rusk to author.

[51] Rusk to author.

[52] CR, vol. 111, part 1, 21 January 1965: pp. 992–993.

[53] CR, vol. 111, part 1, 26 January 1965: p. 1192.

[54] Rusk testimony to SFRC Executive Session, 27 January 1965. National Archives, Legislative Branch.

[55] Hickenlooper, Pastore comments in SFRC Executive Session, 27 January 1965. National Archives, Legislative Branch.

[56] Ball testimony in United States Department of State *Bulletin*, 22 February 1965, pp. 261–263.

[57] *New York Times*, 2 February 1965.

[58] *New York Times*, 4 February 1965.

[59] See United States Department of State *Bulletin*, 22 February 1965, p. 264.

[60] The House voted 198–181 to support the Senate version. See CR, vol. 111, part 2, 8 February 1965: pp. 2098–2105.

[61] Kamel to author. See also Robert Komer to Averell Harriman, 19 January 1965. Johnson Library, NSF, Countries, UAR, vol. 2.

[62] See Glassman, pp. 27–28; Yitzhak Rabin, *The Rabin Memoirs* (London: Weidenfeld and Nicolson, 1979), pp. 49–51; *New York Times*, 4 March 1965; and Peter Solbert (Deputy Secretary of Defense) to McGeorge Bundy, 8 March 1965. Johnson Library, Israel, Harriman Israel Mission.

[63] See text of Johnson letter in Heikal, *Cairo Documents*, p. 233.

[64] See, for example, Nasser's speeches of 1 May and 31 May 1965 in *Nasser's Speeches 1965*, pp. 23–28. See also Heikal, *Cairo Documents*, p. 236.

[65] See text of 1 May speech in *Nasser's Speeches 1965*, pp. 23–25.

[66] See Wallerstein, p. 128.

[67] Battle to author. See also Kleeman, pp. 112–113.

[68] Cairo Embtel 4214, 31 May 1965. Johnson Library, NSF, Countries, UAR, vol. 3.

[69] See United States Department of State *Bulletin*, 12 July 1965, p. 70; and *Washington Post*, 23 June 1965.

[70] Deptel 115 to Cairo, 27 June 1965. Johnson Library, NSF, Countries, UAR, vol. 3.

[71] The Soviet grain shipments, which totalled about 300,000 tons, were designed partly to offset an emergency shipment of 250,000 tons of corn from the People's Republic of China to Egypt. Both the Soviet Union and the PRC hoped to solicit Nasser's support at the forthcoming Algerian Conference of Afro-Asian Nations. In the end, the conference was postponed to prevent it becoming a forum for Sino-Soviet squabbles, but Nasser had

once again managed to benefit from Great Power rivalry for his affections. See Goldman, pp. 73–79; and *New York Times*, 2 July 1965.

[72] Quoted in *New York Times*, 2 July 1965.

[73] Rusk testimony in SFRC Executive Session, 13 October 1965. National Archives, Legislative Branch.

[74] On the Jidda Agreement, see Stookey, p. 186. The appointment of Mohieddin—described by Harold Beeley as "probably the ablest and most sympathetic to Western interests of Nasser's advisers"—was seen in Western diplomatic circles as an important sign of the Nasser regime's newfound moderation. Mohieddin firmly opposed Egyptian involvement in Yemen, and hoped to concentrate Egyptian resources upon domestic economic development. Beeley, Bergus to author. See also "Statement of El Sayed Zakaria Mohieddin," 2 October 1965 (Cairo: Ministry of Information, October 1965).

[75] Rusk testimony to SFRC, 13 October 1965.

[76] See Walt Rostow's memcon with Kaissouny, 7 October 1965. Johnson Library, White House Central File, Confidential File, Box 304.

[77] Cairo Embtel 4214, 31 May 1965.

[78] On 10 January 1966, the U.S. government supplemented the Title I agreement with a hard currency loan of $14.6 million. See *New York Times* 4,11 January 1966; and United States Department of State *Bulletin*, 24 January 1966, p. 123.

[79] For a detailed account of the Sadat visit, see *New York Times*, 27 February 1966.

[80] See *New York Times*, 11 April 1966.

[81] See Cairo Radio broadcasts of 21 and 24 February 1966 in BBC, *Summary of World Broadcasts*, iv, 22 and 25 February 1966.

[82] See *New York Times*, 9 January 1966,.

[83] See *New York Times*, 17 April 1966.

[84] See *New York Times*, 12 May 1966.

[85] Parker to author.

[86] *New York Times*, 27 February 1966.

[87] See Faulkner, p. 132 (table 4.2).

[88] Battle, Parker, and Hedrick Smith to author. Nasser confided his fears of a CIA counteroffensive in the developing world to Chou En-lai, Sukarno, Pakistani President Ayub Khan, and Indian Premier Shastri at a meeting in Cairo in early July 1965. CIA Intelligence Information Cable, 3 July 1965.

[89] In a series of reports on the Egyptian economy in 1966, Barclay's Bank concluded that the diversion of resources from the development program to the Egyptian military and the bloated government bureaucracy made it unlikely that Egyptian economic development could keep pace with the rapid growth of the Egyptian population. See Economic Intelligence Department reports of 11 February and 22 August 1966, Barclay's Bank.

[90] Kamel to author. See also oral history of Representative L.H. Fountain (D-N.C.), JOH, p. 26.

[91] PL480 exports declined steadily in proportion to total American agricultural exports in the late 1950s and 1960s. In 1957, for example, PL480 exports accounted for 33 percent of total farm exports; in 1967, PL480 exports accounted for only 19 percent of total farm exports. This shift was caused

partly by a rise in Third World income, which permitted more dollar sales, and partly by the gradual reduction of domestic price supports in the Kennedy-Johnson era. See USDA, *1978 Annual Food for Peace Report,* pp. 19–22; and Wallerstein, p. 9.

[92] Anderson, p. 201.

[93] Wallerstein, p. 10.

[94] *Nasser's Speeches 1966,* p. 25.

[95] See *New York Times,* 14 September 1966.

[96] See Winston Burdett, p. 191; and *New York Times,* 28 April 1967. The Yemeni civil war continued to be the chief source of friction between Nasser and the Saudis; when the British government announced in February 1966 that it would withdraw from Aden by 1968, Nasser apparently resolved to continue the Egyptian intervention in Yemen, as a means of influencing the political future of South Arabia. See Stookey, p. 186.

[97] Battle to author.

[98] Heikal in *Al Ahram,* 17 March 1967.

[99] Heikal's lengthy essays on the development of U.S.-Egyptian relations since 1952 appeared each Friday in *Al Ahram* between 3 March and 12 May 1967.

[100] Broadcast on Radio Cairo, 2 May 1967. See *Summary of World Broadcasts,* 4 May 1967.

[101] Michael Howard and Robert Hunter, *Israel and the Arab World: The Crisis of 1967* (London: International Institute for Strategic Studies, 1967) and William Quandt, *Decade of Decisions* (Berkeley: University of California Press, 1977), chapter 2, provide detailed accounts of the origins of the 1967 War.

[102] Parker to author; Burdett, pp. 190–192.

[103] Bergus to author.

[104] See "U.S. AID/UAR Interim Termination and Evaluation Report," 22 July 1967.

[105] A Senate Appropriations Committee staff study concluded in 1965 that "Egypt has withheld almost completely from its people the facts regarding U.S. PL480 assistance and what it has accomplished for Egypt and its people." See "Report on PL480 Aid to Egypt," 4 August 1965. See also C.A. Cabooris (Regional Food for Peace Officer, 1963–65), "End of Tour Report," 25 September 1965. Cabooris remarked: "Except for USDA container markings, the presence of AID personnel in the field, and an occasional newspaper article, no other media were used in the UAR to inform recipients that the foods were furnished by the people of the United States."

[106] CR, vol. 111, part 1, 23 January 1965: p. 1187.

[107] "U.S. AID/UAR Interim Termination and Evaluation Report," 22 July 1967.

[108] See Fouad Ajami, *The Arab Predicament* (New York: Cambridge University Press, 1982, Paperback Edition), p. 85.

Chapter Seven

[1] Gail Sheehy, "The Riddle of Sadat," *Esquire*, 30 January 1979.

[2] Henry Kissinger, *Years of Upheaval* (Boston: Little, Brown and Company, 1982), p. 201.

[3] Lucius D. Battle, "Anwar Sadat Remembered", *SAIS Review*, Winter 1981–1982, p. 44.

[4] Roger Morris, *Uncertain Greatness: Henry Kissinger and American Foreign Policy* (London: Quartet Books, 1977), p. 134.

[5] See Kissinger, pp. 210–216; and Hermann F. Eilts, "Sadat: The Making of an American Popular Image: A Personal Evaluation," *International Insight*, July/August 1981, pp. 2–3.

[6] See, for example, Kissinger, pp. 804–805.

[7] Kissinger, p. 615.

[8] Marvin G. Weinbaum provides detailed consideration of the post-1973 U.S. aid program in Egypt in "Politics and Development in Foreign Aid: U.S. Economic Assistance to Egypt, 1975–82–", *Middle East Journal*, Autumn 1983, pp. 636–655.

[9] Eilts to author.

[10] "Economic Support Fund Programs in the Middle East," House Foreign Affairs Committee Staff Study, (Washington: GPO, April 1979), p. 4.

[11] John Waterbury, *Egypt: Burdens of the Past/Options for the Future* (Bloomington, Indiana: Indiana University Press, 1978), p. 207.

[12] See Quandt, *Decade of Decisions*, pp. 260–267.

[13] See Quandt, *Decade of Decisions*, pp. 271–276, for details of the Sinai II accord.

[14] Eilts, "Sadat: The Making of an American Popular Image," pp. 4–5.

[15] Eilts, "Sadat: The Making of an American Popular Image," p. 5.

[16] U.S. economic aid to Israel amounted to $775 million in fiscal year 1976 and $735 million in fiscal year 1977. See "Economic Support Fund Programs in the Middle East," p. 6.

[17] "Economic Support Fund Programs in the Middle East," p. 9.

[18] Eilts to author.

[19] "Economic Support Fund Programs in the Middle East," pp. 15–16.

[20] "Economic Support Fund Programs in the Middle East," pp. 16–17.

[21] Economic Support Fund legislation authorizes the President to furnish assistance to foreign countries "in order to support or promote economic or political stability." See "Economic Support Fund Programs in the Middle East," p. 18.

[22] See appendix 4 for detailed statistics on ESF programs in Egypt in the period 1975–1981.

[23] "Economic Support Fund Programs in the Middle East," p. 28.

[24] See Henry F. Jackson, *From the Congo to Soweto: United States Foreign Policy Toward Africa Since 1960* (New York: William Morrow, 1982), p. 103. Sadat did not, however, completely sever Egypt's ties to the Soviet Union. In April 1976, for example, the Egyptian government concluded a trade agreement worth more than $800 million with the USSR.

[25] Jimmy Carter, *Keeping Faith* (New York: Bantam Books, 1982), p. 429.

[26] See "President Carter's Remarks at Clinton, Massachusetts, Town Meeting," U.S. Department of State Bulletin, 11 April 1977, p. 335.

[27] Senator Henry Jackson, for example, warned that "the fox is back in the chicken coop. The American people must certainly raise the question of why bring the Russians in at a time when the Egyptians have been throwing them out." See Harvey Sicherman, *Broker or Advocate? The US. Role in the Arab-Israeli Dispute 1973-1978* (Philadelphia: Foreign Policy Research Institute, Monograph No. 25, 1978), p. 59.

[28] Eilts, "Sadat: The Making of an American Popular Image," p. 6; and Eilts to author.

[29] See David Hirst and Irene Beeson, *Sadat* (London: Faber and Faber, 1981), p. 218.

[30] Waterbury, *Egypt*, p. 314.

[31] "Economic Support Fund Programs in the Middle East," p. 12.

[32] Ghali Shoukri, *Egypt: Portrait of a President* (London: Zed Press, 1981), p. 316.

[33] Waterbury, *Egypt*, p. 318.

[34] Sadat and Begin were the joint recipients of the 1978 Nobel Peace Prize. Sadat, convinced that he had sought an Arab-Israeli peace settlement with far greater courage and vision than his Israeli counterpart, was unhappy about sharing the award with Begin. See Hirst and Beeson, p. 315.

[35] Jimmy Carter, p. 361.

[36] Carter, pp. 319–403.

[37] The Gulf Organization for the Development of Egypt (GODE), set up after the October War to provide economic assistance to Egypt, furnished about $2.5 billion to the Sadat government between 1977 and 1979. See "Supplemental 1979 Middle East Aid Package to Israel and Egypt," House Foreign Affairs Subcommittee on Europe and the Middle East Hearings, April–May 1979 (Washington: Government Printing Office, 1979), p. 66.

[38] Quoted in Hirst and Beeson, p. 312.

[39] Sudan, Oman, and Somalia were the only members of the Arab League to retain diplomatic relations with Egypt after the signing of the Egyptian-Israeli peace treaty.

[40] Quoted in Hirst and Beeson, p. 335.

[41] "Foreign Assistance Act for 1981," Hearings, House Foreign Affairs Committee, January–March 1980 (Washington: Government Printing Office, 1980), p. 90.

[42] Israel received about $3 billion in supplemental post-treaty aid from the United States. "Supplemental 1979 Middle East Aid Package to Israel and Egypt," p. 5.

[43] Supplemental 1979 Middle East Aid Package to Israel and Egypt," p. 157; and Jackson, p. 104.

[44] Jackson, p. 103.

[45] "Foreign Assistance Act for 1982," Hearings, House Foreign Affairs Committee, February-April 1981 (Washington: Government Printing Office, 1981), p. 148.

[46] *Al-Ahram* of 5, 8, 9, 16 November 1978, quoted in Hirst and Beeson, p. 313.

[47] "Supplemental 1979 Middle East Aid Package to Israel and Egypt," p. 48.

[48] See Hirst and Beeson, pp. 341–342.

[49] Mohamed Hakki, *Egypt Under Mubarak*, Middle East Problem Paper No. 25, The Middle East Institute, Washington, 1983, p. 2.

[50] Hakki, p. 1.

[51] Hirst and Beeson, p. 335.

[52] John G. Merriam, "Egypt after Sadat," *Current History*, p. 5.

[53] See "Economic Support Fund Programs in the Middle East," pp. 12–15, 33; and Weinbaum, p. 644.

[54] See "Foreign Assistance Act for 1982," Hearings, Senate Foreign Relations Committee, March–May 1981(Washington: Government Printing Office, 1981), pp. 81–82.

[55] See AID audit report of Suez Cement Project, reproduced in "Foreign Assistance Act for 1983," Hearings, House Foreign Affairs Committee, March–April 1982, (Washington: Government Printing Office, 1982), pp. 246–290.

[56] "Economic Support Fund Programs in the Middle East," p. 29.

[57] "Foreign Assistance Act for 1982," Hearings, House Foreign Affairs Committee, p. 152.

[58] "Foreign Assistance Act for 1982," pp. 133–134.

[59] *International Herald Tribune*, 15 May 1979. See also Weinbaum, p. 654.

[60] *International Herald Tribune*, 17 November 1982.

Chapter Eight

[1] The Aswan Dam repair bill in 1981–82 amounted to about $80 million. See *Jordan Times*, 24/25 February 1983.

[2] Mohamed Hakki, p. 12.

[3] See "Inside Egypt: The Next Five Years," *Business International* (Weekly Report), 6 August 1982, pp. 254–255.

[4] See Lee Hamilton, "Foreign Aid's Purpose," *New York Times*, 20 March 1983.

[5] Cross reference: see p. 203.

[6] See Hermann F. Eilts, "Sadat: The Making of an American Popular Image: A Personal Evaluation," p. 8.

[7] Quoted in Vatikiotis, p. 357.

[8] Quoted in *New York Times*, 27 July 1980.

[9] Cairo Embtel 70, 13 July 1956.

[10] See Karen Dawisha, pp. 168–174, 178–182.

[11] *Egyptian Economic and Political Review* (September 1961), pp. 9–10.

[12] *Egyptian Economic and Political Review* (September 1961), pp. 9–10; and Faulkner, p. 219.

[13] Badeau, *American Approach to the Arab World*, p. 73.

Selected Bibliography

I. A Note on Documentary Sources

This study is based largely on hundreds of government documents declassified under Executive Orders 11652 and 12065, which went into effect in 1972, and under the Freedom of Information Act amendments of 1975. Many of the documents cited were declassified as a result of specific requests by the author; many others had already been declassified by the early 1980s and are reposited in the Eisenhower, Kennedy, and Johnson Presidential Libraries, in the John Foster Dulles Collection at Princeton University, and in the National Archives. The order of elements in documentary citations is as follows:

1. Actual title/inserted subject heading
2. Source
3. Type of document
4. Document identification number
5. Date
6. Archival citation for documents in Presidential libraries

Example: "Nasser Comments on Arab Summit," CIA Information Cable #113, 25 January 1964, Johnson Library, National Security File (NSF), Countries, UAR, volume 3.

II. Interviews and Correspondence

Personal interviews and correspondence provided a valuable supplement to documentary evidence. Listed below are the names of those persons who graciously consented to interviews or who responded to my questions by letter, brief descriptions of their professional backgrounds, and the places and dates of interviews or the dates of correspondence.

Sir Philip Adams
British Ambassador to Egypt, 1973–75
Personal interview, Ditchley (Oxfordshire), 9 December 1979

Sir Geoffrey Arthur
Political Counselor, British Embassy Cairo, 1961–63
Personal interview, Oxford, 17 November 1980

John Badeau
U.S. Ambassador to Egypt, 1961–64
Telephone interview, from Jamesburg, New Jersey, 10 September 1979

Lucius Battle
U.S. Ambassador to Egypt, 1964–67
Personal interview, Washington, 25 July 1979

Sir Harold Beeley
British Ambassador to Egypt, 1961–64
Personal interview, London, 19 November 1980

Donald Bergus
Political Counselor, American Embassy Cairo, 1962–65; Principal officer, U.S. Interests Section, Spanish Embassy Cairo, 1967–72
Personal interview, Washington, 9 January 1981

Donald S. Brown
AID Mission Director, Cairo, 1976–1982
Personal interview, Washington, 12 August 1982

Henry Byroade
U.S. Assistant Secretary of State for Near Eastern Affairs, 1952–55; Ambassador to Egypt, 1955–56
Personal interview, Washington, 9 March 1981

Miles Copeland
CIA officer, Cairo, 1953–55
Personal interview, Washington, 13 December 1980

Sir Colin Crowe
British Chargé d'Affaires, Cairo, 1959–1961; Ambassador to Saudi Arabia, 1963–64
Personal interview, London, 19 June 1979

Hermann Eilts
U.S. Ambassador to Saudi Arabia, 1965–1970; Ambassador to Egypt, 1974–79
Personal interviews, Washington, 26 July 1979 and Boston, 1 August 1982.

Maha Fahmy
Political Secretary, Egyptian Embassy London, 1980–1983
Personal interview, London, 27 November 1980

Myer Feldman
Deputy Special Counsel, White House Staff, 1961–63; Counsel, 1964–65
Telephone interview, Washington, 19 January 1981

J. William Fulbright
United States Senator, 1945–1974; Chairman, Senate Foreign Relations Committee
Telephone interview, Washington, 12 December 1980

Raymond Hare
U.S. Ambassador to Egypt, 1956–1960
Personal interview, Washington, 26 July 1979

Parker Hart
Political Counselor, American Embassy Cairo, 1955–58
Personal interview, Washington, 13 March 1981

Roger Hilsman
Director, State Department Bureau of Intelligence and Research, 1961–64
Letter, 3 July 1979

Mustapha Kamel
Egyptian Ambassador to the United States, 1958–1967
Personal interview, London, 1 April 1981

Isaiah Kenen
President, America Israel Public Affairs Committee, 1952–1978
Personal interview, Washington, 3 January 1981

William Langdon
Assistant Director, Program Development, CARE
Letter, 30 August 1979

Sir Roger Makins (Lord Sherfield)
British Ambassador to the United States, 1953–56
Personal interview, London, 19 November 1980

Edward Mason
Professor of Economics, Harvard University; Consultant to President Kennedy
Telephone interview, from Cambridge, Massachusetts, 6 September 1979

Albert Mercker
Assistant Director, Office of Food for Peace, Agency for International Development
Letter, 30 August 1979

Sir Willie Morris
Political Secretary, British Embassy Washington, 1955–1960; Ambassador to Egypt, 1975–79
Personal interview, Oxford, 8 November 1980

Richard Parker
Political Counselor, American Embassy Egypt, 1965–67
Personal interview, Washington, 12 February 1981

Kermit Roosevelt
CIA Near East specialist
Personal interview, Washington, 5 January 1981

Dean Rusk
U.S. Secretary of State, 1961–69
Letter, 13 April 1981

Francis Russell
Chief, State Department "Alpha" Group, 1954–56
Letter, 12 February 1981

Hedrick Smith
New York Times Cairo correspondent, 1964–66
Personal interview, Washington, 10 February 1980

Fraser Wilkins
Chief, State Department Office of Near East Affairs, 1956
Personal interview, Washington, 3 March 1981

Evan Wilson
Political Secretary, American Embassy London, 1953–57
Personal interview, Washington, 4 March 1981

Ahmed al-Zant
Career Egyptian diplomat
Personal interviews, Washington, 17 December 1980 and 9 January 1981

III. Oral Histories

John Foster Dulles Oral History Collection, Princeton University

Winthrop Aldrich
George Allen
Eugene Black
Robert Bowie
Maurice Couve de Murville
Abba Eban
Dwight Eisenhower
Loy Henderson
John Hollister
George Humphrey
Jacob Javits
William Macomber
Roger Makins
William Rountree
Francis Russell

John F. Kennedy Oral History Collection, Kennedy Library

John Badeau
George McGovern
Richard Reuter
James Symington

Lyndon B. Johnson Oral History Collection, Johnson Library

Lucius Battle
David Bell
L.H. Fountain
William Gaud
William Macomber

Columbia Oral History Collection, Columbia University

George Aiken
George Allen
John Badeau
Robert Bowie
Earl Butz
Andrew Goodpaster
Raymond Hare
Donald Paarlberg

IV. United States Government Publications

Agency for International Development. "U.S. Economic Assistance to Egypt."
    Washington: Government Printing Office (GPO), 15 February 1978.

Congressional Record

Department of Agriculture. Food for Peace *Annual Reports*, 1961–78. Wash-
    ington: GPO, 1961–1978.
———. "Public Law 480 and Other Economic Assistance to Egypt." Economic
    Research Service (ERS) Foreign Report #83. Washington: GPO, June
    1964.
———. "United States Agricultural Exports Under Public Law 480." ERS
    Foreign Report #395. Washington: GPO, October 1974.
———. "PL480 Concessional Sales." ERS Foreign Report #142. Washington:
    GPO, December 1977.
———. "Egyptian Agriculture and the U.S. Assistance Program." Washing-
    ton: GPO, June 1979.

Foreign Broadcast Information Service

House of Representatives, Agriculture Committee. Hearings: Public Law 480 Extension, 1964. Washington: GPO, 1964.
Senate, Appropriations Committee. Hearings: "Financing of the Aswan High Dam in Egypt," 26 January 1956. Washington: GPO, 1956.
————. Hearings: "Mutual Security Appropriations for 1957." Washington: GPO, 1956.
————. "Report on PL480 Aid to Egypt," 9 August 1965. Washington: GPO, 1965.
Senate, Foreign Relations Committee. *Executive Sessions* (Historical Series), Volumes IV–IX (1953–57). Washington: GPO, 1977–79.
Senate, Government Operations Committee. "Report of Study on U.S. Foreign Aid to Ten Middle Eastern Countries." Washington: GPO, 1963.

V. Egyptian Government Publications

Aswan High Dam Authority. "Aswan High Dam." Aswan, 1964.
Ministry of Information. *Nasser's Speeches and Press Interviews, 1958–1967.* Cairo, 1959–1968.

VI. Unpublished Monographs and Dissertations

Abu-Jaber, Faiz Saley. "Egypt and the Cold War, 1952–56: Implications for American Policy." Syracuse University Ph.D. Thesis, 1966.
Anderson, William D. "The Intersection of Foreign and Domestic Policy: The Examples in Public Law 480." University of Illinois Ph.D. Thesis, 1970.
Balboni, Alan Richard. "A Study of the Efforts of the American Zionists to Influence the Formulation and Conduct of United States Policy during the Roosevelt, Truman, and Eisenhower Administrations." Brown University Ph.D. Thesis, 1973.
Balfe, Harry. "An Inquiry into the United States Foreign Policy with Egypt During the Tenure of John Foster Dulles as Secretary of State." American University M.A. Thesis, 1964.
Bardes, Barbara. "Senatorial Realignment on Foreign Aid, 1953–1972." University of Cincinnati Ph.D. Thesis, 1975.
Biali, Abdel Muhsin. "A Comparative Analysis of the Reactions of the Countries of Egypt, Iraq, and Syria to the USSR and USA Foreign Aid Programs." American University Ph.D. Thesis, 1967.
Blessing, James. "The Suspension of Foreign Aid by the United States, 1948–1972." State University of New York at Albany Ph.D. Thesis, 1975.

Cortada, James. "The Yemen Crisis." Paper presented to UCLA Institute of International and Foreign Studies, 1965.

EBS Management Consultants. "Terminal Report: AID Contract #37." New York: EBS, October 1967.

Faulkner, Constance. "The Economic Effects of U.S. PL480 in the UAR." University of Utah Ph.D. Thesis, 1969.

Fouad, Mahmoud Hassan. "The Economics of Foreign Aid: The UAR Experience with the U.S. and USSR Programs, 1952–1965." University of Southern California Ph.D. Thesis, 1968.

Harrell, Don W. "The Attitudes of the Congress Toward the Middle East." American University M.A. Thesis, 1963.

Huff, Earl Dean. "Zionist Influences Upon U.S. Foreign Policy: A Study of American Policy Toward the Middle East from the Time of the Struggle for Israel to the Sinai Conflict." University of Idaho Ph.D. Thesis, 1971.

Kefauver, W. Tyler. "The Influence of Foreign Policy in the Election of 1956." American University M.A. Thesis, 1968.

Kerr, Malcolm. "Egyptian Foreign Policy and the Revolution." Middle East Centre Library, St. Antony's College, Oxford.

Maheshwari, Bhanwar Lal. "Foreign Aid and the Policy Process: A Study of the Struggle over Foreign Aid in Congress, 1961–65." University of Pennsylvania Ph.D. Thesis, 1966.

Murad, Ahmad. "Egypt's Economic Relations with the Soviet Bloc and the United States." University of Wisconsin Ph.D. Thesis, 1961.

Olmstead, Cecil. "Foreign Aid as an Effective Means of Persuasion." Paper presented to American Society of International Law, 1964.

Perry, Glenn Earl. "United States Relations with Egypt, 1951–1963: Egyptian Neutralism and the American Alignment Policy." University of Virginia Ph.D. Thesis, 1964.

Rice, Andrew Eliot. "Building a Constituency for the Foreign Aid Program: The Record of the Eisenhower Years." Syracuse University Ph.D. Thesis, 1963.

Rubin, Barry. "America and the Egyptian Revolution, 1950–57." Paper presented to the Middle East Studies Association, 1980.

Trice, Robert. "Domestic Political Interests and American Policy in the Middle East: Pro-Arab and Corporate Non-Governmental Actors and the Making of American Foreign Policy, 1966–1971." University of Wisconsin Ph.D. Thesis, 1974.

Waterbury, John. "The Implications of *Infitah* for U.S.-Egyptian Relations." Paper presented to colloquium on "The Middle East and the United States," Shiloah Centre for Middle Eastern and African Studies, Tel Aviv University, 1978.

Windmueller, Steven Fred. "American Jewish Interest Groups: Their Roles in Shaping United States Foreign Policy in the Middle East: A Study of Two Time Periods: 1945–48, 1955–58." University of Pennsylvania Ph.D. Thesis, 1973.

VII. Books

Abu-Jaber, Faiz. *American-Arab Relations From Wilson to Nixon*. Washington: University Press of America, 1979.

Adams, Sherman. *First-Hand Report*. London: Hutchinson, 1962.

Ajami, Fouad. *The Arab Predicament*. New York: Cambridge University Press, 1982.

Amin, Galal. *Food Supply and Economic Development with Special Reference to Egypt*. London: Frank Cass, 1966.

Badeau, John. *The American Approach to the Arab World*. New York: Harper and Row, 1968.

Baker, Raymond. *Egypt's Uncertain Revolution under Nasser and Sadat*. Cambridge, Mass.: Harvard University Press, 1978.

Baldwin, David A. *Economic Development and American Foreign Policy, 1943–62*. Chicago: University of Chicago Press, 1966.

———. *Foreign Aid and American Foreign Policy*. New York: Praeger, 1966.

Beal, John Robinson. *John Foster Dulles*, second edition. New York: Harper, 1959.

Berding, Andrew. *Dulles on Diplomacy*. Princeton: Van Nostrand, 1965.

Berkowitz, Morton; Bock, P.G.; and Fuccillo, Vincent J. *The Politics of American Foreign Policy*. Englewood Cliffs, N.J.: Prentice-Hall, 1977.

Bowles, Chester. *Promises to Keep*. New York: Harper and Row, 1971.

Braddon, Russell. *The Splitting of a Nation*. London: Collins, 1973.

British Broadcasting Corporation, Third Programme. *Suez Ten Years After*. Edited and introduced by Anthony Moncrieff. London: BBC, 1967.

Brown, Seyom. *The Faces of Power*. New York: Columbia University Press, 1968.

Bryson, Thomas. *United States/Middle East Diplomatic Relations, 1784–1978: An Annotated Bibliography*. Metuchen, N.J.: Scarecrow Press, 1979.

Burdett, Winston. *Encounter With the Middle East*. London: André Deutsch, 1970.

Burrel, R. Michael and Abbas Kelidar. *Egypt: The Dilemmas of a Nation, 1970–77*. The Washington Papers, #48. London: Sage Publications, 1977.

Caldwell, Dan. *Food Crises and World Politics*. Sage Professional Papers in International Studies, 5, 02–049. London: Sage Publications, 1977.

Carlton, David. *Anthony Eden: A Biography*. London: Allen Lane, 1981.

Carter, Jimmy. *Keeping Faith*. New York: Bantam Books, 1982.

Cater, Douglass. *Power in Washington*. London: Collins, 1965.

Childs, Marquis. *Eisenhower: Captive Hero*. New York: Harcourt-Brace, 1958.

Chubin, Shahram. *The United States and the Third World: Motives, Objectives, Policies*. Adelphi Paper #167, part II. London: IISS, 1981.

Coffin, Frank. *Witness for AID*. Boston: Houghton-Mifflin, 1964.

Cohen, Warren. *Dean Rusk*. Totawa, N.J.: Cooper Square, 1980.

Cooke, M.L. *Nasser's High Aswan Dam*. Washington: Public Affairs Institute, 1956.

Cooper, Chester. *The Lion's Last Roar*. New York: Harper and Row, 1978.

Copeland, Miles. *The Game of Nations.* London: Weidenfeld and Nicolson, 1969.

Dann, Uriel. *Iraq under Qassem.* London: Pall Mall, 1969.

Dawisha, Adeed. *Egypt in the Arab World: The Elements of Foreign Policy.* London: Macmillan, 1976.

Dawisha, Karen. *Soviet Foreign Policy Towards Egypt.* London: Macmillan, 1979.

Dayan, Moshe. *Diary of the Sinai Campaign 1956.* London: Sphere Books, 1967.

———. *Story of My Life.* New York: William Morrow, 1976.

Declassified Documents Reference System. Washington: Carrollton Press, 1975–1980.

Dekmejian, R. Hrair. *Egypt Under Nasir.* London: University of London Press, 1972.

Domhoff, G. William. *Fat Cats and Democrats: The Role of the Rich in the Party of the Common Man.* Englewood Cliffs, N.J.: Prentice-Hall, 1972.

Donovan, Robert J. *Eisenhower: The Inside Story.* London: Hamish Hamilton, 1956.

Drummond, Roscoe and Gaston Coblentz. *Duel at the Brink.* London: Weidenfeld and Nicolson, 1960.

Dulles, Allen. *The Craft of Intelligence.* London: Weidenfeld and Nicolson, 1963.

Eddine, Mon'im Nasser. *Arab-Chinese Relations 1950–71.* Beirut: The Arab Institute for Research and Publishing, 1972.

Eden, Sir Anthony. *Full Circle.* London: Cassell, 1960.

Eisenhower, Dwight D. *Mandate for Change, Memoirs 1953–56.* London: Heinemann, 1963.

———. *Waging Peace, Memoirs 1956–61.* London: Heinemann, 1965.

Eveland, Wilbur Crane. *Ropes of Sand: America's Failure in the Middle East.* New York: Norton, 1980.

Ewald, William Bragg, Jr. *Eisenhower the President: Crucial Days 1951–60.* Englewood Cliffs, N.J.: Prentice-Hall, 1981.

Finer, Herman. *Dulles over Suez.* Chicago: Quadrangle Books, 1964.

Fullick, Roy and Geoffrey Powell. *Suez: The Double War.* London: Hamish Hamilton, 1979.

Geyelin, Philip. *Lyndon B. Johnson and the World.* New York: Praeger, 1966.

Glassman, Jon D. *Arms for the Arabs.* Baltimore: The Johns Hopkins University Press, 1975.

Glubb, Sir John Bagot. *A Soldier with the Arabs.* London: Hodder and Stoughton, 1957.

Goldman, Eric F. *The Tragedy of Lyndon Johnson.* New York: Knopf, 1969.

Goldman, Marshall I. *Soviet Foreign Aid.* New York: Praeger, 1967.

Goold-Adams, Richard. *The Time of Power.* London: Weidenfeld and Nicolson, 1962.

Guhin, Michael. *John Foster Dulles: A Statesman and His Times.* New York: Columbia University Press, 1972.

Hakki, Mohamed. *Egypt under Mubarak.* Washington: Middle East Institute, Middle East Problem Paper No. 25, 1983.

Halperin, Samuel. *The Political World of American Zionism*. Detroit: Wayne State University Press, 1961.

Hansen, Bent and Girgis Marzouk. *Development and Economic Policy in the UAR*. Amsterdam: North Holland Publishing Company, 1965.

Heikal, Mohamed Hassanein. *The Cairo Documents*. Garden City, N.Y.: Doubleday, 1973.

———. *The Sphinx and the Commissar*. New York: Harper and Row, 1978.

———. *Autumn of Fury*. London: André Deutsch, 1983.

Heller, Deane and David. *John Foster Dulles: Soldier for Peace*. New York: Holt, Rinehart and Winston, 1960.

Hilsman, Roger. *To Move a Nation*. Garden City, N.Y.: Doubleday, 1967.

Hirst, David and Irene Beeson. *Sadat*. London: Faber and Faber, 1981.

Hoopes, Townsend. *The Devil and John Foster Dulles*. London: André Deutsch, 1974.

Hopwood, Derek. *Egypt: Politics and Society 1945-1981*. London: Allen and Unwin, 1982.

Howard, Michael and Robert Hunter. *Israel and the Arab World: The Crisis of 1967*. London: IISS, 1967.

Howe, Russell Warren and Sarah Hays Trott. *The Power Peddlers*. Garden City, N.Y.: Doubleday, 1977.

Hughes, Emmet John. *The Ordeal of Power*. London: Macmillan, 1963.

Humphrey, George. *The Basic Papers of George Humphrey, 1953-57*. Edited by Nathaniel R. Howard. Cleveland: The Western Reserve Historical Society, 1965.

Huntington, Samuel. *Political Order in Changing Societies*. New Haven: Yale University Press, 1968.

Hurewitz, J.C. *Diplomacy in the Near and Middle East: A Documentary Record, 1914-56*, 2 volumes. Princeton: Van Nostrand, 1956.

Hussein I, King of Jordan. *Uneasy Lies the Head*. New York: Bernard Geis Associates, 1963.

Isaacs, Stephen D. *Jews and American Politics*. Garden City, N.Y.: Doubleday, 1974.

Jabber, Paul. *Not By War Alone: Security and Arms Control in the Middle East*. Berkeley: University of California Press, 1981.

Jackson, Henry F. *From the Congo to Soweto: U.S. Foreign Policy Toward Africa Since 1960*. New York: William Morrow, 1982.

Joesten, Joachim. *Nasser: The Rise to Power*. Westport, Conn.: Greenwood Press, 1974.

Kaplan, Jacob J. *The Challenge of Foreign Aid*. New York: Praeger, 1967.

Karanjia, R.K. *Arab Dawn*. Bombay: Blitz, 1958.

Kerr, Malcolm. *The Arab Cold War, 1958-70*, third edition. London: Oxford University Press, 1971.

Kissinger, Henry. *Years of Upheaval*. Boston: Little, Brown and Company, 1982.

Komzin, Ivan. *The High Aswan Dam*. Moscow: Foreign Languages Publishing House, n.d.

Lacouture, Jean and Simone. *Egypt in Transition*. London: Methuen, 1962.

Lacouture, Jean. *Nasser*. London: Secker and Warburg, 1973.

Lappé, Frances and Joseph Collins. *Food First.* Boston: Houghton-Mifflin, 1977.

Liska, George. *The New Statecraft.* Chicago: University of Chicago Press, 1960.

Little, Tom. *High Dam at Aswan: The Subjugation of the Nile.* New York: John Day, 1965.

———. *Modern Egypt.* London: Ernest Benn, 1967.

Loeber, Thomas. *Foreign Aid: Our Tragic Experiment.* New York: Norton, 1961.

Love, Kennett. *Suez: The Twice-Fought War.* New York: McGraw-Hill, 1969.

Lyon, Peter. *Eisenhower: Portrait of the Hero.* Boston: Little Brown, 1974.

Macmillan, Sir Harold. *Tides of Fortune, Memoirs 1945–55.* London: Macmillan, 1969.

———. *Riding the Storm, Memoirs 1956–59.* London: Macmillan, 1971.

———. *At the End of the Day, Memoirs 1961–63.* London: Macmillan, 1973.

McGovern, George. *War against Want.* New York: Walker, 1964.

———. *Grassroots.* New York: Harper, 1977.

Mabro, Robert. *The Egyptian Economy 1952–72.* London: Oxford University Press, 1974.

Mansfield, Peter. *Nasser's Egypt.* Middlesex: Penguin, 1969.

Mason, Edward S. *Foreign Aid and Foreign Policy.* New York: Harper and Row, 1964.

Mason, Edward S. and Robert E. Asher. *The World Bank Since Bretton Woods.* Washington: Brookings Institute, 1973.

Meyer, Gail E. *The United States and Egypt: The Formative Years.* Rutherford, N.J.: Fairleigh Dickinson University Press, 1980.

Millikan, Max F. and Walt W. Rostow. *A Proposal: Key to an Effective Foreign Policy.* New York: Harper, 1957.

Montgomery, John D. *The Politics of Foreign Aid.* New York: Praeger, 1962.

Morgan, Dan. *Merchants of Grain.* New York: Viking, 1979.

Morris, Roger. *Uncertain Greatness: Henry Kissinger and American Foreign Policy.* London: Quartet Books, 1977.

Mosley, Leonard. *Dulles: A Biography of Eleanor, Allen, and John Foster Dulles and their Family Network.* New York: Dial Press, 1978.

Murphy, Robert. *Diplomat among Warriors.* Garden City, N.Y.: Doubleday, 1964.

Nadich, Judah. *Eisenhower and the Jews.* New York: Twayne Publishers, 1953.

Naguib, Mohamed. *Egypt's Destiny.* Garden City, N.Y.: Doubleday, 1955.

Nasser, Gamal Abdel. *The Philosophy of the Egyptian Revolution.* Translated by Richard H. Nolte. Cairo: American Universities Field Staff, March 1954.

Neff, Donald. *Warriors at Suez.* New York: Simon and Schuster, 1981.

Nelson, Joan M. *Aid, Influence, and Foreign Policy.* New York: Macmillan, 1968.

Neustadt, Richard. *Alliance Politics.* New York: Columbia University Press, 1970.

Noble, G. Bernard. *Christian A. Herter.* New York: Cooper Square, 1970.

Nutting, Anthony. *I Saw For Myself.* London: Hollis and Carter, 1958.

————. *No End of a Lesson*. London: Constable, 1967.

————. *Nasser*. London: Constable, 1972.

O'Leary, Michael Kent. *The Politics of American Foreign Aid*. New York: Atherton Press, 1967.

Packenham, Robert A. *Liberal America and the Third World*, paperback edition. Princeton: Princeton University Press, 1973.

Paddock, William and Paul. *Famine 1975*. Boston: Little Brown, 1967.

Pineau, Christian. *1956/Suez*. Paris: Robert Laffont, 1976.

Polk, William. *The United States and the Arab World*, third edition. Cambridge, Mass.: Harvard University Press, 1975.

————. *The Elusive Peace: The Middle East in the Twentieth Century*. London: Croom Helm, 1979.

Quandt, William. *Decade of Decisions*. Berkeley: University of California Press, 1977.

Ra'anan, Uri. *The USSR Arms the Third World*. Cambridge, Mass.: The MIT Press, 1969.

Rabin, Yitzhak. *The Rabin Memoirs*. London: Weidenfeld and Nicolson, 1979.

Rafael, Gideon. *Destination Peace*. London: Weidenfeld and Nicolson, 1981.

Riad, Mahmoud. *The Struggle for Peace in the Middle East*. London: Quartet Books, 1981.

Robertson, Terence. *Crisis: The Inside Story of the Suez Conspiracy*. New York: Atheneum, 1965.

Rubin, Barry. *The Arab States and the Palestine Conflict*. Syracuse: Syracuse University Press, 1981.

Sadat, Anwar. *In Search of Identity*. New York: Harper and Row, 1977.

Safran, Nadav. *The United States and Israel*. Cambridge, Mass.: Harvard University Press, 1963.

————. *From War to War*. New York: Pegasus, 1969.

————. *Israel The Embattled Ally*. Cambridge, Mass.: Harvard University Press, 1978.

Schlesinger, Arthur, Jr. *A Thousand Days*. London: André Deutsch, 1965.

Schmidt, Dana Adams. *Yemen: The Unknown War*. London: The Bodley Head, 1968.

Seale, Patrick. *The Struggle for Syria*. London: Oxford University Press, 1965.

Selwyn Lloyd. *Suez 1956*. New York: Mayflower Books, 1978.

Shibl, Yusuf A. *The Aswan High Dam*. Beirut: The Arab Institute for Research and Publishing, 1971.

Shichor, Yitzhak. *The Middle East in China's Foreign Policy 1949–77*. New York: Cambridge University Press, 1979.

Shoukri, Ghali. *Egypt: Portrait of a President*. London: Zed Press, 1981.

Sicherman, Harvey. *Broker or Advocate? The U.S. Role in the Arab-Israeli Dispute 1973–1978*. Philadelphia: Foreign Policy Research Institute, Monograph No. 25, 1978.

Snetsinger, John. *Truman, the Jewish Vote, and the Creation of Israel*. Stanford: Hoover Institute Press, 1974.

Stanley, Robert G. *Food for Peace*. New York: Gordon and Breech, 1973.

Stephens, Robert. *Nasser: A Political Biography*. London: Penguin, 1971.

St. John, Robert. *The Boss*. New York: McGraw-Hill, 1960.

Stookey, Robert. *America and the Arab World.* New York: John Wiley, 1975.
————. *Yemen.* Boulder, Colorado: Westview Press, 1978.
Teslik, Kennan. *Congress, the Executive Branch, and Special Interests.* Westport, Conn.: Greenwood, 1982.
Thomas, Hugh. *Suez.* New York: Harper and Row, 1966.
Toma, Peter. *The Politics of Food for Peace.* Tucson: Arizona State University Press, 1967.
Trevelyan, Humphrey. *The Middle East in Revolution.* Boston: Gambit, 1970.
Tully, Andrew. *CIA: The Inside Story.* New York: William Morrow, 1962.
Vatikiotis, P.J. *Nasser and His Generation.* London: Croom Helm, 1978.
Wallerstein, Mitchel B. *Food for War—Food for Peace.* Cambridge, Mass.: MIT Press, 1980.
Walters, Robert S. *American and Soviet Aid.* Pittsburgh: University of Pittsburgh Press, 1970.
Walton, Richard. *Cold War and Counterrevolution: The Foreign Policy of John F. Kennedy.* New York: Viking, 1972.
Waterbury, John. *Hydropolitics of the Nile Valley.* Syracuse: Syracuse University Press, 1979.
————. *Egypt: Burdens of the Past/Options for the Future.* Bloomington, Indiana: Indiana University Press, 1978.
Weintraub, Sidney. Editor. *Economic Coercion and U.S. Foreign Policy.* Boulder, Colorado: Westview Press, 1982.
Weissman, Steve. *The Trojan Horse: A Radical Look at Foreign Aid.* Palo Alto, California: Ramparts Press, 1975.
Wenner, Manfred. *Modern Yemen.* Baltimore: The Johns Hopkins University Press, 1967.
Wheelock, Keith. *Nasser's New Egypt.* New York: Praeger, 1960.
Wilson, Sir Harold. *The Chariot of Israel.* London: Weidenfeld and Nicolson and Michael Joseph, 1981.
Wynn, Wilton. *Nasser of Egypt: The Search for Dignity.* Cambridge, Mass.: Arlington Books, 1959.

VIII. Articles

Ajami, Fouad. "The Struggle for Egypt's Soul." *Foreign Policy* (Summer 1979).
Badeau, John S. "Crisis in Confidence." *Foreign Affairs* (January 1965).
Battle, Lucius. "Anwar Sadat Remembered". *SAIS Review* (Winter 1981/82).
Brown, Donald S. "Egypt and the United States: Collaborators in Economic Development." *Middle East Journal* (Winter 1981).
Castleberry, H.P. "The Arabs' View of Postwar American Foreign Policy: Retrospect and Prospect." *Western Political Quarterly* (March 1959).
Deney, Nicole. "Les États-Unis et le Financement du Barrage d'Assouan." *Revue Française de la Science Politique* (Juin 1962).
Dougherty, James. "The Aswan Decision in Perspective." *Political Science Quarterly* (March 1959).

Eilts, Hermann Fr. "Sadat: The Making of an American Popular Image: A Personal Evaluation." *International Insight* (July/August 1981).

Ellis, Harry B. "Nasser's Economy." *The New Leader* (26 December 1960).

Frank, Lewis. "Nasser's Missile Program." *Orbis* (Fall 1967).

Galtung, Johan. "On the Effects of International Economic Sanctions, With Examples from the Case of Rhodesia." *World Politics* (April 1967).

Gelb, Leslie and Anthony Lake. "Less Food, More Politics." *Foreign Policy* (Winter 1974–75).

Graebner, Norman. "Foreign Aid and American Policy." *Current History* (xxxi, 1956).

Haviland, H. Field. "Foreign Aid and the Policy Process: 1957." *American Political Science Review* (September 1958).

Hazlitt, Henry. "That Egyptian Dam." *Newsweek* (2 April 1956).

Hourani, Albert. "The Middle East and the Crisis of 1956." *St. Antony's Papers*, #4, 1958.

Huntington, Samuel P. "Foreign Aid: For What and For Whom?" *Foreign Policy* (Winter 1970–71 and Spring 1971).

Hurewitz, J.C. "Our Mistakes in the Middle East." *Atlantic Monthly* (December 1956).

Jackson, Henry F. "Sadat's Perils." *Foreign Policy* (Spring 1981).

Johnson, Joseph E. "Arab and Israeli: A Persistent Challenge." *Middle East Journal* (Winter 1964).

Kent, George. "Congress and American Middle East Policy" in *The Middle East: Quest for an American Policy*. Edited by Willard A. Beling. Albany, N.Y.: State University of New York Press, 1973.

Kerr, Malcolm. "Coming to Terms With Nasser." *International Affairs* (January 1967).

Kraft, Joseph. "Those Arabists in the State Department." *New York Times Magazine* (7 November 1971).

Lichtblau, J.H. "Is the Tank Running Low?" *The Reporter* (21 March 1957).

McLean, Neil. "The War in the Yemen." *Journal of the Royal Central Asian Society* (April 1964).

Merriam, John G. "U.S. Wheat to Egypt: The Use of an Agricultural Commodity as a Foreign Policy Tool" in *The Role of U.S. Agriculture in Foreign Policy*. Edited by Richard Fraenkel. New York: Praeger, 1979.

————. "Egypt after Sadat." *Current History* (January 1983).

Nasser, Gamal Abdel. "The Egyptian Revolution." *Foreign Affairs* (January 1955).

Peretz, Don. "The United States, the Arabs, and Israel: Peace Efforts of Kennedy, Johnson, and Nixon." *The Annals of the American Academy of Political and Social Science* (May 1972).

Pye, Lucian. "Soviet and American Styles in Foreign Aid." *Orbis* (June 1968).

Quandt, William B. "Domestic Influences in United States Foreign Policy in the Middle East: The View From Washington" in *The Middle East: Quest for an American Policy*. Edited by Willard A. Beling. Albany, N.Y.: State University of New York Press, 1973.

————. "Middle East Crises." *Foreign Affairs* (America and the World 1979).

Rosenfeld, Stephen. "The Politics of Food." *Foreign Policy* (Spring 1974).

Rothschild, Emma. "Food Politics." *Foreign Affairs* (January 1976).

Rycroft, Robert and Joseph Szyliowicz. "The Technological Dimension of Decision-Making: The Case of the Aswan High Dam." *World Politics* (October 1980).

Seale, Patrick. "The War in Yemen." *New Republic* (26 January 1963).

Sheehy, Gail. "The Riddle of Sadat." *Esquire* (30 January 1979).

Sid-Ahmed, Mohamed. "Shifting Sands of Peace in the Middle East." *International Security* (Summer 1980).

Slade, Shelley. "The Image of the Arab in America: Analysis of a Poll of American Attitudes." *Middle East Journal* (Spring 1981).

Sterling, Claire. "Superdams: The Perils of Progress." *The Atlantic* (June 1972).

Suleiman, Michael. "National Stereotypes as Weapons in the Arab-Israeli Conflict." *Journal of Palestine Studies* (Spring 1974).

Thimmesch, Nick. "These Men Have a Pipeline to the Heartland." *Potomac* (20 June 1976).

Trice, Robert. "The American Elite Press and the Arab-Israeli Conflict." *Middle East Journal* (Summer 1979).

Truman, David. "The Domestic Politics of Foreign Aid." *Proceedings of the Academy of Political Science* (January 1962).

Wallenstein, Peter. "Scarce Goods as Political Weapons: The Case of Food." *Journal of Peace Research* (xiii, 1976).

Warner, Geoffrey. " 'Collusion' and the Suez Crisis of 1956." *International Affairs* (April 1979).

Weinbaum, Marvin G. "Politics and Development in Foreign Aid: U.S. Economic Assistance to Egypt, 1975–82–." *Middle East Journal* (Autumn 1983).

IX. Newspapers

Al Ahram, Cairo.
Al Akhbar, Cairo.
The Egyptian Gazette, Cairo.
The Financial Times, London.
The Guardian, Manchester and London.
International Herald Tribune, Paris.
Le Journal d'Egypte, Cairo.
Le Monde, Paris.
New York Herald Tribune, New York.
New York Times, New York.
The Observer, London.
The Sunday Times, London.
The Times, London.
Washington Post, Washington.

Index